Frances Power Cobbe, Theodore Parker

Discourses of Slavery

Frances Power Cobbe, Theodore Parker

Discourses of Slavery

ISBN/EAN: 9783744796576

Printed in Europe, USA, Canada, Australia, Japan

Cover: Foto ©ninafisch / pixelio.de

More available books at **www.hansebooks.com**

THE

COLLECTED WORKS

OF

THEODORE PARKER,

MINISTER OF THE TWENTY-EIGHTH CONGREGATIONAL
SOCIETY AT BOSTON, U.S.

CONTAINING HIS

THEOLOGICAL, POLEMICAL, AND CRITICAL WRITINGS,
SERMONS, SPEECHES, AND ADDRESSES,
AND LITERARY MISCELLANIES.

EDITED BY

FRANCES POWER COBBE.

VOL. V.

DISCOURSES OF SLAVERY.

LONDON:
TRÜBNER & CO., 60, PATERNOSTER ROW.
1863.

DISCOURSES

OF

SLAVERY

BY
THEODORE PARKER.

LONDON:
TRÜBNER & CO., 60, PATERNOSTER ROW.
1863.

PREFACE.

THERE can hardly fail at the present time to attach a mournful interest to these Discourses on Slavery by Theodore Parker. Few will read them and see how deeply their author's heart was engaged in the cause of Negro Emancipation, without being touched by the thought that in the great struggle now passing in America, the voice which would have spoken loudest for right and justice has been silent, and the brave soul which would have exulted in the triumph of freedom has passed away from earth beyond the tidings of the conflict, perhaps beyond the echoes of that last glad *Te Deum* which shall arise from an enfranchised race and a regenerated land.

Another and a brighter interest will doubtless cling to these Discourses in times to come, when slavery shall have been swept from the world, and men look back to its stupendous wrong with the same wondering horror wherewith we now regard the tyrannies of feudalism and the cruelties of the Inquisition. It will then be remembered with joy that the first preacher of pure Theism was also the fearless denouncer of the great National Crime of his age—that crime which the Churches of his land were rarely found to condemn, and often to justify and defend.

F. P. C.

Switzerland, August, 1863.

CONTENTS.

	PAGE
Sermon of Slavery	1
Letter touching the matter of Slavery	17
Speech on the Abolition of Slavery by the French Republic	85
Speech at Faneuil Hall before the New England Anti-slavery Convention, May 31, 1848	93
Speech in Boston, May 29, 1850, on Slave Power in America	103
The Function of Conscience in Relation to the Laws of Men	134
Speech at the Ministerial Conference at Boston, May 29, 1851	164
On the Boston Kidnapping	172
On the Law of God and the Statutes of Men	225
Thoughts on the Nebraska Question	245
Address on the Condition of America	257

A SERMON OF SLAVERY.*

DELIVERED JANUARY 31, 1841, REPEATED JUNE 4, 1843.

Know ye not that to whom ye yield yourselves servants to obey, his servants ye are whom ye obey; whether of sin unto death, or of obedience unto righteousness?—ROM. vi. 16.

IN our version of the New Testament the word *servant* often stands for a word in the original, which means *slave*. Such is the case in this passage just read, and the sense of the whole verse is this :—" If a man yields unconditional service to sin, he is the *slave* of sin, and gets death for his reward." Here, however, by a curious figure of speech, not uncommon in this apostle, he uses the word *slave* in a good sense—*slave* of obedience unto righteousness. I now ask your attention to a short sermon of slavery.

A popular definition has sometimes been given of common bodily slavery, that it is the holding of property in man. In a kindred language it is called body-property. In this case, a man's body becomes the possession, property, chattel, tool, or thing of another person, and not of the man who lives in it. This foreign person, of course, makes use of it to serve his own ends, without regard to the true welfare, or even the wishes, of the man who lives in that body, and to whom it rightfully belongs. Here the relation is necessarily that of force on one side and suffering on the other, though the force is often modified and the suffering sometimes disguised or kept out of sight.

Now man was made to be free, to govern himself, to be

* Reprinted from the Boston edition of 1843.

his own master, to have no cause stand between him and God, which shall curtail his birthright of freedom. He is never in his proper element until he attains this condition of freedom; of self-government. Of course, while we are children, not having reached the age of discretion, we must be under the authority of our parents and guardians, teachers, and friends. This is a natural relation. There is no slavery in it; no degradation. The parents, exercising rightful authority over their children, do not represent human caprice, but divine wisdom and love. They assume the direction of the child's actions, not to do themselves a service, but to benefit him. The father restrains his child, that the child may have more freedom, not less. Here the relation is not of force and suffering, but of love on both sides; of ability, which loves to help, and necessity, which loves to be directed. The child that is nurtured by its parent gains more than the parent does. So is it the duty of the wise, the good, the holy, to teach, direct, restrain the foolish, the wicked, the ungodly. If a man is wiser, better, and holier than I am, it is my duty, my privilege, my exaltation to obey him. For him to direct me in wisdom and love, not for his sake but for my own, is for me to be free. He may gain nothing by this, but I gain much.

As slavery was defined to be holding property in man, so freedom may be defined as a state in which the man does, of his own consent, the best things he is capable of doing at that stage of his growth. Now there are two sorts of obstacles which prevent, or may prevent, men from attaining to this enviable condition of freedom. These are:—

I. Obstacles external to ourselves, which restrict our freedom; and

II. Obstacles internal to ourselves, which restrict our freedom.

A few words may be said on the condition to which men are brought by each of these classes of objects.

I. Of the slavery which arises from a cause external to ourselves. By the blessing of Providence, seconding the efforts, prayers, tears of some good men, there is no bodily, personal slavery sanctioned by the law amongst us in New England. But at the South we all know that some millions of our fellow-citizens are held in bondage; that men, women, and children are bought and sold in the shambles of the national capital; are owned as cattle; reared as cattle; beaten as cattle. We all know that our fathers fought through the War of Independence with these maxims in their mouths and blazoned on their banners: that all men are born free and equal, and that the God of eternal justice will at last avenge the cause of the oppressed, however strong the oppressor may be; yet it is just as well known that the sons of those very fathers now trade in human flesh, separating parent and child, and husband and wife, for the sake of a little gain; that the sons of those fathers eat bread not in the sweat of their own brow, but in that of the slave's face; that they are sustained, educated, rendered rich, and haughty, and luxurious by the labour they extort from men whom they have stolen, or purchased from the stealer, or inherited from the purchaser. It is known to you all, that there are some millions of these forlorn children of Adam, men whom the Declaration of Independence declares "born free and equal" with their master before God and the Law; men whom the Bible names "of the same blood" with the prophets and apostles; men "for whom Christ died," and who are "statues of God in ebony"—that they are held in this condition and made to feel the full burden of a corrupt society, and doomed from their birth to degradation and infamy, their very name a mock-word; their life a retreat, not a progress,—for the general and natural effect of slavery is to lessen the qualities of a man in the slave as he increases in stature or in years,—their children, their wives, their own bones and sinews at the mercy of a master! That these things are so, is known to all of us; well known from our childhood.

Every man who has ever thought at all on any subject, and has at the same time a particle of manhood in him, knows that this state of slavery would be to him worse than a thousand deaths; that set death in one scale, and hopeless slavery for himself and children in the other, he would not hesitate in his choice, but would say, "Give me death, though the life be ground out of me with the most exquisite tortures of lingering agony that malice can invent or tyranny inflict." To the African thus made the victim of American cupidity and crime, the state of slavery, it will be said, may not appear so degrading as to you and me, for he has never before been civilized, and though the untaught instinct of man bid him love freedom, yet Christianity has not revealed to him the truth, that all men are brothers before God, born with equal rights. But this fact is no excuse or extenuation of our crime. Who would justify a knave in plundering a little girl out of a fortune that she inherited, on the ground that she was a little girl "of tender years," and had never enjoyed or even beheld her birthright? The fact, that the injured party was ignorant and weak, would only enhance and aggravate the offence, adding new baseness and the suspicion of cowardice to guilt. If the African be so low, that the condition of slavery is tolerable in his eyes, and he can dance in his chains—happy in the absence of the whip—it is all the more a sin, in the cultivated and the strong, in the Christian (!) to tyrannize over the feeble and defenceless. Men at the South with the Bible in one hand—with the Declaration of Independence in the other hand—with the words of Jesus, "Love your neighbour as yourself," pealing upon them from all quarters, attempt to justify slavery; not to excuse, to cloak, or conceal the thing, but to vindicate and defend it. This attempt, when made by reflecting men in their cool moments, discovers a greater degree of blackness of heart than the kidnapping of men itself. It is premeditated wickedness grown conscious of itself. The plain truth of the matter is this :—Men who wish for wealth and luxury, but hate the toil and sweat, which are their natural price, brought the African to America; they make his chains; they live by his tears; they dance to the piping of his groans; they fatten on his sweat and are pampered by his blood. If these men spoke as plainly as they must needs think, they would say openly; "our sin captured these men on the African sands; our sin fettered them in slavery; and, please God, our sin shall keep them in slavery till the world ends." This has been thought long enough, it is high time it was said also, that we may know what we are about and where we stand.

Men at the North sometimes attempt to gloss the matter over, and hush it up by saying the least possible on the subject. They tell us that some masters are "excellent

Christians." No doubt it is so, estimating these masters by the common run of Christians,—you find such on the deck of pirate ships; in the dens of robbers. But suppose some slaveholders are as good Christians as Fenelon or St Peter; still a sin is sin, though a Christian commit it. Our fathers did not think "taxation without representation" any the less an evil because imposed by "his most Christian Majesty," a King of Christians.

Then, too, it is said, "the slaves are very happy, and it is a great pity to disturb them," that "the whole mass are better fed and clothed, and are troubled with fewer cares, than working men at the North." Suppose this true also, what then? Do you estimate your welfare in pounds of beef; in yards of cloth; in exemption from the cares of a man! If so all appeal to you is vain, your own soul has become servile. The Saviour of the world was worse fed and clothed, no doubt, than many a Georgian slave, and had not where to lay his head, wearied with many cares; but has your Christianity taught you that was an evil, and the slave's hutch at night, and pottage by day, and exemption from a man's cares by night and day, are a good, a good to be weighed against freedom! Then are you unworthy the soil you stand on; you contaminate the air of New England, which free men died to transmit to their children free!

Still further it is said, "the sufferings of slaves are often exaggerated." This may be true. No doubt there have been exaggerations of particular cases. Every slave-owner is not a demon, not a base man. No doubt there are what are called good Christians, men that would be ornaments to a Christian church, among slaveholders. But though there have been exaggerations in details, yet the awful sum of misery, unspeakable wretchedness, which hangs over two millions of slaves is such that eye hath not seen it; nor ear heard it; nor heart conceived of it. It were so if all their masters were Christians in character, in action, still retaining slaves. How much deeper and wilder must swell that wide weltering sea of human agony, when the masters are what we know so many are, hard-hearted and rapacious, insolent and brutal!

This attempt to gloss the matter over and veil the fact, comes from two classes of men.

1. Some make the attempt from a real design to promote peace. They see no way to abate this mischief; they see "the folly and extravagance" of such as propose "dangerous measures," and therefore they would have us say nothing about it. The writhing patient is very sick; the leech more venturesome than skilful; and the friends, fearful to try the remedy, unwilling to summon wiser advice, declare the sick man is well as ever if you will only let him alone! These men mourn that any one should hold another in bondage; they think our fathers were illustrious heroes, for fighting dreadful wars with the parent country rather than pay a little tax against their will, but that this evil of slavery can never be healed; therefore, in the benevolence of their heart, they refuse to believe all the stories of suffering that reach their ears. The imagination of a kind man recoils at the thought of so much wretchedness; still more, if convinced that it cannot be abated. Now these men are governed by the best of motives, but it does not follow that their opinions are so just as their motives are good.

2. But there are others, who are willing to countenance the sin and continue it, well knowing that it is a sin. They would not have it abated. They tell you of the stupidity of the African; that he is made for nothing but a slave; is allied to the baboon and the ape, and is as much in his place when fettered, ignorant and savage, in a rice field, to toil under a taskmaster's whip, as a New Englander, free and educated, is in his place, when felling forests, planning railroads, or "conducting" a steam-engine. Hard treatment and poor fare, say they, are the black man's due. Besides, they add, there is a natural antipathy between the black race and the white, which only the love of money, or the love of power, on the part of the white is capable of overcoming; that the blacks are an inferior race, and therefore the white Saxons are justified in making them slaves. They think the strong have a right to the services of the weak, forgetting that the rule of reason, the rule of Christianity, is just the other way; "We that are strong ought to bear the infirmities of the weak." They would have us follow the old rule, "that they should get who have the power, and they should keep who can." Of this class nothing further need be said save this: that they

are very numerous, and quote the New Testament in support of slavery, thus contriving to pass for Christians, and have made such a stir in the land that it is scarce safe to open one's mouth and strip the veil from off this sin.

If some one should come and tell us that a new race of men had been discovered living at the bottom of the sea, who had a government which declared that all men were "born free," and a religion which laid down these excellent maxims: that all men were brothers; that God was no respecter of persons; and that man's chief earthly duty was to love and serve his fellow-mortals, keeping the law God Himself had made for man; we should say, what an admirable government! what a beautiful religion! what a free, religious, and blessed people they must be! "Happy is the people that is in such a case. Yea, happy is that people whose God is the Lord." But if we were told that a part of that nation had seized certain men weaker than themselves, whom their government had declared "free," whom their religion called "brothers" to the best of men; that they held these men in bondage, making them do all their masters' work, and receive no recompense, but a wretched life which they were to transmit to their children; and that in the mean time the other part of the nation looked on, and said nothing against this shameful wrong; they encouraged the crime and lent their wisdom, their wealth, and their valour to support and perpetuate this infamous institution; what should we say? Certainly that these men were liars! Liars before their government! Liars before their God! Such is the fact. This people does not live at the bottom of the sea, but on the firm land, and boasts the name of Republic, and Christian Commonwealth!

The opinion of good and religious men here amongst us seems to be, that slavery is a great sin and ought to be abolished as soon as possible; that the talent and piety of the nation cannot be better employed than in devising the speediest and most effectual way of exterminating the evil. Such of them as see a way to abolish the wrong cry aloud and publish the tidings; others who see no way state that fact also, not failing to express their dread of all violent measures. Such is the conviction of good and religious men at the North. But there is another opinion a little different, which is held by a different class of men at the North;—they think that slavery is a great sin, and ought to be kept up so long as men can make money by it. But if the suppression of slavery could be effected—not as our fathers won their freedom, by blood and war—so gently as not to ruffle a sleeping baby's eyelid, yet if it diminished the crop of rice, or cotton, or tobacco, or corn, a single quintal a year, it would be a great mistake to free, cultivate, Christianize, and bless these millions of men! No one, I take it, will doubt this is a quite common opinion here in New England. The cause of this opinion will presently be touched upon. To show what baseness was implied in holding such opinions, would be simply a waste of time.

We all know there is at the North a small body of men, called by various names, and treated with various marks of disrespect, who are zealously striving to procure the liberation of slaves, in a peaceable and quiet way. They are willing to make any sacrifice for this end. They start from the maxim, that slavery is sin, and that sin is to be abandoned at once, and for ever, come what will come of it. These men, it is said, are sometimes extravagant in their speech; they do not treat the "patriarchal institution" with becoming reverence; they call slave-holders hard names, and appeal to all who have a heart in their bosoms, and to some who find none there, to join them and end the patriarchal institution by wise and Christian measures. What wonder is it that these men sometimes grow warm in their arguments! What wonder that their heart burns when they think of so many women exposed to contamination and nameless abuse; of so many children reared like beasts, and sold as oxen; of so many men owning no property in their hands, or their feet, their hearts, or their lives! The wonder is all the other side, that they do not go to further extremities, sinful as it might be, and like St John in his youth, pray for fire to come down from heaven and burn up the sinners, or like Paul, when he had not the excuse of youthful blood, ask God to curse them. Yet they do none of these things; never think of an appeal to the strong arm, but the Christian heart. When a man in this land of ours begins to feel this desperate iniquity and sees the deadness of those around him; the silly game played over his head by political parties and political leaders; the game yet sillier played by theological parties and theological leaders, while the land lies overgrown with "trespasses and sins,"—he may be pardoned if he shrieks over human sufferings and human crime; if he cries out and spares not, but wishes he had a mouth in his hands, and a mouth in his feet, and was speech all over, that he might protest in every limb against this abomination which maketh the heart desolate. There is no doubt that these men are sometimes extravagant! There need be no wonder at that fact. The best of men have their infirmities, but if this extravagance be one of them, what shall we call the deadness of so many more amongst us? An infirmity? What shall we say of the sin itself? An infirmity also? Honest souls engaged in a good work, fired with a great idea, sometimes forget the settled decorum of speech, commonly observed in forum and pulpit, and call sin SIN. If the New Testament tell truth, Paul did so, and it was thought he would "turn the world upside down," while he was only striving to set it right. John the Baptist and Jesus of Nazareth did the same thing, and though one left his head in a charger, and the other his body on a cross, yet the world thinks at this day they did God's great work with their sincerity of speech.

The men who move in this matter encounter opposition from two classes of men; from the moderate, who do not see the wisdom of their measures, and who fear that the slave if set free will be worse off than before, or who think that the welfare of the masters is not sufficiently cared for. These moderate men think "we had better not meddle with the matter at present," but by and by, at a convenient season, they will venture to look into it. Now these moderate men it is not likely would ever think of doing the work until it is all done, yet deserve the gratitude of the public, of the more enthusiastic Abolitionists. A balance wheel is useful to a machine; though it renders more force necessary at first to start the machine, it gives it stability and power when once set a moving. In certain stages of vegetation a chilly day is a most auspicious event.

Then too they encounter opposition from the selfish, who see, or think they see, that the white masters will lose some thousands of millions of dollars, if slavery be abolished! Who has forgotten the men that opposed the introduction of Christianity at Ephesus,—the craftsmen that made silver shrines for Diana!

I know some men say, "we have nothing to do with it. Slavery is the affair of the slave-owners and the slaves, not yours and mine. Let them abate it when they will." A most unchristian saying is this. Slavery! we have something to do with it. The sugar and rice we eat, the cotton we wear, are the work of the slave. His wrongs are imported to us in these things. We eat his flesh and drink his blood. I need not speak of our political connection with slavery. You all know what that is, and its effect on us here. But socially, individually, we are brought into contact with it every day. If there is a crime in the land known to us, and we do not protest against it to the extent of our ability, we are partners of that crime. It is not many years since it was said, temperate men had nothing to do with the sin of drunkenness; though they paid for it out of their purse! When they looked they found they had much to do with it, and sought to end it. I have no doubt, to go back to the Hebrew mythical tale, that when God called Cain, "Where is Abel?" he said, "I have nothing to do with it; that is Abel's affair. Am I my brother's keeper?" If the Law of Moses made it the duty of a Hebrew to lift up the beast of a public enemy which had stumbled in the street, how much more does the Law of God make it a Christian's duty to tell his brother of his sin, and help him out of it; how much more to rescue the oppressed,—"to bind up the broken-hearted; to proclaim liberty to the captives, the opening of the prison to them that are bound?"

Such then is slavery at the South; such the action of men at the North to attack or to defend it. But look a moment at the cause of this sin, and of its defence. It comes from the desire to get gain, comfort, or luxury; to have power over matter, without working or paying the honest price of that gain, comfort, luxury, and power; it is the spirit which would knowingly and of set purpose injure another for the sake of gaining some benefit to yourself. Such a spirit would hold slaves everywhere, if it were possible. Now when the question is put to any fair man,—Is not this spirit active at the North as well as the

South? there is but one answer. The man who would use his fellow-man as a tool merely, and injure him by that use; who would force another in any way to bend to his caprice; who would take advantage of his ignorance, his credulity, his superstition, or his poverty, to enrich and comfort himself; in a word, who would use his neighbour to his neighbour's hurt,—that man has the spirit of slaveholding, and were circumstances but different, he would chain his brethren with iron bonds. If you, for your own sake, would unjustly put any man in a position which degrades him in your eyes, in his own eyes, in the eyes of his fellow-men, you have the spirit of the slave-holder. There is much of this spirit with us still. This is the reason that slavery finds so many supporters amongst us; that we deliver up the fugitives, and "bewray him that wandereth," sheltering ourselves under the plea, that we keep the law of the land, written by man on parchment, half a century ago, while we violate the law of nature, written everlastingly by God on the walls of the world. It was through this spirit,—so genial to our Anglo-Saxon blood,—that our fathers slew the Indians, who would not work, and the Southern planter enslaves the African, who will work. Both acted from the same motives, at North and South; killing or enslaving. That spirit is still with us, and shows itself in many shapes that need not be touched on now. It is not owing so much to our superior goodness, perhaps, as to a fortunate accident, that we have no slaves here at this day. They are not profitable. The shrewd men of our land discerned the fact long ago, and settled the question. Doubtless we have still social institutions which eyes more Christian than ours shall one day look upon as evils, only less than that of slavery itself. But it is gradually that we gain light; he that converts it to life as fast as it comes, does well.

II. Let a word be said on the other kind of slavery; that which comes from a cause internal to ourselves. This is common at the North, and South, and East, and West. In this case the man is prevented from doing what is best for him, not by some other man who has bound him, but by some passion or prejudice, superstition or sin. Here the mischief is in his own heart. If you look around you, you find many that bear the mark of the beast; branded on the forehead and the right hand; branded as slaves. "He that committeth sin is the slave of sin." The avaricious man is a slave. He cannot think a thought but as his master bids. He cannot see a truth if a dollar intervene. He cannot relieve the poor, nor sympathize with the distressed, nor yield to the humane impulse of his natural heart. If he sees in the newspaper a sentence on the wastefulness or the idleness of the poor, he remembers it for ever; but a word in the Bible to encourage charity,— he never finds that.

The passionate man is a slave; he lies at the mercy of the accidents of a day. If his affairs go well he is calm and peaceful; but if some little mistake arise he is filled with confusion, and the demon that rules him draws the chain. This master has many a slave under his yoke. He is more cruel than any planter in Cuba or Trinidad. He not only separates friend from friend, parent from child, and husband from wife, but what is worse yet, prevents their loving one another while they are together. This makes man a tyrant, not a husband; woman a fiend, not an angel, as God made her to be. This renders marriage a necessary evil, and housekeeping a perpetual curse, for it takes the little trifles which happen everywhere, except between angels, and makes them very great matters; it converts mistakes into faults, accidents into vices, errors into crimes; and so rends asunder the peace of families, and in a single twelvemonth disturbs more marriages than all the slave-holders of Carolina in a century.

So the peevish man is a slave. His ill humour watches him like a demon. Ofttimes it casteth him into the fire, and often into the water. In the morning he complains that his caprice is not complied with; in the evening that it is. He is never peaceful except when angry; never quiet but in a storm. He is free to do nothing good, so he acts badly, thinks badly, feels badly,—three attributes of a devil. A yoke of iron and fetters of brass were grievous to bear, no doubt; the whip of a task-master makes wounds in the flesh; but God save us from the tyranny of the peevish, both what they inflict and what they suffer.

The intemperate man also is a slave; one most totally subjugated. His vice exposes him to the contempt and insult of base men, as well as to the pity of the good. Not only this, but his master strips him of his understanding; takes away his common sense, conscience, his reason, religion,—qualities that make a man differ from a beast; on his garments, his face, his wife and child, is written in great staring letters, so that he may read that runs — This man also has sold his birthright and become a slave. The jealous planter forbids his slave to learn; but he cannot take from him the understanding he has got. This refinement of torture it was left for intemperance to exercise, levelling at once the distinctions between rude and polished.

Bodily slavery is one of the greatest wrongs that man can inflict on man; an evil not to be measured by the external and visible woe which it entails on the victim, but by the deep internal ruin which it is its direct tendency to produce. If I had the tongue of the Archangel I could not give utterance to the awfulness of this evil. There is no danger that this be exaggerated,—no more than that the sun in a picture be painted too bright. A wise man would do anything within the compass of righteousness, or suffer a hundred deaths, if that were possible, rather than yield himself a slave, to be the tool and chattel of a master, who views him as a dog. A religious man will do all within the compass of religion to rescue others from a fate so hard. What we can do for this, then, let us do with faith in Him who brings good out of evil. You and I cannot move multitudes of men, but we can each move one, and so contribute our mite to remove the outward obstacles that oppose the freedom of man.

I know men say that you and I ought not to move in this matter; that we have nothing to do with it. They urge in argument that the Constitution of the United States is the supreme law of the land, and that sanctions slavery. But it is the supreme law made by the voters, like the statutes denouncing capital punishment. What voters have made can voters unmake. There is no supreme law but that made by God; if our laws contradict that, the sooner they end or the sooner they are broken, why, the better. It seems to be thought a very great thing to run counter to a law of man, written on parchment; a very little thing to run counter to the law of Almighty God, Judge of the quick and the dead. Has He sanctioned slavery? "Oh yes," say some, and cite Old Testament and New Testament in proof thereof. It has been said, "The devil can quote Scripture for his purpose." We need not settle that question now, but it is certain that men can quote it to support despotism when that is the order of the day,—or freedom when that is the "law of the land;" certain that men defend drunkenness and war, or sobriety and peace, out of its pages. A man finds what he looks for. Now some tell us that Paul said, "Let every soul be subject unto the higher powers," meaning the "law of the land,"—"for the powers that be are ordained of God." Did Paul do so? Not at all; he resisted the very religion established by the powers that were. But it will be said, he did not war directly with slavery, yet lived in the midst of slave-holders. Paul had work enough to do, no doubt, without that of abolishing slavery; perhaps he had not his eyes open to this great sin,—not seeing it as a sin. This is certain, that he thought the world was to end in his own lifetime, and therefore if he did see the wickedness of the "institution," he may have thought it not worth while to attempt to remove what would so soon perish, at the "coming of the Lord." But it is said still further, Jesus himself did not forbid slavery in set speech. Did he forbid by name any one of a hundred other vices that might be mentioned? He did not forbid the excessive use of intoxicating liquors in that way. Nay, we are told in the fourth Gospel that he made three or four barrels of wine—of superior quality too—for a single wedding in a little country town, in Cana of Galilee! Does his silence or his alleged action afford any excuse for that sin also? It is a very sad state of mind in which a man can forget all the principles which Jesus laid down, all the spirit of his doctrine and his life, and then quibble about this,—that he did not forbid slavery in words! Men that cite him in defence of slavery seem to forget the "Sermon on the Mount;" yes, all of his teachings, and would do well to read for their special edification, what is said to their prototypes in the twenty-third chapter of Matthew, and elsewhere.

Bodily slavery, though established by the powers that be, is completely in the hands of the voters, for they are

the powers that be, is no more sanctioned by the supreme law of the land than stealing or murder. No enactment of man can make that right which was wrong before. It can never be abstractly right in any circumstances to do what is abstractly wrong.

But that other slavery, which comes from yourself, that is wholly within your power. And which, think you, is the worse, to be unwillingly the slave of a man and chained and whipped, or to be the voluntary slave of avarice, passion, peevishness, intemperance! It is better that your body be forcibly constrained, bought and sold, than that your soul, yourself, be held in thraldom. The spirit of a slave may be pure as an angel's; sometimes as lofty and as blessed too. The comforts of religion, when the heart once welcomes them, are as beautiful in a slave's cabin as in a king's court. When death shakes off the slave's body, the chain falls with it, and the man, disenthralled at last, goes where the wicked cease from troubling, where the weary are at rest, where the slave is free from his master; yes, where faithful use of the smallest talent and humblest opportunity has its reward, and unmerited suffering finds its ample recompense. But the voluntary slavery under sin—it has no bright side. None in life; in death no more. You may flee from a taskmaster, not from yourself.

Body-slavery is so bad that the sun might be pardoned if it turned back, refusing to shine on such a sin; on a land contaminated with its stain. But soul-slavery, what shall we say of that? Our fathers bought political freedom at a great price; they sailed the sea in storms; they dwelt here aliens on a hostile soil, the world's outcasts; in cold and hunger, in toil and want they dwelt here; they fought desperate wars in freedom's name! Yet they bought it cheap. You and I were base men, if we would not give much more than they paid, sooner than lose the inheritance.

But freedom for the soul to act right, think right, feel right, you cannot inherit; that you must win for yourself. Yet it is offered you at no great price. You may take it who will. It is the birthright of you and me and each of us; if we keep its conditions it is ours. Yet it is only to be had by the religious man—the man true to the nature

God gave him. Without His Spirit in your heart you have no freedom. Resist His law, revealed in nature, in the later scripture of the Bible, in your own soul; resist it by sin, you are a slave, you must be a slave. Obey that law, you are Christ's freeman; nature and God are on your side. How strange it would be that one man should be found on all the hills of New England, of soul so base, of spirit so dastardly, that of his own consent took on him the yoke of slavery; went into the service of sin; toiled with that leprous host, in hopeless unrecompensed misery, without God, without heaven, without hope. Strange, indeed, that in this little village there should be men who care not for the soul's freedom, but consent to live, no, to die daily, in the service of sin.

A LETTER

TO THE PEOPLE OF THE UNITED STATES
TOUCHING
THE MATTER OF SLAVERY.*

FELLOW-CITIZENS OF THE UNITED STATES:

It may seem strange and presumptuous that an obscure man, known even by name to but very few in the land, should write you a public letter on a theme so important as this of slavery. You may call it foolish and rash. Say that if you will; perhaps you are right. I have no name, no office, no rank amongst men, which entitle my thoughts to your consideration. I am but one of the undistinguished millions, who live unnoticed, and die remembered only by their family and friends; humble and obscure. If any of the famous men accustomed to sway the opinions of the political parties and the theological sects, had suitably treated this matter, showing you the facts and giving manly counsel, I should not have presumed to open my mouth. It is their silence which prompts me to speak. I am no aspirant for office or for fame; have nothing to gain by your favour; fear nothing from your frown. In writing this letter I obey no idle caprice, but speak from a sense of duty, in submission to the voice of conscience. I love my country, and my kind; it is patriotism and humanity which bid me speak. I ask you to read and consider, not to read without your prejudices, but with them, with them all; then to consider, to decide, to act, as you may or must. I address myself to no party, to no sect,

* Reprinted from the Boston edition of 1848.

but speak to you, as Americans and as men, addressing my thoughts to all the citizens of the Slave States and the Free.

I am to speak of a great evil, long established, wide spread, deeply rooted in the laws, the usages, and the ideas of the people. It affects directly the welfare of three millions of men, one sixth part of the nation: they are slaves. It affects directly half the States: they are slave-holders. It has a powerful influence on the other half, though more subtle and unseen. It affects the industry, laws, morals, and entire prosperity of the whole nation to a degree exceeding the belief of men not familiar with its history and its facts. The evil increases with a rapid growth; with advancing flood it gains new territory, swells with larger volume; its deadly spray and miasma gradually invade all our institutions. The whole nation is now legally pledged to its support; the public legislation for the last sixty years has made slavery a federal institution. Your revenue boats and your navy are bound to support it: your army acts for its defence. You have fought wars, spending money and shedding blood, to gain new soil wherein to plant the tree of slavery. You have established it in your districts and your territories. You have recently annexed to your realm a new territory as large as the kingdom of France, and extended slavery over that soil whence a semi-barbarous people had expelled it with ignominy. You are now fighting a war in behalf of slavery, a war carried on at great cost of money and of men. The national capital is a great slave market; in her shambles your brothers are daily offered for sale. Your flag floats over the most wicked commerce on earth—the traffic in men and women. Citizens of the United States breed youths and maidens for sale in the market, as the grazier oxen and swine.

The Bey of Tunis has abolished slavery as a disgrace to Africa and the Mahometan religion. Your Constitution of the United States supports this institution, and binds it upon the free States; the South fondly clings to it; the free men of the North bend suppliant necks to this yoke. With a few exceptions, your representatives and senators in Congress give it their countenance and their vote; their hand and their heart. Your great and famous men are pledged to this, or their silence practically purchased. Seven Presidents of your Christian Democracy have been holders of slaves; three only free from that taint. You will soon be called on to elect another slave-holder to sit in the presidential chair, and rule over a republic containing twenty millions of men.

In all the Union there is no legal asylum for the fugitive slave; no soil emancipates his hurrying feet. The States which allow no slavery within their limits legally defend the slave-holder: catch and retain the man fleeing for his manhood and his life.

I cannot call upon the political leaders of the nation. You know what they look for, and how they would treat a letter exposing a national evil, and talking of truth and justice. I do not address you as members of the political parties; they have their great or petty matters to deal with, differing in regard to free trade or protection, but are united in one policy as it respects slavery. Demagogues of both parties will play their little game, and on your shoulders ride into fame, and ease, and wealth, and power, and noise. The sects also have their special work, and need not be addressed on the subject of slavery—of human wrong.

I speak to the people, not as sectarians, Protestant or Catholic—not as Democrats or Whigs, but as Americans and as men. I solemnly believe if you all knew the facts of American slavery and its effects, as I know them, that you would end the evil before a twelvemonth had passed by. I take it for granted that you love justice and truth. I write to you, having confidence in your integrity and love of men, having confidence also in the democratic ideas on which a government should rest.

In what I write you will doubtless find mistakes—errors of fact or of reasoning. I do not ask to be screened from censure even for what no diligence could wholly escape, only that you will not reject nor refuse to consider the truth of fact and of reasoning which is presented to you. A few mistakes in figures or in reasoning will not affect the general argument of this letter. Read with what prejudice you may, but decide and act according to reason and conscience.

I.

STATISTICS AND HISTORY OF SLAVERY.

I WILL first call your attention to the statistics and history of slavery. In 1790 there were but 697,897 slaves in the Union; in 1840, 2,487,355. At the present day their number probably is not far from 3,000,000. In 1790, Mr Gerry estimated their value at $10,000,000; in 1840 Mr Clay fixed it at $1,200,000,000. They are owned by a population of perhaps about 300,000 persons, and represented by about 100,000 voters.

At the time of the Declaration of Independence slavery existed in all the States; it gradually receded from the North. In the religious colonies of New England it was always unpopular and odious. It was there seen and felt to be utterly inconsistent with the ideas and spirit of their institutions, their churches, and their State itself. After the revolution therefore it speedily disappeared—here perishing by default, there abolished by statute. Thus it successively disappeared from Rhode Island, Massachusetts, New Hampshire, New York, Pennsylvania, and New Jersey. By the celebrated Ordinance of 1787, involuntary servitude, except as a punishment after legal conviction of crime, was for ever prohibited in the North-West Territory. Thus the new States, formed in the western parallels, were, by the action of the Federal Government, at once cut off from that institution. Besides, they were mainly settled by men from the eastern States, who had neither habits nor principles which favoured slavery. Thus Ohio, Indiana, Illinois, Michigan, Wisconsin, and Iowa, have been without any legal slaves from the beginning.

In the South the character of the people was different; their manners, their social and political ideas, were unlike those of the North. The Southern States were mainly colonies of adventurers, rather than establishments of men who for conscience' sake fled to the wilderness. Less pains were taken with the education—intellectual, moral, and religious—of the people. Religion never held so prominent a place in the consciousness of the mass as in the sterner and more austere colonies of the North. In the Southern States—New Jersey, Delaware, Maryland, Virginia, the Carolinas, and Georgia,—slavery easily found a footing at an early day. It was not at all repulsive to the ideas, the institutions, and habits of Georgia and South Carolina. The other Southern States protested against it;—they never.

Consequences follow causes; it is not easy to avoid the results of a first principle. The Northern States, in all their constitutions and social structure, consistently and continually tend to Democracy—the government of all, for all, and by all;—to equality before the State and its laws; to moral and political ideas of universal application. In the mean time the Southern States, in their constitutions and social structure, as consistently tend to Oligarchy—the government over all, by a few, and for the sake of that few;—to privilege, favouritism, and class-legislation; to conventional limitations; to the rule of force, and inequality before the law. In such a state of things when slavery comes, it is welcome. In 1787, South Carolina and Georgia refused to accept the Federal Constitution unless the right of importing slaves was guaranteed to them for twenty years. The new States formed in the Southern parallels—Kentucky, Tennessee, Alabama, Mississippi—retaining the ideas and habits of their parents, kept also the institution of slavery.

At the time of forming the Federal Constitution some of the Southern statesmen were hostile to slavery, and would gladly have got rid of it. Economical considerations prevailed in part, but political and moral objections to it extended yet more widely. The Ordinance of 1787, the work mainly of the same man who drafted the Declaration of Independence, passed with little opposition. The proviso for surrendering fugitive slaves came from a Northern hand. Subsequently opposition to slavery, in the North and the South, became less. The culture of cotton, the wars in Europe creating a demand for the productions of American agriculture, had rendered slave labour more valuable. The day of our own oppression was more distant and forgotten. So in 1802, when Congress purchased from Georgia the western part of her territory, it was easy for the South to extend slavery over that virgin soil. In 1803, Louisiana was purchased from France; then, or in 1804, when it was organized into two territories, it would have been easy to apply the Ordinance of 1787, and prevent slavery from extending beyond the original thirteen States. But though some provisions restricting slavery were made, the ideas of that Ordinance were forgotten. Since that time five new States have been formed out of territory acquired since the revolution,—Louisiana, Missouri, Arkansas, Florida, Texas,—all slave States; the last two with constitutions aiming to make slavery perpetual. The last of these was added to the Union on the 22nd of December, 1845, two hundred and twenty-five years after the day when the Forefathers first set foot on Plymouth Rock; while the sons of the Pilgrims were eating and drinking and making merry, the deed of Annexation was completed, and slavery extended over nearly 400,000 square miles of new territory, whence the semi-barbarous Mexicans had driven it out.

Slavery might easily have been abolished at the time of the Declaration of Independence. Indeed in 1744 the Continental Congress, in their celebrated "non-importation Agreement," resolved never to import or purchase any slaves after the last of December in that year. In 1775, they declare in a "Report" that it is not possible "for men who exercise their reason to believe that the Divine Author of our existence intended a part of the human race to hold an absolute property in and unbounded power over others." Indeed the Declaration itself is a denial of the national right to allow the existence of slavery: "We hold these truths to be self-evident, that all men are created equal; that they are endowed by their Creator with certain unalienable rights; that among these are [the right to] life, liberty, and the pursuit of happiness;—that to secure these rights governments are instituted among men deriving their just powers from the consent of the governed."

But the original draft of this paper contained a condemnation yet more explicit: "He [the king of England] has waged cruel war against human nature itself; violating its most sacred rights of life and liberty in the persons of a distant people who never offended him; captivating and carrying them into slavery.... Determined to keep open a market where men should be bought and sold, he has prostituted his negative for suppressing every legislative attempt to prohibit or restrain this execrable commerce." This clause, says its author himself, "was struck out in compliance to South Carolina and Georgia, who had never attempted to restrain the importation of slaves, and who, on the contrary, still wished to continue it. Our northern brethren also, I believe, felt a little tender under these censures; for though their people have very few slaves themselves, yet they had been pretty considerable carriers of them to others."

These were not the sentiments of a single enthusiastic young Republican. Dr Rush, in the Continental Congress, wished "the colonies to discourage slavery and encourage the increase of the free inhabitants." Another member of the American Congress declared, in 1779, "Men are by nature free;" "the right to be free can never be alienated." In 1776, Dr Hopkins, the head of the New England divines, declared that "slavery is, in every instance, wrong, unrighteous, and oppressive; a very great and crying sin."

In the articles of Confederation, adopted in 1778, no provision is made for the support of slavery; none for the delivery of fugitives. Slavery is not once referred to in that document. The General Government had nothing to do with it. "If any slave elopes to those States where slaves are free," said Mr Madison in 1787, "he becomes emancipated by their laws."

In the Convention of 1787, which drafted the present Constitution of the United States, this matter of slavery was abundantly discussed; it was the great obstacle in the way of forming the Union, as now of keeping it. But for the efforts of South Carolina, it is probable slavery would have been abolished by the Constitution. The South claimed the right of sending Representatives to Congress on account of their slaves. Mr Patterson, of New Jersey, contended that as the slaves had no representative or vote at home, their masters could not claim additional votes in Congress on account of the slaves. Nearly all the speakers in that Convention, except the members from South

Carolina and Georgia, referred to the slave-trade with horror. Mr Gerry, of Massachusetts, declared in the Convention, that it was " as humiliating to enter into compact with the slaves of the Southern States, as with the horses and mules of the North." It was contended, that if slaves were men, then they should be taxed as men, and have their vote as men; if mere property, they should not entitle their owners to a vote, more than other property. It might be proper to tax slaves, " because it had a tendency to discourage slavery, but to take them into account in giving representatives tended to encourage the slave-trade, and to make it the interest of the States to continue that infamous traffic." It was said, that " we had just assumed a place among independent nations, in consequence of our opposition to the attempts of Great Britain to enslave us; that this opposition was grounded upon the preservation of those rights to which God and Nature had entitled us, not in particular, but in common with all the rest of mankind. That we had appealed to the Supreme Being for his assistance, as the God of heaven, who could not but approve our efforts to preserve the rights which he had imparted to his creatures; that now, when we had scarcely risen from our knees from supplicating his aid and protection in forming our government over a free people,—a government formed pretendedly on the principles of liberty, and for its preservation,—in that government to have a provision, not only putting it out of its power to restrain or prevent the slave-trade, even encouraging that most infamous traffic, and giving States power and influence in the Union in proportion as they cruelly and wantonly sport with the rights of their fellow-creatures,—ought to be considered as a solemn mockery of, and insult to, that God, whose protection we had then implored, and could not fail to hold us up in detestation, and render us contemptible to every true friend of liberty in the world.

Luther Martin, the attorney-general of Maryland, thought it " inconsistent with the principles of the revolution, and dishonourable to the American character," to have the importation of slaves allowed by the Constitution.

The Northern States, and some of the Southern, wished to abolish the slave-trade at once. Mr Pinckney, of South Carolina, thought that State " would never accede to the

Constitution, if it prohibits the slave-trade;" she "would not stop her importation of slaves in any short time." Said Mr Rutledge, of South Carolina, "the people of the Carolinas and Georgia will never be such fools as to give up so important an interest." "Religion and humanity have nothing to do with this question. Interest alone is the governing principle with nations." In apportioning taxes, he thought three slaves ought to be counted as but one free man; while in apportioning representatives, his colleagues—Messrs Butler and Pinckney—declared, "the blacks ought to stand on an equality with the whites." Mr Pinckney would "make blacks equal to whites in the ratio of representation;" he went further,—he would have "some security against an emancipation of slaves;" and, says Mr Madison, "seemed to wish some provision should be includ 'd [in the Constitution] in favour of property in slaves." "South Carolina and Georgia," said Mr Pinckney, "cannot do without slaves." "The importation of slaves would be for the interest of the whole Union; the more slaves, the more produce to employ the carrying trade, the more consumption also."

On the other hand, Mr Bedford of Delaware thought "South Carolina was puffed up with her wealth and her negroes." Mr Madison, cool and far-sighted, always referring to first principles, was unwilling to allow the importation of slaves till 1808:—"So long a term will be more dishonourable to the American character than to say nothing about it in the Constitution."

Mr Williamson of North Carolina, in 1783, thought "slaves an encumbrance to society," and was "both in opinion and practice against slavery." Col. Maun, of Virginia, in the Convention, called the slave-trade an "infernal traffic," and said that "slavery discourages arts and manufactures; the poor despise labour when performed by slaves." "They produce the most pernicious effect on manners. Every master of slaves is born a petty tyrant. They bring the judgment of Heaven on a country." Mr Dickinson, of Delaware, thought it "inadmissible on every principle of honour and safety that the importation of slaves should be authorized." Gouverneur Morris, of Pennsylvania, "never would concur in upholding domestic slavery." It was a "nefarious institution;" "the curse of Heaven was on the States where it prevailed!" "Are the slaves men? then make them citizens, and let them vote. Are they property? why then is no other property included [in the ratio of representation]? The houses in this city [Philadelphia] are worth more than all the wretched slaves who cover the rice-swamps of South Carolina." Mr Gerry declared we "ought to be careful not to give any sanction to it."

All the North was at first opposed to slavery and the slave-trade. Both parties seemed obstinate; the question of "taxes on exports" and of "navigation laws" remained to be decided. Gouverneur Morris recommended that the whole subject of slavery might be referred to a committee, "including the clauses relating to the taxes on exports and to the navigation laws. These things may form a bargain among the Northern and Southern States." Says Luther Martin, "I found the Eastern States, notwithstanding their aversion to slavery, were very willing to indulge the Southern States, at least with a temporary liberty to prosecute the slave-trade, provided the Southern States would in their turn gratify them by laying no restriction on navigation acts." The North began to understand if the contemplated navigation laws should be enacted, that, as Mr Grayson afterwards said, "all the produce of the Southern States will be carried by the Northern States on their own terms, which must be high." Mr Clymer, of Pennsylvania, declared, "The Western and Middle States will be ruined, if not enabled to defend themselves against foreign regulations;" will be ruined if they do not have some navigation laws giving Americans an advantage over foreign vessels. Mr Gorham of Massachusetts said, "The Eastern States had no motives to union but a commercial one." The proffered compromise would favour their commercial interests. It was for the commercial interest of the South, said Mr Pinckney, to have no restrictions upon commerce, but "considering the loss brought on the Eastern States by the revolution, and their liberal conduct towards the views of South Carolina, [in consenting to allow slavery and the importation of slaves,] he thought that no fetters should be imposed on the power of making commercial regulations, and his constituents would be reconciled to the liberality." So the North took the boon, and winked at the "infernal traffic." When the question was put, there were in favour of the importation of slaves, Georgia, the two Carolinas, and Maryland, with New Hampshire, Massachusetts, and Connecticut. Opposed to it were Pennsylvania, New Jersey, Delaware, and Virginia! Subsequently Mr Ames, in the Massachusetts Convention for the adoption of the Constitution, said the Northern States "have great advantages by it in respect of navigation;" in the Virginia Convention Patrick Henry said, "Tobacco will always make our peace with them," for at that time cotton was imported from India, not having become a staple of the South. When the article which binds the free States to deliver up the fugitive slaves came to be voted on, it was a new feature in American legislation; not hinted at in the "articles of confederation;" hostile to the well-known principles of the common law of England—which always favours liberty—and the usages and principles of modern civilized nations. Yet new as it was and hostile, it seems not a word was said against a the Convention. It "was agreed to, *nem. con.*" Yet "The Northern delegates," says Mr Madison, "owing to their particular scruples on the subject of slavery, did not choose the word slave to be mentioned." In the Conventions of the several States it seems no remonstrance was made to this article.

Luther Martin returning home, said to the House of Delegates in Maryland, "At this time we do not generally hold this commerce in so great abhorrence as we have done; when our liberties were at stake, we warmly felt for the common rights of men; the danger being thought to be past, we are daily growing more insensible to their rights."

When the several States came to adopt the Constitution, some hesitancy was shown at tolerating the slave-trade or even slavery itself. In the Massachusetts Convention, Mr Neal would not "favour the making merchandise of the bodies of men." General Thompson exclaimed, "Shall it be said, that after we have established our own independence and freedom we make slaves of others?" Washington has immortalized himself, "but he holds those in slavery who have as good a right to be free as he has." All parties deprecated the slave-trade in most pointed terms. "Slavery was generally detested." It was thought that the new States could not claim the sad privilege of their parents, that the South itself would soon hate and abolish it. "Slavery is not smitten by an apoplexy," said Mr Dawes, "yet it has received a mortal wound, and will die of consumption." This reflection, with the "tobacco" and "navigation laws," turned the scale. Patrick Henry was no son of New England, but knew well on what hinges her political morality might turn, by what means and which way.

In the New York Convention, Mr Smith could "not see any rule by which slaves were to be included in the ratio of representation, the very operation of it was to give certain privileges to men who were so wicked as to keep slaves;" to which Mr Hamilton replied, that "without this indulgence no union could possibly have been formed. But . . . considering those peculiar advantages which we derived from them, [the Southern States,] it is entirely just that they should be gratified. The Southern States possess certain staples, tobacco, rice, indigo, &c., which must be capital objects in treaties of commerce with foreign nations; and the advantage . . . will be felt in all the States."

In the Pennsylvania Convention, Mr Wilson considered that the Constitution laid the foundation for abolishing slavery out of this country," though the period was more distant than he could wish. Yet "the new States . . . will be under the control of Congress in this particular, and slavery will never be introduced amongst them;" "yet the lapse of a few years, and Congress will have power to exterminate slavery from within our borders."

In the Virginia Convention Gov. Randolph regarded the slave-trade as "infamous" and "detestable." Slavery was one of our vulnerable points. "Are we not weakened by the population of those whom we hold in slavery?" he asked. Col. Mason thought the trade "diabolical in itself and disgraceful to mankind." He would "not admit the Southern States [Georgia and the Carolinas] into the Union unless they agreed to the discontinuance of this disgraceful trade." Mr Tyler thought "nothing could justify it." Patrick Henry, who contended for slavery, confessed "slavery is detested,—we feel its fatal effects,—

we deplore it with all the pity of humanity." "It would rejoice my very soul that every one of my fellow-beings was emancipated." Said Mr Johnson, "Slavery has been the foundation of that impiety and dissipation which have been so much disseminated among our countrymen. If it were totally abolished it would do much good."

In the North Carolina Convention, it was found necessary to apologize for the pro-slavery character of the Constitution. Mr Iredell in defence said, the matter of slavery "was regulated with great difficulty, and by a spirit of concession which it would not be prudent to disturb for a good many years." "It is probable that all the members reprobated this inhuman traffic [in slaves], but those of South Carolina and Georgia would not consent to an immediate prohibition of it." "Were it practicable to put an end to the importation of slaves immediately, it would give him the greatest pleasure." "When the entire abolition of slavery takes place it will be an event which must be pleasing to every generous mind and every friend of human nature." Mr McDowall looked upon the slave-trade "as a very objectionable part of the system." Mr Goudy did not wish "to be represented with negroes."

In the South Carolina Convention, Gen. Pinckney admitted that the Carolinas and Georgia were so weak that they "could not form a union strong enough for the purpose of effectually protecting each other;" it was their policy therefore "to form a close union with the Eastern States who are strong;" the Eastern States had been the greatest sufferers in the revolution, they had "lost everything but their country and their freedom;" "we," the Carolinas and Georgia, "should let them, in some measure, partake of our prosperity." But the union could come only from a compromise; "we have secured an unlimited importation of negroes for twenty years." "We have obtained a right to recover our slaves in whatever part of America they shall take refuge, which is a right we had not before." "We have made the best terms for the security of this species of property it was in our power to make; we would have made better if we could, but on the whole I do not think them bad." No one in South Carolina, it seems, thought slavery an evil.

Thus the Constitution was assented to as " the result of

accommodation," though containing clauses confessedly "founded on unjust principles." The North had been false to its avowed convictions, and in return "higher tonnage duties were imposed on foreign than on American bottoms," and goods imported in American vessels "paid ten per cent. less duty than the same goods brought in those owned by foreigners." The "navigation laws" and the "tobacco" wrought after their kind; South Carolina and Georgia had their way. The North, said Gouverneur Morris, in the national Convention, for the "sacrifice of every principle of right, of every impulse of humanity," had this compensation, "to bind themselves to march their militia for the defence of the Southern States, for their defence against those very slaves of whom they complain. They must supply vessels and seamen in case of foreign attack. The legislature will have indefinite power to tax them by excises and duties on imports."

Still, with many there lingered a vague belief that slavery would soon perish. In the first Congress Mr Jackson, of Georgia, admitted that "it was an evil habit." Mr Gerry and Mr Madison both thought that Congress had "the right to regulate this business," and, "if they see proper, to make a proposal to purchase all the slaves." But the most obvious time for ending the institution had passed by; the feeling of hostility to it grew weaker and weaker as the nation became united, powerful, and rich; its "mortal wound" was fast getting healed.

II.

CONDITION AND TREATMENT OF SLAVES.

I WILL next consider the general condition and treatment of the slaves themselves. The slave is not theoretically considered as a person; he is only a thing, as much so as an axe or a spade; accordingly he is wholly subject to his master, and has no rights—which are an attribute of persons only, not of things. All that he enjoys therefore is but a privilege. He may be damaged but not wronged. However ill treated, he cannot of himself, in his own name and right, bring a formal action in any court, no more than an axe or a spade, though his master may bring an action for damages. The slave cannot appear as a witness when a freeman is on trial. His master can beat, maim, mutilate, or mangle him, and the slave has, theoretically, no complete and legal redress; practically, no redress at all. The master may force him to marry or forbid his marriage; can sell him away from wife and children. He can force the lover to beat his beloved; the husband his wife, the child his parent. "A slave is one who is in the power of his master, to whom he belongs. The master may sell him, dispose of his person, his industry, and his labour; he can do nothing, possess nothing, nor acquire anything but what must belong to his master." No contract between master and slave, however solemnly made and attested, is binding on the master. Is the freeborn child of the freeman likewise theoretically subject to his father?—natural and instinctive affection prevent the abuse of that power. The connection between father and child is one of guardianship and reciprocal love, a mutual gain; that of master and slave is founded only on the interest of the owner; the gain is only on the master's side.

The relation of master and slave begins in violence; it must be sustained by violence—the systematic violence of general laws, or the irregular violence of individual caprice. There is no other mode of conquering and subjugating a man. Regarding the slave as a thing, "an instrument of husbandry," the master gives him the least, and takes the most that is possible. He takes all the result of the slave's toil, leaving only enough to keep him in a profitable working condition. His work is the most he can be made to do; his food, clothing, shelter, amusement, the least he can do with. "A Southern Planter," in his "Notes on Political Economy as applicable to the United States," says to his fellow slave-holders: "You own this labour, can regulate it, work it many or few hours in the day, accelerate it, stimulate it, control it, avoid turn-outs and combinations, and pay no wages. You can dress it plainly, feed it coarsely and cheap, lodge it, on simple forms, as the plantations do, house it in cabins costing little." "The slaves live without beds or houses worth so calling, or family cares, or luxuries, or parade or show; have no relaxations, or whims, or frolics, or dissipations; instead of sun to sun, in their hours are worked from daylight till nine o'clock at night. Where the freeman or labourer would require a hundred dollars a year for food and clothing alone, the slave can be supported for twenty dollars a year, and often is." "Let us bestow upon them the worst, the most unhealthy and degrading sort of duties and labour." Said Mr Jefferson, "the whole commerce between master and slave is a perpetual exercise of the most boisterous passions, the most unremitting despotism on the one part, and degrading submission on the other."

The idea of slavery is to use a man as a thing, against his nature and in opposition to his interests. The consequences of such a principle it is impossible to escape; the results of this idea meet us at every step. Man is certainly not cruel by nature; even in the barbarous state. In our present civilization man is far from being brutal. There are many kind and considerate slave-holders whose aim is to make their slaves as comfortable and happy as it is possible while they are slaves; men who feel and know that slavery is wrong, and would gladly be rid of it; who are not consistent with the idea of slavery. Let us suppose, in this argument, there are ten thousand such who are heads of families in the United States, and ninety thousand of a different stamp, men who have at least the average of human selfishness.

Now under the mildest and most humane of masters, slavery commonly brings intensity of suffering. The slave feels that he is a man, a person, his own person, born with all a man's unalienable rights; born with the right to life, to liberty, and the pursuit of happiness. He sees himself cut off from these rights, and that too amid the wealth, the refinement, and culture of this country and this age. He feels his degradation, born a man to be treated as a thing, bought and sold, beaten as a beast. Here and there is one with a feeble nature, with affections disproportionately strong, attached to an owner who never claimed all the legal authority of master, and this man may not desire his freedom. Some hear of the actual sufferings of the free blacks, or exaggerated reports thereof, and fear that by becoming free in America they might exchange a well-known evil for a greater or a worse. Others have become so debased by their condition that the man is mainly silenced in their consciousness, the animal alone surviving, contented if well fed and not over-worked, and they do not wish to be free. Suppose that these three classes, the feeble-minded, the timid, and the men overwhelmed and crushed by their condition, are as numerous as the humane portion of the masters, are one-tenth of the whole, or 300,000. The rest are conscious of the qualities of a man. They desire their freedom, and are kept in slavery only by external force—the systematic force of public law, the irregular force of private will. The number of this class will be about 2,700,000, a greater number than the whole population of the colonies in 1776.

The condition of the majority of the slaves is indeed terrible. They have no rights, and are to be treated not as men, but only as things; this first principle involves continual violence and oppression, with all the subordinate particulars of their condition, which shall now be touched on as briefly as possible. A famous man said in public, that his "slaves were sleek and fat;" the best thing he could say in defence of his keeping men in bondage. But even this is not always true. Take the mass of slaves together, and an abundance of testimony compels the conviction that they are miserably clad, and suffer bitterly from hunger. So far as food, clothing, and shelter are concerned, the physical condition of the mass of fieldslaves is far worse than that of condemned criminals, in the worst prison of the United States. House-slaves and mechanics in large towns fare better; they are under the eye of the public. Farm-slaves feel most the poignant smart. The plantations are large, the dwellings distant, the ear of the public hears not the oppressor's violence. "The horse fattens on his master's eye," says the proverb; but the farm-slaves are committed mainly to overseers, the Swiss of slavery, whom Mr Wirt calls "the most abject, degraded, and unprincipled race."

Let us pass over the matter of food, clothing, shelter, and toil, to consider other features of their condition. They are treated with great cruelty; often branded with a red-hot iron on the breast, or the shoulder, the arm, the forehead, or the cheek, though the Roman law forbid it fifteen centuries ago. They are disfigured and mutilated, now by the madness of anger, then by the jealous malice of revenge; their backs and sides scored with the lash, or bruised with the " paddle," bear marks of the violence needful to subdue manhood still smouldering in the ashes of the negro slave. Drive Nature out with whips and brands—she will come back. These abuses can be proved from descriptions of run-aways in the newspapers of the South.

The slave-holder's temptation to cruelty is too much for common men. His power is irresponsible. 'Tis easy to find a stick if you would beat a dog. The lash is always at hand; if a slave disobeys,—the whip; if he is idle,—the whip; does he murmur,—the whip; is he sullen and silent, —the whip; is the female coy and reluctant,—the whip. Chains and dungeons also are at hand. The slave is a thing; judge and jury no friends to him. The condition of the weak is bad enough everywhere, in Old England and in New England. But when the strong owns the very bodies of the weak, making and executing the laws as he will—it is not hard to see to what excess their wrongs will amount, wrongs which cannot be told.

It is often said that the evils of slavery are exaggerated. This is said by the masters. But the story of the victim when told by his oppressor—it is well known what that is. The few slaves who can tell the story of their wrongs, show that slavery cannot easily be represented as worse than it is. Imagination halts behind the fact. The lives of Moses Roper, of Lunsford Lane, of Moses Grundy, Frederic Douglas, and W. W. Brown, are before the public, and prove what could easily be learned from the advertisements of Southern newspapers, conjectured from the laws of the Southern States, or foretold outright from a knowledge of human nature itself:—that the sufferings of three millions of slaves form a mass of misery which the imagination can never realize, till the eye is familiar with its terrible details. Governor Giles, of Virginia, calls slavery "a punishment of the highest order." And Mr Preston says, "Happiness is incompatible with slavery."

In the most important of all relations, that of man and

wife, neither law nor custom gives protection to the slave. Their connection may at any moment be dissolved by the master's command, the parties be torn asunder, separated for ever, husband and wife, child and mother; the infant may be taken from its mother's breast, and sold away out of her sight and power. The wife torn from her husband's arms, forced to the lust of another, for the slave is no person, but a thing. For the chastity of the female there is no defence; no more than for the chastity of sheep and swine. Many are ravished in tender years. So is the last insult, and outrage the most debasing, added to this race of Americans. By the laws of Louisiana, all children born of slaves are reckoned as "natural and illegitimate." Marriage is "prostitution;" sacred and permanent neither in the eyes of the churches nor the law. The female slave is wholly in her master's power. Mulattoes are more valuable than blacks. So in the slave States lust now leagues with cupidity, and now acts with singleness of aim. The South is full of mulattoes; its "best blood flows in the veins of the slaves"—masters owning children white as themselves. Girls, the children of mulattoes, are sold at great price, as food for private licentiousness, or public furniture in houses of ill-fame. Under the worst of the Roman emperors this outrage was forbidden, and the Prefect of the city gave such slaves their freedom. But republican parents not rarely sell their own children for that abuse.

After the formal and legal abolition of the African slave trade, it became more profitable to breed slaves for sale in the northern slave-holding States. Their labour was of comparatively little value to the declining agriculture of Delaware, Maryland, Virginia, and North Carolina. From planting they have become, to a great degree, slave-breeding States. The reputed sons of the "Cavaliers" have found a new calling, and the "chivalry of the Old Dominion" betakes itself, not to manufactures, commerce, or agriculture,—but to the breeding of slaves for the southern market. Kentucky and Tennessee have embarked largely in the same adventure. It would be curious to ascertain the exact annual amount of money brought into those States from the sale of their children, but the facts are not officially laid before the public, and a random conjecture, or even a shrewd estimate, is not now to the purpose.

In the latter half of the last century Virginia displayed such an array of talent and statesmanship, of eloquence, of intelligent and manly life in a noble form, as few States with the same population could ever equal; certainly none in America. There were Randolph and Mason, Wythe, Henry, Madison, Jefferson, Marshall, Washington; her very "tobacco" could purchase the peace of New England and New York. Now Virginia is eminent as a nursery of slaves, bred and begotten for the Southern market. Ohio sends abroad the produce of her soil—flour, oxen, and swine; Massachusetts the produce of her mills and manual craft—cottons and woollens, hardware and shoes; while Virginia, chivalrous Virginia, the "Old Dominion," sells in the world's market the produce of her own loins—menservants and maidens; her choicest exports are her sons and daughters. She has borne for the nation five presidents, three of them conspicuous men, famous all over the world; and God knows how many slaves to till the soil of the devouring South. In 1832, it was shown in her legislature that slaves were "all the productive capacity," and "constitute the entire available wealth of Eastern Virginia." The president of William and Mary's College says, "Virginia is a negro-raising State for other States." Thomas Jefferson Randolph pronounced it "one grand menagerie where men are raised for the market like oxen for the shambles." In 1831, it was maintained in her legislature by Mr Gholson, that "the owner of land had a reasonable right to its annual profits; the owner of orchards to their annual fruits; the owner of brood-mares to their products; and the owner of female slaves to their increase."

Is any man born a slave? The Declaration of Independence says, all men are born "equal;" their natural rights "unalienable." It is absurd to say a man was born free in Africa, and his son born a slave in Virginia. The child born in Africa is made a slave by actual theft and personal violence; by what other process can he be made a slave in America? The fact that his father was stolen before him makes no difference. By the law of the United States it is piracy to enslave a man born in Africa; by the law of justice is it less piracy to enslave him when born in Baltimore?

The domestic slave trade is carried on continually in all

the great cities of the South; the capital of the Union, called after "the father of his country," is a great slave mart. Droves of slaves, chained together, may often be seen in the streets of Washington; the advertisements of the dealers are in the journals of that city. There the great demagogues and the great drovers of slaves meet together, and one city is common to them all. If there be degrees in such wrong-doing, it seems worse to steal a baby in America than a man in Guinea; worse to keep a gang of women in Virginia, breeding children as swine for market, than to steal grown men in Guinea; it is cowardly no less than inhuman. But so long ago as 1829, it was said in the Baltimore Reporter, "Dealing in slaves has become a large business, establishments are made in several places in Maryland, at which they are sold like cattle; these places of deposit are strongly built, and well supplied with iron thumb-screws and gags, and ornamented with cowskins and other whips, often bloody.

The African slave trader perhaps even now is not unknown at Baltimore or New Orleans, but he is a pirate; he shuffles and hides, goes sneaking and cringes to get along amongst men, while the American slave-trader goes openly to work, advertises "the increase of his female slaves," erects his jail, and when that is insufficient, has those of the nation thrown open for his use, and all the States solemnly pledged to deliver up the fugitives who escape from his hands. He marches his coffles where he will. The laws are on his side, "public sentiment" and the "majesty of the Constitution." He looks in at the door of the Capitol and is not ashamed.

There are mean men engaged in that traffic who "are generally despised even in the slave-holding States," but men of property and standing are also concerned in this trade. Mr Erwin, the son-in-law of Mr Clay, it is said, laid the foundation of a large fortune by dealing in slaves; General Jackson was a dealer in slaves, and so late as 1811, bought a coffle and drove them to Louisiana for sale.

In this transfer of slaves, the most cruel separation of families takes place. In the slave-breeding States it is a common thing to sell a boy or a girl while the mother is kept as a "breeder." Does she complain of the robbery? —There is the scourge, there are chains and collars. Will the husband and father resent the wrong?—There are handcuffs and jails; the law of the United States, the Constitution, the Army and Navy, all the able-bodied men of the free States, are legally bound to come, if need be, and put down the insurrection. Yet, more than fifteen hundred years ago, a Roman Emperor forbid the separation of families of slaves, and ordered all which had been separated to be reunited. "Who can bear," said the Emperor to his heathen subjects, "who can bear that children should be separated from their parents, sisters from their brothers, wives from their husbands?"

In 1836, the Presbyterian Synod of Kentucky said to the world: "Brothers and sisters, parents and children, husbands and wives, are torn asunder and permitted to see each other no more. These acts are daily occurring in the midst of us. There is not a neighbourhood where these heart-rending scenes are not displayed. There is not a village or road which does not behold the sad procession of manacled outcasts, whose chains and mournful countenances tell that they are exiled by force from all that their hearts held dear." The affections are proportionally stronger in the Negro than the American; his family is his all. The terror of being sold and thus separated from the companion of his sad misfortune, hangs over the slave for ever, at least till too old for service in that way. The most able-minded are of course the most turbulent, the most difficult to manage, and therefore the most commonly sold. But the angel of death—to them the only angel of mercy—benignantly visits these poor Ishmaels in the hot swamps of Georgia and Alabama. Thou-God-seest-me, were fitting inscription over the spot where the servant thus becomes free from his master and the weary is at rest.

III.

EFFECTS OF SLAVERY ON INDUSTRY.

LET us examine the effects of slavery on industry in all its forms. In the South, manual labour is considered menial and degrading; it is the business of slaves. In the free States the majority work with their hands, counting it the natural business of a man, not a reproach, but a duty and a dignity. | Thus in Boston—the richest city of its population in America, and perhaps in the world—out of 19,037 private families in 1845, there were 15,744 who kept no servant, and only 1069 who had more than one assistant to perform their household labour. In the South the freeman shuns labour; "in a slave country every freeman is an aristocrat," and of course labour is avoided by such. Where work is disgraceful, men of spirit will not submit to it. So the high-minded but independent freemen are continually getting worse off, or else emigrating out of the slave States into the new free States,—not as the enterprising adventurer goes from New England, because he wants more room, but because his condition is a reproach.

Most of the productive work of the South is done by slaves. But the slave has no stimulus; the natural instinct of production is materially checked. The master has the mouth which consumes, the slave only the hand which earns. He labours not for himself, but for another; for another who continually wrongs him. His aim, therefore, is to do the least he can get along with. He will practise no economy; no thrift; he breaks his tools. He will not think for his master; it is all hand-work, for he only gives what the master can force from him, and he cannot conceal; there is no head-work. There is no invention in the slave; little among the masters, for their business is to act on men, not directly on things. This circumstance may fit the slave-holder for politics—of a certain character; it unfits him for the great operations of productive industry. They and all labour-saving contrivances come from the North. In 1846 there were seventy-six patents granted by the national office for inventions made in fourteen slave States, with a population of 7,334,431, or one for each 96,505 persons; at the same time there were 564 granted to the free States with a population of 9,728,922, or one for each 17,249 persons. Maryland, by her position, partakes more of the character of the free States than most of her sisters, and accordingly made twenty-one inventions—more than a fourth part of all made in the South. But Massachusetts had made sixty-two; and New York, with a population of only 2,428,921, had received two hundred and forty-seven patent-rights—more than three times as many as the whole South. Works which require intelligence and skill require also the hand of the freeman. The South can grow timber, it is the North which builds the ships. The South can rear cotton, the free intelligence of the North must weave it into cloth.

In the North the freeman acts directly upon things by his own will; in the South, only through the medium of men reduced to the rank of things, and they act on material objects against their will. Half the moral and intellectual effect of labour is thereby lost; half the productive power of the labour itself. All the great movements of industry decline where the aristocracy own the bodies of the labouring class. No fertility of soil or loveliness of climate can ever make up for the want of industry, invention, and thrift in the labouring population itself. Agriculture will not thrive as under the freeman's hand. Slave labour can only be profitably employed in the coarse operations of field-work. It was so in Italy 2000 years ago; the rich gardens of Latium, Alba, Tuscany, were the work of freemen. When their owners were reduced to slavery by the Roman conqueror, those gardens became only pastures for buffalos and swine. Only coarse staples, sugar, cotton, rice, corn, tobacco, can be successfully raised by the slave of America. His rude tillage impoverishes the soil; the process of tilth "consists in killing the land." They who will keep slavery as a "patriarchal institution," must adopt the barbarism of the patriarchs, become nomadic, and wander from the land they have exhausted to some virgin soil. The freeman's fertilizing hand enriches the land the longer he labours.

In Maryland, Virginia, and the Carolinas, the soil is getting exhausted; the old land less valuable than the new. In 1787, said Gouverneur Morris, in the national Convention, "Compare the free regions of the Middle States, where a rich and noble cultivation marks the prosperity and happiness of the people, with the misery and poverty which overspread the barren wastes of Virginia, Maryland, and the other States having slaves. Travel through the whole Continent, and you behold the prospect continually varying with the appearance and disappearance of slavery. The ւ oment you leave the Eastern States and enter New York, the effects of the institution ˛become visible. Passing through the Jerseys and entering Pennsylvania, every criterion of superior improvement witnesses the change. Proceed southwardly, and every step you take through the great regions of slaves, presents a desert increasing with the increasing proportion of these wretched beings." At this day, sixty years later, the contrast is yet more striking, as will presently appear. Slavery has wrought after its way. Every tree bears its own fruit.

Slavery discourages the immigration of able but poor men from the free States. They go elsewhere to sell their labour; all the Southern States afford proof of this. The freeman from the North will not put himself and his intelligent industry on a level with the slave, degraded and despised. In the free States the farmer buys his land and his cattle; hires men to aid him in his work—he buys their labour. Both parties are served—this with labour, that with employment. There is no degradation, but reciprocal gain. In a few years the men who at first sold their labour will themselves become proprietors, and hire others desirous of selling their services. It requires little capital to start with. So the number of proprietors rapidly increases, and the amount of cultivated land, of wealth, of population, of comfort. In the South the proprietor must also buy his workmen; the poor man who seeks a market for his work, not his person, must apply elsewhere.

This cause has long impeded the agriculture of the South; it will also hinder the advance of manufactures. At Lowell the manufacturer builds his mill, buys his cotton, and reserves a sufficient sum for his "floating capital;" he hires five hundred men and women to work his machinery, paying t n from week to week for the labour he has bought. In South Carolina he must buy his operatives also; five hundred slaves at $600 each, amount to $300,000. This additional sum is needed before a wheel can turn. To start, it requires large capital; but capital is what is not so easily obtained in a slave State, where there is no natural stimulus urging the labouring mass to production. Men of small capital are kept out of the field; business is mainly in the hands of the rich; property tends to accumulate in few hands.

Compare a slave and a free State: in the free population of the former there is less enterprise; less activity of body and mind; less intelligence; less production; less comfort, and less welfare. In the free States an enterprising man whose own hands are not enough for him to work out his thoughts with, can trade in human labour, buying men's work and seeing the result of that work. That is the business of the merchant-manufacturer in all departments. In the present state of society both parties are gainers by the operation. In the South, such a man must buy the labourers before he can use their work, but intelligent labour he cannot thus buy.

Men are born with different tastes and tendencies—some for agriculture, others for commerce, navigation, manufactures, for science, letters, the arts, useful or elegant. The master is able to command the muscles, not to develope the mind. He directs labour mainly to the coarser operations c husbandry, and makes work monotonous. Uniformity . labour involves a great loss. Political economists know well the misery which happens to Ireland from this source—not to mention others and worse.

In Connecticut, every farmer and day-labourer, in his family or person, is a consumer not only of the productions of his own farm or handiwork, but also of tea, coffee, sugar, rice, molasses, salt, and spices; of cotton, woollen, and silk goods, ribbons and bonnets; of shoes and hats; of beds and other furniture; of hard-ware, tin-ware, and cutlery; of crockery and glass ware; of clocks and jewelry; of books, paper, and the like. His wants stimulate the mechanic and the merchant; they stimulate him in return, all grow up together; each has a market ome, a market continually enlarging and giving vent to superior wares. The young man can turn his hand to the art he likes best. Industry, activity, intelligence, and comfort are the result.

In a slave population the reverse of all this takes place. The "Southern planter" thinks $20 adequate for the yearly support of a slave. Add twenty-five per cent. to his estimate, making the sum $25: then the 3,000,000 slaves are consumers to the amount of dls 75,000,000 a year. In 1845 the annual earnings of the State of Massachusetts were dls 114,492,636. This does not include the improvements made on the soil, nor bridges, nor railroads, highways, houses, shops, stores, and factories that were built—these things form a permanent investment for future years. It cannot reasonably be supposed that, in addition, so large a sum as fourteen per cent. of the annual earnings is saved and laid by. But on that supposition, the 737,699 inhabitants of Massachusetts are consumers to the amount of dls 100,000,000 a year; that is, dls 25,000,000 more than four times that number of slaves would consume. The amount of additional energy, comfort, and happiness is but poorly indicated even by these figures.

In the present age, slavery can compete successfully with free labour only under rare circumstances. The population must be sparse; perhaps not exceeding fifty persons to the square mile. But in the nice labour and minute division of employment, in the economy and the improved methods of cultivation, consequent on a dense population, slavery ceases to be profitable; the slave will not pay for rearing. It must be on a soil extraordinarily fertile, which the barbarous tillage of the slave cannot exhaust. Some of the rich lands of Georgia, Alabama, Louisiana, and Mississippi are of this character. Then it must have the monopoly of some favourite staple, which cannot be produced elsewhere. A combination of those three conditions may render slavery profitable even at this day, yet by no means so profitable as the work of the freeman. Mr Rutledge was not far from right in 1787, when he contended that, in direct taxation, a slave should pay but one third as much as a freeman, his labour being only of one third the value of a freeman's.

In the Northern States, the freeman comes directly in contact with the material things which he wishes to convert to his purpose. To shorten his labour he makes his head save his hands. He invents machines. The productive capacity of the free States is extended by their use of wind, water, and steam for the purposes of human labour. That is a solid gain to mankind. Wind-mills, water-mills, steam-engines, are the servants of the North; homebred slaves born in their house, the increase of fertile heads.

These are an important element in the power and wealth of a nation. While South Carolina has taken men from Africa, and made slaves, New England has taken possession of the winds, of the waters; she has kidnapped the Merrimack, the Connecticut, the Androscoggin, the Kennebeck, the Penobscot, and a hundred smaller streams. She has caught the lakes of New Hampshire, and holds them in thrall. She has seized fire and water, joined them with an iron yoke, and made an army of slaves, powerful, but pliant. Consider the machinery moved by such agents in New England, New York, Pennsylvania; compare that with the human machines of the South, and which is the better drudge? The " Patriarchal Institution of slavery" and the economic institution of machinery stand side by side,—this representing the nineteenth century before Christ, and that the nineteenth century after Christ. They run for the same goal, though slavery started first and had the smoother road. It is safe to say, that the machinery of the free States has greater productive ability than the 3,000,000 bondmen of the South. While slavery continues, the machinery will not appear. Steam-engines and slaves come of a different stock.

The foreign trade of the South consists mainly in the export of the productions of the farm and the forest; the domestic trade, in collecting those staples and distributing the articles to be consumed at home. Much of the domestic trade is in the hands of Northern men—though mainly "with Southern principles." The foreign trade is almost wholly in the hands of foreigners, or men from the North, and is conducted by their ships. In the South, little is demanded for home consumption; so the great staples of Southern production find their market chiefly in the North, or in foreign ports. The shipping is mainly owned by the North. Of the Atlantic States seven have no slaves: Maine, New Hampshire, Massachusetts, Rhode Island, Connecticut, New York, and New Jersey; in 1846, they, with Pennsylvania, had 2,160,501 tons of shipping. In 11 the slaves States which lie on the seaboard, there are owned but 401,583 tons of shipping. In 1846, the young State of Ohio, two thousand miles from the sea, had 39,917 tons; the State of South Carolina, 32,588. Even Virginia, full of bays and harbours, had but 53,441 tons. The single district of the city of New York had 572,522 tons, or 70,939 more than all the Southern States united.

The difference in the internal improvements of the two sections is quite as remarkable. In general, the public highways in the slave-holding States are far inferior to those of the North, both in extent and character. If the estimates made are correct, in 1846 there were, omitting the fractions, 5663 miles of railroad actually in operation in the United States. In all the slave States together there were 2090 miles. Taking the cost of such as are described in trustworthy sources, and estimating the value of those not so described by the general cost per mile of railroads in the same State, then the slave States have invested dls 43,910,183 in this property. In the free States there were 3573 miles of railroad, which had cost dls 112,914,465 Thus the ^ree States have 1483 miles of railroad more than the South, the value of which is dls 69,004,282 above the value of all the railroads of the slave States. The railroads in Pennsylvania have cost dls 43,426,385 ; within less than half a million of the value of all the railroads in all the slave States. Maryland, from her position, resembles the free States in many respects. Besides those of this State, all the railroads of the South are worth only dls 27,717,835, while those of Massachusetts alone have cost dls 30,341,444, and are now, on the average, five or six per cent. above par. The State of South Carolina has only paid dls 5,671,452 for her railroad stock. I will not undertake to estimate its present value. Nor need I stop to inquire how many miles of the Southern roads have been planned by Northern skill, paid for by the capital of the free States, and are owned by their citizens!

Let us next consider the increase of the value of the landed property in the free and the slave States. In 1798, the value of all the houses and lands in the eight slave States, that is, Delaware, Maryland, Virginia, North and South Carolina, Georgia, Kentucky, and Tennessee, was estimated at dls 197,742,557 ; that of the houses and lands in the eight free States—New Hampshire, Vermont, Massachusetts, Connecticut, Rhode Island, New Jersey, New York, and Pennsylvania—was dls 422,235,780. It is not easy to ascertain exactly the value of real property in all these States at this moment. But in 1834-6, the government of New York, and in 1839, that of Virginia, made a new valuation of all the real property in their respective States. In 1798, all the real estate in Virginia was worth $71,225,127; in 1839, $211,930,538. In 1798, all the real property in the State of New York was worth $100,380,707; in 1835, $430,751,273. In Virginia there had been an increase of 195·7 per cent. in forty one years; in New York, an increase of 329·9 per cent. in thirty-seven years.

For convenience' sake let us suppose each of the eight Southern States has gained as rapidly as Virginia, and each of those eight Northern, in the same ratio with New York—and what follows? In 1798, the real estate in South Carolina was valued at $17,465,013; that of Rhode Island at $11,066,358. By the above ratios, the real estate in South Carolina was worth $51,958,393 in 1839; and in 1835, that of Rhode Island was worth $47,574,288. Thus the real property in the leading slave State of the Union, with a population of 594,398, was worth but $4,384,105 more than the real property of Rhode Island, with a population of only 108,830. In 1840 the aggregate real property in the city of Boston was valued at $60,424,200, and in 1847 at $97,764,500, — $45,271,120 more than the computed value of all the real estate in South Carolina. In 1798, the value of the aggregate real property of the eight slave States was $197,742,557; of the eight free, $422,235,780; in 1839, by the above ratios, the real estate of the Southern States would be worth $588,289,107, and that of the Northern $1,715,201,618. Thus the real property of these eight free States would be almost three times more valuable than the eight slave States, yet the free contain but 170,150 square miles, while the slave States contain 212,920. But this, in part, is a matter of calculation only, and liable to some uncertainty, as the ratio of Virginia and New York may not represent the increase of any either South or North. Let us come to public and notorious facts.

In 1839, the value of all the annual agricultural products of the South, as valued by the last census, was $312,380,151; that of the free States $342,007,446. Yet in the South there were 1,984,866 persons engaged in agriculture, and in the North only 1,785,086, and the South has the advantage of raising tropical productions, which cannot be grown in Europe. The agricultural products of the South which find their way to foreign lands, are mainly cotton, sugar, rice, and tobacco. The entire value of these articles raised in the fifteen slave States in that year, was $74,866,310; while the agricultural productions, the single State of New York amounted in the year to $108,275,281.

The value of articles manufactured in the South was $42,178,184; in the free States $197,658,040. In the slave States there were, in various manufactories, 246,601 spindles; in Rhode Island, the smallest of the free States, 518,817. The aggregate annual earnings of all the slave States was $403,429,718; of the free, $658,705,108. The annual earnings of six slave States—North Carolina, South Carolina, Georgia, Alabama, Mississippi, and Louisiana, amount to $189,321,719; those of the State of New York to $193,806,433, more than $4,000,000 above the income of six famous States. The annual earnings of Massachusetts alone are more than $9,000,000 greater than the united earnings of three slave States,—South Carolina, Georgia, and Florida. The earnings of South Carolina, with her population of 594,398, about equals that of the county of Essex, in Massachusetts, with less than 95,000.

In 1839, in the South there were built houses to the value of $14,421,441; and in the North, to the value of $27,496,560. The ships built by the South that year were valued at $704,289; by the North, at $6,301,805.

In 1846, the absolute debt of all the free States was $109,176,527. The actual productive State-property of those States, including the school fund, was $96,630,285,—leaving the actual indebtedness above their State-property only $10,546,242. The absolute debt of the slave States was $55,948,373; their productive State-property, including their school funds, $30,294,428—leaving their actual indebtedness above their State-property $25,653,945, more than twice the corresponding indebtedness of the North.

Besides this, it must be remembered that in the free States there are 45,569 men engaged in the learned professions, while in the slave States there are but 20,292. In addition to that, in all the free States there are many employed in teaching common schools. Thus, in 1847, in Massachusetts, there were 7,582 engaged in the common schools. In the slave States this class is much smaller. Still more, in all the free States there are many, not ranked in the learned professions, who devote themselves to science, literature, and the fine arts; in the South but few. In the South, the female slaves are occupied in hard field-labour, which is almost unheard-of in the free States. Thus the difference in the earnings of the two, great as it is, is not an adequate emblem of the actual difference or productive capacity, or even of the production, in the two sections of the country.

IV.

EFFECTS OF SLAVERY ON POPULATION.

LET us next consider the effects of slavery on the increase of numbers, as shown by the great movements of the population in the North and South.

In 1790, the present free States—New England, New York, New Jersey, and Pennsylvania—contained 1,968,455 persons; the slave States 1,961,372. In 1840 the same slave States—Delaware, Maryland, Virginia, North Carolina, South Carolina, Georgia, Kentucky—contained 5,479,860; the same free States, 6,767,082. In 50 years those slave States had increased 179 per cent.; those free States 243 per cent., or with 64 per cent. greater rapidity.

In 1790 the entire population of all the slave States was 1,961,372; in 1840, including the new slave States, 7,334,431; while the population of the free States—including the new ones—was 9,728,922. The slave States had increased 279 per cent.; the free, 394, the latter increasing with a rapidity 115 per cent. greater than the former.

In 1810 the new slave States—Louisiana, Mississippi, Alabama, Arkansas, Tennessee, Missouri, and Kentucky—contained 805,991 persons; the new free States—Ohio, Indiana, Illinois, Michigan—contained but 272,324. But in 1840 those new slave States, with the addition of Florida, contained 3,409,132, while the population of the new free States—with the addition of Wisconsin and Iowa —contained 2,937,840. In 50 years the new slave States had increased 323 per cent., and the new free States 1090 per cent.

In 1790, the whole free population of the present free States was 1,930,125; the free population of the present slave States and territories was 1,394,847. The difference in the number of free persons in the North and South was only 535,278. But in 1840 the free population of the free States and territories was 9,727,893; the free population of the slave States and territories only 4,848,105; the difference between the two was 4,879,788. In 50 years the free persons in the slave States had increased 247 per cent.; the free persons of the free States 404 per cent. It is true something has been added to the North by immigrations from abroad, but the accessions which the South has received by the purchase of Louisiana and Florida, by the immigration of enterprising men from the North, and by the importation of slaves, is perhaps more than adequate to balance the Northern increase by foreign immigration.

The Southern States have great advantages over the Northern in soil, climate, and situation; they have a monopoly of the tropical productions so greatly sought by all northern nations; they have superior facilities for the acquisition of wealth, and through that for the rapid increase of population. In some countries the advance of both is retarded by oppressive legislation. Of this the South cannot complain, as it will by and by appear. The new land lay nearer to the old Southern States than the old free States, and that not "infested with Indians" to the same extent with the soil since conquered and colonized by the emigrants from the Northern States. The difference of the increase of the two in wealth and numbers is to be ascribed, therefore, to the different institutions of the two sections of the land.

V.

EFFECTS OF SLAVERY ON EDUCATION.

LET us now look at the effects of slavery on the intellectual, moral, and religious development of the people. The effect on the intellectual, moral, and religious condition of the slave is easily understood. He is only continued in slavery by restraining him from the civilization of mankind in this age. His mind, conscience, soul—all his nobler powers—must be kept in a state of inferior development, otherwise he will not be a slave in the nineteenth century, and in the United States. In comparison with the intellectual culture of their masters the slaves are a mass of barbarians; still more emphatically, when compared with the free institutions of the North, they are savages. This is not a mere matter of inference, the fact is substantiated by the notorious testimony of slave-holders themselves. In 1834 the Synod of South Carolina and Georgia reported that the slaves "may justly be considered the heathen of this country, and will bear comparison with the heathen of any part of the world." "They are destitute of the privileges of the Gospel, and ever will be under the present state of things." "In all the slave States," says the Synod, "there are not twelve men exclusively devoted to the religious instruction of the Negroes." Of the regular ministers " but a very small portion pay any attention to them." "We know but of five churches in the slave-holding States built exclusively for their use," and " there is no sufficient room for them in the white churches for their accommodation." "They are unable to read, as custom, or law, and generally both, prohibit their instruction. They have no Bible—no family altars; and when in affliction, sickness, or death, they have no minister to address to them the consolations of the Gospel, nor to bury them with solemn and appropriate services." They may sometimes be petted and caressed as children and toys, they are never treated as men.

"Heathenism," says another Southern authority, "is as real in the slave States as in the South Sea Islands." "Chastity is no virtue among them [the slaves]; its violation neither injures female character in their own estimation nor that of their mistress." Where there is no marriage recognized by the State or Church as legal or permanent between slaves; where the female slave is wholly in her master's power—how can it be otherwise? Said the Roman proverb, "Nothing is unlawful for the master to his slave." When men are counted as things, instruments of husbandry, separable limbs of the master, and retained in subjugation by external force and the prohibition of all manly culture, the effect of slavery on its victim is so obvious that no more need be said thereof.

The effect of slavery on the intellectual, moral, and religious condition of the free population of the South is not so obvious perhaps at first sight. But a comparison with the free States will render that also plain.

All attempts at the improvement of the humbler and more exposed portions of society, the perishing and dangerous classes thereof, originate in the free States. It is there that men originate societies for the Reform of Prisons, the Prevention of Crime, Pauperism, Intemperance, Licentiousness, and Ignorance. There spring up Education Societies, Bible Societies, Peace Societies, Societies for teaching Christianity in foreign and barbarous lands. There, too, are the learned and philosophical societies, for the study of Science, Letters, and Art. Whence come the men of superior education who occupy the pulpits, exercise the professions of Law and Medicine, or fill the chairs of the Professors in the Colleges of the Union? Almost all from the North, from the free States. There is preaching everywhere. But search the whole Southern States for the last seven-and-forty years, and it were hard to show a single preacher of any eminence in any pulpit of a slave-holding State; a single clergyman remarkable for ability in his calling, for great ideas, for eloquence, elsewhere so cheap —or even for learning! Even Expositions and Commentaries on the Bible, the most common clerical productions, are the work of the North alone.

Whence come the distinguished authors of America? the Poets—Bryant, Longfellow, Whittier; Historians—

Sparks, Prescott, Bancroft; Jurists—Parsons, Wheaton, Story, Kent! Whence Irving, Channing, Emerson;—whence all the scientific men, the men of thought, who represent the nation's loftier consciousness? All from the free States; north of Mason and Dixon's line!

Few works of any literary or scientific value have been written in this country in any of the slave States; few even get reprinted there. Compare the works which issue from the press of New Orleans, Savannah, Charleston, Norfolk, Baltimore, with such as come from Philadelphia, New York, and Boston—even from Lowell and Cincinnati; compare but the booksellers' stock in those several cities, and the difference between the cultivation of the more educated classes of the South and North is apparent at a glance.

But leaving general considerations of this sort, let us look at facts. In 1671, Sir William Berkely, Governor of Virginia, said, "I thank God that there are no free schools nor printing-presses [in Virginia], and I hope we shall not have them these hundred years." In 1840, in the fifteen slave States and territories there were at the various primary schools 201,085 scholars; at the various primary schools of the free States 1,626,028. The State of Ohio alone had 218,609 scholars at her primary schools, 17,524 more than all the fifteen slave States. South Carolina had 12,520 such scholars, and Rhode Island 17,355. New York alone had 502,367.

In the higher schools there were in the South, 35,935 "scholars at the public charge," as they are called in the census; in the North, 432,388 similar scholars. Virginia, the largest of the slave States, had 9791 such scholars; Rhode Island, the smallest of the free States, 10,749. Massachusetts alone had 158,351, more than four times as many as all the slave States.

In the slave States, at academies and grammar schools, there were 52,906 scholars; in the free states, 97,174. But the difference in numbers here does not represent the difference of fact, for most of the academies and grammar schools of the South are inferior to the "schools at public charge" of the North; far inferior to the better portion of the northern "district schools."

In 1840 there were at the various colleges in the South,

7106 pupils, and in the free States, 8927. Here, too, the figures fail to indicate the actual difference in the numbers of such as receive a superior education; for the greater part of the eighty-seven "Universities and Colleges" of the South are much inferior to the better Academies and high schools of the North.

In the libraries of all the Universities and Colleges of the South there are 223,416 volumes; in those of the North, 593,897. The libraries of the Theological schools of the South contain 22,800 volumes; those of the North, 102,080. The difference in the character and value of these volumes does not appear in the returns.

In the slave States there are 1,368,325 free white children between the ages of five and twenty; in the free States, 3,536,689 such children. In the slave States, at schools and colleges, there are 301,172 pupils; in the free States, 2,212,444 pupils, at schools or colleges. Thus, in the slave States, out of twenty-five free white children between five and twenty, there are not quite five at any school or college; while out of twenty-five such children in the free States, there are more than fifteen at school or college.

In the slave States, of the free white population that is over twenty years of age, there is almost one tenth part that are unable to read and write; while in the free States there is not quite one in one hundred and fifty-six who is deficient to that degree.

In New England there are but few born therein and more than twenty years of age, who are unable to read and write; but many foreigners arrive there with no education, and thus swell the number of the illiterate, and diminish the apparent effect of her free institutions. The South has few such emigrants; the ignorance of the Southern States therefore is to be ascribed to other causes. The Northern men who settle in the slave-holding States, have perhaps about the average culture of the North, and more than that of the South. The South therefore gains educationally from immigration as the North loses.

Among the Northern States, Connecticut, and among the Southern States, South Carolina, are to a great degree free from disturbing influences of this character. A comparison between the two will show the relative effects of the respective institutions of the North and South. In Connecticut, there are 163,843 free persons over twenty years of age; in South Carolina but 111,663. In Connecticut, there are but 526 persons over twenty who are unable to read and write, while in South Carolina there are 20,615 free white persons over twenty years of age unable to read and write. In South Carolina, out of each 626 free whites more than twenty years of age, there are more than 58 wholly unable to read or write; out of that number of such persons in Connecticut, not quite two! More than the sixth part of the adult freemen of South Carolina are unable to read the vote which will be deposited at the next election. It is but fair to infer that at least one third of the adults of South Carolina, if not of much of the South, are unable to read and understand even a newspaper. Indeed, in one of the slave States, this is not a matter of mere inference, for in 1837 Gov. Clarke, of Kentucky, declared, in his message to the legislature, that "one third of the adult population were unable to write their names;" yet Kentucky has a "school-fund," valued at $1,221,819, while South Carolina has none.

One sign of this want of ability even to read, in the slave States, is too striking to be passed by. The staple reading of the least cultivated Americans is the newspapers, one of the lowest forms of literature, though one of the most powerful, read even by men who read nothing else. In the slave States there are published but 377 newspapers, and in the free 1135. These numbers do not express the entire difference in the case, for as a general rule the circulation of the Southern newspapers is 50 to 75 per cent. less than that of the North. Suppose, however, that each Southern newspaper has two thirds the circulation of a Northern journal, we have then but 225 newspapers for the slave States! The more valuable journals—the monthlies and quarterlies—are published almost entirely in the free States.

The number of churches, the number and character of the clergy who labour for these churches, are other measures of the intellectual and moral condition of the people. The scientific character of the Southern clergy has been already touched on. Let us compare the more external facts.

In 1830, South Carolina had a population of 581,185

souls; Connecticut, 297,675. In 1836, South Carolina had 364 ministers; Connecticut, 498.

In 1834, there were in the slave States but 82,532 scholars in the Sunday schools; in the free States 504,835; in the single State of New York, 161,768.

A cause which keeps 3,000,000 men in bondage in America and in the nineteenth century, has more subtle influences than those just now considered. It not only prevents the extension of education among the people, but affects the doctrines taught them, even the doctrines taught in the name of God. Christianity is nominally the public religion of America; not of the Government, which extends protection alike to all modes of worship, of the Indian, the Mormon, and the Jew, but of the people. I will not touch the doctrines of the sects, in which Christian differs from Christian, but come to what is general among Christians—a part of the universal religion implied also in human nature itself. All sects, as such, theoretically agree that the most important practical doctrine of Christianity is LOVE TO MEN; to all men, of all ages, races, and conditions. As the Christian idea of God rises far above the Heathen or Hebrew conception thereof, so the Christian idea of man's relation to man far transcends the popular notions of human duty which formerly had prevailed. God is "OUR FATHER," the God of love; Man OUR BROTHER, whom we are bound to love as ourselves, and treat as we would be treated. Christian piety, or love of God, involves Christian morality, or love of man.

I lay aside the peculiar theoretical doctrines of the sects, that are preached everywhere, and ask: can the Christian relations of human brotherhood, the Christian duty of love to men, be practically preached in the slave States? I only publish an open secret in saying it is impossible. The forms of Christianity may be preached, not its piety, not its morality, not even its philosophy, or its history. If a man holds slaves in practice and justifies the deed in theory, how can he address an audience of slave-holders and teach them the duty of loving others as themselves? He cannot consistently teach that doctrine, nor they consistently hear.

The doctrines of the public religion are always modified by national habits, history, institutions, and ideas. Christianity, as taught in New England, has modifications unknown in Old England. The great rational and peculiar ideas of America—of which I shall soon speak—are among the truths of Christianity. We began our national career by declaring all men born with equal rights. In such a people we might look for a better and more universal development of Christianity, than in a nation which knows no unalienable rights, or equality of all men, but robs the many of their rights, to squander privileges on the few.

In some lands monarchy, aristocracy, prelacy, appear in the public teaching as parts of Christianity. In America it is not so. But it is taught that slavery is an ordinance of God,—justified by Christianity. Thus as the public religion is elsewhere made to subserve the private purposes of kings, nobles, priests—so here is it made to prove the justice of holding men in bondage. There are no claims like those wrought in the name of God, and welded upon their victim by the teachers of religion.

Most of the churches in the United States exercise the power of excluding a man from their communion for such offences as they see fit; for any unpopular breach of the moral law;—for murder, robbery, theft, public drunkenness, seduction, licentiousness, for heresy. Even dancing is an offence for which the churches sometimes deal with their children. But, with the exception of the Quakers and the United Brethren, no religious bodies in the United States now regard slave-holding or slave-dealing as an ecclesiastical offence. Church-members and clergymen are owners of slaves. Even churches themselves in some instances have, in their corporate capacity, been owners of men. In Turkey, when a man becomes a Mahometan, he ceases to be a slave. But in America a clergymen may own a member of his own church, beat him, sell him, and grow rich on "the increase of his female slaves."

Few productions of the Southern clergy find their way to the North. Conspicuous among those few are sermons in defence of slavery; attempts to show that if Christ were now on earth he might consistently hold property in men!

The teachings of the Southern pulpit become more and more favourable to slavery. Oppressed, America promulgated the theory of freedom;—free, she established the practice of oppression. In 1780 the Methodist Episcopal

Church declared "slavery is contrary to the laws of God," and "hurtful to society;" in 1784 it refused to admit slave-holders to its communion—passing a vote to exclude all such. But in 1836 the general conference voted "not to interfere in the civil and political relations between master and slave," and exhorted its ministers "to abstain from all abolition movements." The general conference since declared that American slavery "is not a moral evil." The conference of South Carolina has made a similar declaration.

In 1794 the Presbyterian Church added a note to the eighth commandment, bringing slavery under that prohibition, declaring it manstealing and a sin. Yet, though often entreated, it did not excommunicate for that offence. In 1816, by a public decree, the note was erased. Numerous Presbyteries and Synods have passed resolutions like these: "Slavery is not opposed to the will of God;" "It is compatible with the most fraternal regard to the best good of those servants whom God may have committed to our charge." Even the Catholic Church in the United States forms no exception to the general rule. The late lamented Dr England, the Catholic bishop of Charleston, South Carolina, undertook in public to prove that the Catholic Church had always been the uncompromising friend of slaveholding, not defending the slaves' right, but the usurped privilege of the masters. What a difference between the present Christian Pope of Rome, and the bishop of a democratic State in a Christian republic!

It has been currently taught in the most popular churches of the land, that slavery is a "Christian institution," sustained by the apostles, and sanctioned by Christ himself. None of the theological parties has been so little connected with slavery as the Unitarians—perhaps from the smallness of the sect itself, and its northern latitude—but, for years, one of its vice-presidents was a slave-holder.

While the Southern churches teach that slavery is Christian, the Northern join in the belief. Here and there a few voices in the North have been lifted up against it; seldom an eminent voice in an eminent place, then to be met with obloquy and shame. Almost all the churches in the land seem joined in opposing such as draw public attention to the fact that a Christian republic holds millions of men in bondage. Not long since a clergyman of the South, who boasted that he owned thirty slaves, and "would wade knee-deep in blood" to defend his right to them, was received by the Northern churches, and, as himself has said, "invited on every hand to pulpits," with no rebuke, but only welcome, from the large and powerful denomination to which he belonged. He returned, as he says, "leaving the hot-beds of abolitionism, without having been once foiled. God be praised for sustaining me. I give Him all the glory, for without Him I am nothing." Even in Boston there is a church of the same denomination, in which no coloured man is allowed to purchase a seat. Coloured men at the North are excluded from colleges and high schools, from theological seminaries and from respectable churches—even from the town hall and the ballot. Doctrines and outward deeds are but signs of sentiments and ideas which rule the life.

The sons of the North, when they settle in the South, as merchants, ministers, lawyers, planters, when they stand in the congress of the nation, when they fill important offices in the federal government—what testimony do they bear to the declaration that "all men are created equal"? I should blush to refresh your memories with Northern shame.

If the clergy find slavery "ordained" in the Bible, and established amongst the "Christian institutions," did not the laymen first find it in the Bible of Rousseau? Important men at the South have taught that slavery is "a moral and humane institution, productive of the greatest political and social advantages;" "the corner-stone of our republican edifice:" "It is the most sure and stable edifice for free institutions in the world." The doctrine that "all men are created equal" in rights is declared "ridiculously absurd." Democratic Mr Calhoun declares that where "common labour is performed by members of the political community a dangerous element is obviously introduced into the body politic." A pagan had taught it two thousand years before.

Thus powerful is the influence of slavery in its action on the intellectual, moral, and religious development of the people at the South; thus subtly does it steal upon the North. As one of your most illustrious citizens, old but not idle, has said, the spirit of slavery "has crept into the philosophical chairs of the schools. Its cloven foot has ascended the pulpits of the churches. Professors of colleges teach it as a lesson of morals; ministers of the gospel seek and profess to find sanctions for it in the Word of God."

The effect of slavery on the industrial, numerical, intellectual, and moral developments of the people may be best shown by a comparison of the condition and history of the two largest States, one slave, the other free. Virginia contains more than 64,000 square miles, or 13,370 more than England. The climate is delightful. The State is intersected by "the finest bay in the world," watered by long and abundant rivers; this inviting navigation, and allowing numerous and easy communications with the interior; that waiting to turn the wheels of the manufacturer, to weave and spin. The soil is rich in minerals. Iron, lead, and limestone are abundant. Nitre is found in her caverns. Salt abounds on the Great Kenawha and the Holston. Fields of coal, anthracite and bituminous, are numerous, rich, and of easy access. The soil is fertile, the sky genial, the air salubrious. She is the oldest State in the Union; long the most important in wealth, population, and political power. The noble array of talent and virtue found there in the last century has already been mentioned. Abundantly blessed with bays, harbours, rivers, mines, no State in the Union had such natural advantages as Virginia in 1790. New York has 49,000 square miles, and was settled somewhat later than Virginia, and under circumstances less propitious. Numerous causes retarded her growth before the Revolution. Though favoured with an excellent harbour, she has but one natural channel of communication with the interior. In 1790 Virginia contained 748,348 inhabitants; New York but 340,120. In 1840 Virginia had 1,239,797; New York 2,428,921, and in 1845, 2,604,495. In fifty years Virginia had not doubled her population, while New York had increased more than four-fold. In 1790, Virginia had more than eleven inhabitants to each square mile, and New York not quite eight; but in 1840, Virginia had only nineteen, and New York fifty-three persons to the square mile. In 1798, the houses and lands of Virginia were valued at

$71,225,127, those of New York at $100,380,707; in 1839 the real estate in Virginia was worth but $211,930,538, while that of New York had increased to $430,751,273. In 1840 the annual earnings of Virginia were $76,769,032; of New York $193,806,433. The population of New York is not quite double that of Virginia, but her annual earnings nearly three times as great. In 1840, at her various colleges and schools, Virginia had 57,302 scholars, and also 58,787 adult free whites unable to read and write—1484 more than the entire number of her children at school or college. New York had 44,452 illiterate adults, and 565,442 children at school or college. Besides that, in Virginia there were 448,987 slaves, with no literary culture at all, shut out from communication with the intelligence of the age. In 1844, in New York, 709,156 children, between four and sixteen, attended the common public schools of the State, and the common school libraries contained over a million of volumes; while in Virginia there were over 100,000 free white children between four and sixteen, who attended no school at all, perpetual vagrants from learning, year out and year in. Shall it always be so? The effect follows the cause. A man loses half his manhood by slavery, said Homer, and it is as true of a State as a man.

VI.

EFFECT OF SLAVERY ON LAW AND POLITICS.

I NOW call your attention to the influence of slavery on law and politics, its local effect on the slave States in special, its general effect on the politics of the Union.

In the settlement of America only the people came over. Nobility and royalty did not migrate. The people, the third estate, of course brought the institutions and laws of their native land—these are the national habits, so to say. But they brought also political sentiments and ideas not represented by the institutions or laws; sentiments and ideas hostile thereto, and which could not be made real in England, but were destined—as are all such ideas—to form institutions and make laws in their own image. There are three such political ideas which have already found a theoretical expression, and have more or less been made facts and become incarnate in institutions and laws. These are, first, the idea, that in virtue of his manhood, EACH MAN HAS UNALIENABLE RIGHTS, not derived from men or revocable thereby, but derived only from God; second, that in respect to these rights ALL MEN ARE CREATED EQUAL; third, that THE SOLE DESIGN OF POLITICAL GOVERNMENT IS TO PLACE EVERY MAN IN THE ENTIRE POSSESSION OF ALL HIS UN-ALIENABLE RIGHTS.

The priesthood, nobility, royalty, did not share these ideas—nor the sentiments which led to them. These ideas were of the people; they must form a democracy, the government of all, for all, and by all—a commonwealth with no privileged class—a state without nobles or kings, a church without prelate or priest.

These ideas, in becoming facts and founding political institutions to represent themselves, modified also the ancient and common law. "The laws of England," said Sir John Fortescue, in the fifteenth century, "the laws of England favour liberty in every case;" "let him who favours not liberty be judged impious and cruel." After the national and solemn expression of the above democratic ideas, the laws must favour liberty yet more, and new institutions likewise come into being. Accordingly, in the free States of the North, where these ideas have always had the fullest practical exposition, ever since the Revolution there has been a continual advance in legislation—laws becoming more humane, universal principles getting established, and traditional exceptions becoming annulled. In law—the theory of these ideas—so far as expressed in institutions and habits; and in society—the practice thereof, so far as they have passed into actual life,—there is a constant levelling upward; the low are raised—the slave, the servant, the non-freeholder; the lofty not degraded. In the constitutions of nearly all the free States it is distinctly stated that all men are created equal in rights, and in all it is implied. They are all advancing towards a realization of that idea—slowly, but constantly. They have lost none of the justice embodied in the common law of their ancestors—but gained new justice, and embodied it in their own forms.

This idea of the natural equality of all men in rights is inconsistent with slavery; accordingly it is expressed in the constitutions of but one slave State—Virginia. It is consistently rejected by the politicians of the South. This difference of ideas must appear in all the institutions of the North and South, and produce continual and conflicting modifications of the common law of England, which they both inherit; if the one idea adds justice thereto, the other takes it away.

Now among the institutions inherited from England were the trial by a jury of twelve men in all matters affecting liberty and life; the presumption in favour of life, liberty, and innocence; the right of every man under restraint to have a legal reason publicly shown for his confinement, by a writ of Habeas Corpus. The form of the latter is indeed modern, but its substance old, and of uncertain date. These three have long been regarded as the great safeguards of public justice, and in the legislation of the free States remain undisturbed in their beneficent action, extending to every person therein. In the slave States the whole class of bondmen is in fact mainly deprived of them all.

By the customs of England and her law, while villainage obtained there, the rule was that the child followed the condition of its father: *Filius sequitur patrem.* Hence the issue of a freeman, though born of a servile mother, was always free. In virtue of this maxim, and the legal presumption in favour of liberty, a presumption extending to all classes of men, the child of a female slave, which was born out of wedlock, was of course free. It was possible the father was a freeman. The child gained nothing but existence from his unknown father, and the law would not make that a curse. The child of a slave father, but born before the father was proved a slave, retained his freedom for ever.

If a freeman married a female slave, she became free during the life of her husband, and the children of course were free.

The slave, under certain circumstances, could possess

property, acquired by devise, by gift, or other means. It was so as a general rule through all the North of Europe; the more cruel maxims of the Roman slave-code never prevailed with the Teutonic race.

The slave could make a contract with his lord, binding as that between peer and peer. He could in his own name bring an action against any one; in some cases even against his master. He could, in all cases and in his own name, demand a trial by jury in a court of record, to determine if he were born a slave, or free. To determine against him, it was necessary not only to show in general that he was a slave, but that he was the slave of some one person in special. If it was simply shown that the man was a slave, but was not shown to the jury's satisfaction that he was the slave of the particular man who claimed him, the slave received his freedom at once, as one derelict by his master, and if legally claimed by nobody, he naturally belonged to himself.

He could be a witness in any court even when his master was an adverse party; though not possessed of all the privileges of a citizen—*legalis homo*—not admitted to hold office or serve on a jury, yet he could testify on oath even in criminal cases, as any other man.

If a slave ran away, and the master for one year neglected to pursue him with public outcry and prosecution of his claim, the slave was free by adverse possession of himself. While he was in flight, and in actual possession of freedom, the master could not seize on his children or on his possessions. He must legally possess the principal, the substance, before he could touch the subordinate and accident thereof. Did the slave flee to another borough or shire, a jury of that place—except in certain cases, when the trial must take place in another county—must not only convict him as a slave before the master could recover his body, but must convict him of being the slave of that special claimant.

If a slave took orders in the church, or became a monk, he was free from his master, though this was an exception to the law in most Catholic countries. If violence were offered to a female slave by her master, she had redress as a free woman. Slaves had all the personal rights of freemen except in regard to their own respective masters, and in some cases even then. There was no hindrance to manumission.

In America the laws relating to slavery are in many respects more severe than the English laws, since the Norman conquest, respecting villains—*regardant* or *in gross*. The child's condition follows that of the mother. This American departure from the common law was early made by statute, and the opposite maxim, the rule of the civil law, extended over the slave States;—*Partus sequitur ventrem*. Illegitimate children of female slaves were of course slaves for ever, though the father was free. But for this alteration, many thousands of men now slaves would have been free.

Contrary to the old common law of England, but in obedience to the Roman code, the American slave, in law, is regarded merely as a thing; "doomed," as Judge Ruffin, of North Carolina, sorrowfully declares, "to live without knowledge and without the capacity to make anything his own, and to toil that another may reap the fruits." In some of the slave States trial by jury is allowed to him in all capital cases; sometimes with the concurrence of a grand jury, sometimes without. Sometimes he is allowed to challenge the jurors "for cause," though not peremptorily. But in South Carolina, Virginia, and Louisiana, the slave is not allowed a jury trial, even when his life is in peril. In some others he has the protection of a jury when arraigned for inferior offences. But in every slave State he may be beaten to the extent of "thirty-nine lashes well laid on," without the verdict of a jury, but by the decision of a body of justices of the peace, varying in number from two to five. In all cases he is tried by men who regard him only as a thing, never by a jury of his peers—not even by a mixed jury of slave-holders and slaves. Some States have made humane provisions to guard against popular excitement, removing the trial to another county; now and then humane decisions are made in their favour by just men. But these are exceptional spots of humanity amidst the general gloom of the slave-code. There is some difference in the legislation of the several States, justifying the remark long ago made in Europe, that the condition of slaves was mildest in the North—hardest in the South.

Since the slave is a thing, he is not allowed his oath; sometimes he may give legal evidence for or against another slave, though without any form of solemn affirmation. There are laws in all the slave States designed to restrain the master from excessive cruelty, still they afford but incomplete protection to the slave; he cannot bring an action against the oppressor in his own name—for, as a thing, he has no rights. No slave, free negro, or mulatto to the fourth degree of descent is allowed to testify against a white man; as if this were not enough in South Carolina and Louisiana, if a slave is injured or killed when only one white person is present—and the presumption of guilt fall on the one white man, he is allowed by statute "to clear or exculpate himself by his own oath." This law is worse than the code of the Romans, "whose history was written in the blood of vanquished nations."

The slave has no legal right of self-defence against his master's assault and battery; the female none against brutal violation. The law of Georgia directs that "if any slave shall presume to strike any white man, such slave shall, for the first offence, suffer such punishment as the justice or justices shall see fit, not extending to life or limb; and, for the second offence, suffer death." In South Carolina, on his owner's account, he is allowed to strike even a white man, and the offence is capital only when twice repeated. In Kentucky, the penalty is less severe, but applied to freemen of colour as well as slaves.

A slave cannot be party to a civil suit. Indeed, when his condition is doubtful, he may apply to a court, and the court authorize some man to act as "guardian," and bring an action in the slave's behalf, and have investigation made of his servitude. But the burthen of proof remains on the slave's shoulders—to show that he is free. The presumption that he is a slave—*presumptio malæ partis*—prevails in all the South except North Carolina,—where the slave-code is perhaps more humane than elsewhere,—and is thus declared by statute in South Carolina and Georgia: "It shall always be presumed that every negro, Indian, mulatto, and mestizo is a slave." No adverse possession of himself, however long, makes a negro free, or his offspring born while he is in that state. In Mississippi, every negro or mulatto, not able to prove that he is free, may be sold by order of the court, as a slave for ever. If an applicant for freedom is cast in his suit, the court is "fully empowered to inflict such punishment not extending to life and limb, as they should think fit;" the "guardian" shall pay the costs; and in South Carolina, double those costs with damages to the owner of the slave. In Virginia, such a guardian, if defeated in his application, may be fined $100. In such a trial in Maryland, the master is allowed to challenge peremptorily twelve jurors. How difficult to find a "guardian" willing to incur the risk! how more than difficult to secure justice when a negro is wrongfully claimed as a slave! Yet notwithstanding the general spirit displayed by such legislation, some decisions have been made in the Southern States remarkable for the nicety of legal distinction and the exactness of their justice even to the slave.

Since the slave is a thing in many States, a conditional contract which the master has solemnly made with a slave, is not binding on the master, even after the slave has fulfilled the contract in spirit and letter. This is notoriously the law in South Carolina, and even in Virginia. A contract made with a spade or a mule binds no man—with a slave no more; the court cannot proceed to "enforce a contract between master and slave, even though the contract should be fully complied with on the part of the slave." This is a departure from the common law of England, and even from the customs of the Saxons and Germans.

The common law of England jealously defends the little property of the slave;—his *Peculium*. By the common law of Villainage, in England and Germany, he could acquire property as it was said above, and could transmit it to his heirs. Something of the sort was allowed even at Rome. But in all the slave States this is strictly forbidden. A slave cannot hold property solemnly devised to him by testament, even by that of his master. This provision, enforced by statute in Virginia, North Carolina, South Carolina, Georgia, Mississippi, Kentucky, and Tennessee, and perhaps all the slave States, is more rigorous even than the black codes of the Spanish and Portuguese colonies.

By the common law, the marriage of a slave was sacred as that of a peer of the realm. The customs of Turkey regard it as inviolable. Even the Roman code respected that, and the common law, by making marriage a sacrament, rendered it perpetual. "Neither bond nor free may be separated from the sacraments of the Church," said the Decretal of Gregory; "the marriages among slaves must not be hindered, and though contracted against their master's will, ought not, on that account, to be dissolved." But in the American law the slave cannot contract marriage. In North Carolina no marriage is legal between whites and persons of colour, including in the latter term all descended from a negro to the fourth generation.

In some States it is a penal offence to teach slaves the elements of common learning. By the recent code of Virginia, any one who undertakes to teach reading or writing to slaves, or even free coloured persons, may be fined from $10 to $100. The same is forbidden in Georgia. In Alabama, the punishment is a fine from $250 to $500; in Mississippi imprisonment for one year. Louisiana forbids the teaching of slaves to read or write, and prohibits any one from using language in public discourse or private conversation, having a tendency to produce discontent among the free coloured population. The latter offence is punishable " with imprisonment or death, at the discretion of the court." This antipathy to the education of the coloured race extends even to the free States. It is not unknown in New England. The State of Ohio established schools in 1829 for " the white youth of every class and grade without distinction."

According to the alleged precept of Mahomet, slaves are supposed to be bound by feebler social and civil obligations than freemen, and thus common offences receive but half the punishment of the free. Such, it is said, is the common law of Mahometans in Turkey and the East. In Virginia there are six capital offences for a freeman, seventy-one for a slave. In Mississippi there are thirty-eight offences for which a slave must be punished with death,—not one of which is a capital crime in a free white man. In some States the law is milder, but in none does the Christian Republican of Anglo-Saxon descent imitate the humanity of the Mussulman, and legally favour the weaker part—correcting slaves as the children of the State.

Many offences for which a slave is severely punished are not wrongs by nature, sins against the universal and divine law, but only crimes by statute. Thus in Mississippi, if a slave be found "fire-hunting" he is punishable "with thirty-nine lashes, well laid on his bare back." In the same State, if a slave be found out of the limits of the town, or off the plantation where he usually works, "any one may apprehend and punish him with whipping on the bare back, not exceeding twenty lashes." If he refuses to submit to the examination of any white person, "such white person may apprehend and moderately correct him, and if he shall assault and strike such white person, he may be lawfully killed." Louisiana has a similar law, and also punishes any slave or free coloured person exercising the functions of a minister of the Gospel, with thirty-nine lashes. In Virginia a slave or free coloured person may be beaten with twenty lashes for being found at any school for teaching reading and writing. In South Carolina he is forbidden to wear any but the coarsest garments.

The Roman code allowed emancipation; the customs of England and Germany favoured it. The Christian Church often favoured and recommended it. In the Roman Empire, the advance of humanity continually rendered it easy and common. A slave sick, and derelict of his master, recovering, claimed legally his freedom for salvage of himself. But in America the laws constantly throw obstacles in its way. In South Carolina, Georgia, Alabama, and Mississippi no man can emancipate any slave, except by authority of the legislature, granted by a special enactment conveying the power. In Georgia, a will, setting free a slave, is so far null and void, and any person attempting to execute it shall be fined $1000. In Kentucky, Missouri, Virginia, Maryland, it is less difficult; but even there no man is allowed to emancipate a slave to the prejudice of his creditors;—or in Virginia, Mississippi, and Kentucky, to the lessening of his widow's dower, the common law favours three things—life, liberty, and dower;—the law of these three States sacrifices the liberty of slaves to the dower of a widow. Emancipation must be made with most formal and technical minuteness, or the act is void. Does the master solemnly covenant with his slave to emancipate him? the contract can be revoked at the master's will. No extraordinary service of the slave, except in North Carolina, would be held "a good consideration" and sufficient to bind the bargain. In some States, as Maryland and Virginia, in fact—no person under thirty nor over five-and-forty can be emancipated.

Take all the slave-laws of the United States together, consider the race that has made them, their religion, the political ideas of their government, that it is in the nineteenth century after Christ, and they form the most revolting work of legislation to be found in the annals of any pacific people. The codes of the Barbarians who sat on the ruins of the Roman Empire—the Burgundians, Bavarians, the Allemanni, with the Visigoths and their northern kin—have left enactments certainly more terrible in themselves. But the darkness of that period shrouds all those barbarian legislations in a general and homogeneous gloom; and here, it is "the freest and most enlightened nation of the world," who keeps, extends, and intensifies the dreadful statutes which make men only things, binds them and sells them as brute cattle. In 1102, the council of London decreed that "hereafter no one shall presume to carry on the nefarious business in which, hitherto, men in England are wont to be sold as brute beasts." The churches of America have no voice of rebuke—no word of entreaty—when Christian clergymen sell their brothers in the market. The flag of America and the majesty of the law defend that "business," which the Anglo-Saxon bishops, seven hundred and forty-five years ago, looked on as "nefarious," *nefarium negotium*. M. de Tocqueville regarded the American slave-code as "Legislation stained by unparalleled atrocities; a despotism directed against the human mind; legislation which forbids the slaves to be taught to read and write, and which aims to sink them as nearly as possible to the level of the brutes."

The effect of slavery appears in the general legislation of the South. In wisdom and humanity it is far behind the North. It is the_ _hat laws are most bloody; punishments most barbarous and vindictive; that irregular violence takes most often the place of legal procedure;

that equity is least sure even for the free whites themselves. One end of the slave's chain is round the master's neck. "Justice," says a proverb, "has feet of wool but iron hands." The slave-driver's whip and the bowie-knife of the American have a near relation.

Some of the Southern States have enacted remarkable laws to this effect: That when any free negro or person of colour arrives in any vessel at a Southern port, he shall be shut up in prison until the departure of the vessel, the owner of the vessel paying the costs. By this law the free citizens of the free States are continually imprisoned in South Carolina and Louisiana. This is not only a violation of the constitution of the United States, but it is contrary to the common customs of Christian nations; a law without a parallel in their codes; a result which Gouverneur Morris did not anticipate in 1787, when he made his satirical calculation of the value of the Union to the North.

The iniquity of the code of the slave States has passed into some enactments of the general government of the Union. In 1793, a law was made by Congress to this effect: A fugitive slave escaping into a free State—and consequently any man claimed to be such—may be seized by the master or his agent, and carried back to slavery without the intervention of a trial by jury to determine whether the man is a slave—simply by a trial before "any judge of the circuit or district courts of the United States residing or being within the State, or before any magistrate of the county, city, or town corporate where such seizure or arrest shall be made." The proof required that the man is a slave is by "oral testimony or affidavit" of the parties interested in the man's capture. This is a departure from the customs of your fathers; a departure which the common law of England would not justify at any time since the Norman conquest. The trial by jury has been regarded the great safeguard of personal freedom; even in the dark ages of English law it was the right of every man, of every fugitive slave, when his person was in peril. Had a slave escaped with his children, and remained some time a freeman—*statu liber;* did the master find the children and not the father, he could not hold them till he caught the father, and by a jury-trial proved his claim. In the United States the laws do not favour liberty in case of men born with African blood in their veins.

The power of the general government has been continually exercised against this class of Americans. It pursues them after they have taken refuge with the Indians; it has sullied the American name by vainly asking the monarch of England to deliver up fugitive American slaves who had fled to Canada and sought freedom under her flag.

The Federal Government established slavery in the District of Columbia, in various Territories, and approved the constitutions of eight new States which aim to perpetuate the institution.

For a long time the House of Representatives refused to receive "all petitions, memorials, resolutions, and propositions relating in any way or to any extent whatever to the subject of slavery." Thus have the "unalienable rights" of man been trampled under foot by the government of the most powerful Republic in the world. But last summer, in the city of Washington two women were sold as slaves, on account of the United States of America, by her marshal, at public auction!

But let us look at the POLITICAL EFFECT of slavery. The existence of 3,000,000 slaves in the heart of the nation, with interests hostile to their masters, weakens the effective force of the nation in a time of war. It was found to be so in the Revolution, and in the late war. The slave States offer a most vulnerable point of attack. Let an enemy offer freedom to all the slaves who would join the standard —they will find "in every negro a decided friend," and the South could not stand with millions of foes scattered through all parts of her territory. Have the slaves arms? There are firebrands on every hearth. During the Revolution many thousands escaped from South Carolina alone. At the conclusion of the last war with England she offered to pay $1,204,000 as the value of the slaves who, in a brief period, had taken shelter beneath her flag. What if England had armed them as soldiers—to revenge the country and burn the towns? Will a future enemy be so reluctant? The feeling of the civilized world revolts at our inhumanity. The English, for reasons no longer existing, took little pains to avail themselves of the weapon thus thrust into their hands. In the time of our troubles with France, when war was expected, General Washington had serious apprehensions from this source. Even in 1756, during the French war, Governor Dinwiddie of Virginia did not "dare venture to part with any of our white men any distance, as we must have a watchful eye over our negro slaves."

The Revolutionary war showed the respective military abilities of North and South, and their respective devotion to their country's cause. It is not easy, perhaps not possible, to ascertain the sums of money furnished by the particular States, for the purposes of that war; the number of men it is easy to learn. Taking the census of 1790 as the standard, the six slave States had a free population of 1,852,504, or, including Kentucky and Tennessee, 1,961,372. Let us suppose, that during the Revolution, from 1775 to 1783, the number was but two-thirds as great, or 1,307,549. In those States there were 657,527 slaves, all the other States had likewise slaves; but in New England there were but 3886, their influence quite inconsiderable in military affairs. Let us therefore compare the number of men furnished for the war by New England and the six slave States. In 1790 the population of New England was 1,009,823. But let us suppose, as before, that from 1775 to 1783, it was, on an average, but two-thirds as large, or 673,215. During the nine years of Revolutionary war, New England furnished for the continental army 119,305 men; while the slave States, with a free population of 1,307,549, furnished but 59,336 men for the continental army. Besides that, the slave States furnished 10,123 militia men, and New England 29,324.

Let us compare a slave State, and a free one, of about equal population. In 1790, South Carolina contained 249,073 persons; Connecticut, 238,141. Supposing the population, during the war, only two-thirds as great as in 1790, then South Carolina contained 166,018, and Connecticut 158,760 persons. During the nine years of the war, South Carolina sent 6417 soldiers to the continental army, and Connecticut 32,039. In 1790, Massachusetts contained 475,257 souls; during the Revolution, according to the above ratio, 316,838. While the six slave States, with their free population of 1,307,549, furnished but 59,336 soldiers for the continental army, and 10,123 militia men, Massachusetts alone sent 68,007 soldiers to the continental army, and 15,155 militia. Thus, shoulder to shoulder, Massachusetts and South Carolina went through the Revolution, and felt the great arm of Washington lean on them both for support.

By the Constitution of the United States, in the apportionment of representatives to Congress, five slaves count the same as three freemen. This is a provision unknown in former national codes, resting on a principle un-democratic, detrimental to liberty, and hitherto unheard of: the principle of allowing parts of a nation political power in proportion to the number of men which they hold in bondage. It would have astonished the heathen democracy of Athens long centuries ago. By this arrangement, from 1789 to 1792, the South gained seven representatives in the first Congress; from 1795 to 1813—fourteen; from 1813 to 1823--nineteen; from 1823 to 1833—twenty-two; from 1833 to 1843—twenty-five. By the last apportionment bill, one representative is allowed for 70,680 freemen, or a proportionate number of slaves. By this arrangement, in a house of only 225 members, the South gains twenty representatives on account of her slaves—more than one-twelfth part of the whole.

At present the North has 138 representatives for 9,728,922 souls; or 9,727,893 freemen; one representative for each 70,492 freemen. The South has 87 representatives. There are within the slave States 4,848,105 freemen; they have one representative for each 55,725 free persons.

In the next Presidential election the North will have 166 electoral votes; the South 117. The North has an electoral vote for each 52,576 freemen; the South one for each 41,436. Part of this difference is due to the fact that in the South there are several small States. But twenty electoral votes are given by the South, on account of her property in slaves. But if slaves are merely property, there is no reason why Southern negroes should be represented in Congress more than the spindles of the North.

But the South pays direct taxes for her slaves in the same proportion. A direct tax has been resorted to only four times since 1789 by the General Government, viz. in 1798, 1813, 1814, and 1816. The whole amount assessed is $14,000,000. Of this about $12,750,000 was actually paid into the treasury of the United States, though part in a depreciated currency. Of that the South paid for her slaves, if the computation be correct, only $1,256,553.

In 1837 the surplus revenue of the Union, amounting to $37,468,859 97, was distributed among the several States in proportion to their electoral votes. By the census of 1830, the North had 7,008,451 free persons, and the South but 3,823,289. The free States received $21,410,777 12, and the slave States $16,058,082 85. Each freeman of the North received but $3 05, while each freeman of the South received $4 20 in that division.

At that time the South had one hundred and twenty-six electoral votes, of which twenty-five were on account of her slave-representation. She therefore received by that arrangement $3,186,127 50 on account of the representation of her slaves. From that if we deduct the $1,256,553 paid by her as direct taxes on her slaves, there is left $1,929,574 50, as the bonus which the South has received from the treasury of the nation on account of the representation of slaves—Southern property represented in Congress. To this we must add $57,556, which the South received in 1842 from the sale of public land on account of her slaves, the sum is $1,987,130 50. Mr Pinckney was right when he said the terms were not bad for the South.

Slavery diverts the freeman from industry, from science, from letters and the elegant Arts. It has been said to qualify him for politics. As political matters have been managed in the United States in this century, the remark seems justified by the facts. Elections are not accidents. Of the eight presidents elected in the nineteenth century, six were born in the South—children of the slave States. No northern man has ever twice been elected to the highest office of the nation. A similar result appears in the appointment of important officers by the President himself. From 1789 to 1845, one hundred and seventy appointments were made of ministers and charges to foreign powers; of these, seventy-eight were filled from the North, ninety-two from the South. Of the seventy-four ministers plenipotentiary sent to Europe before 1846, forty-three were from the slave States. There have been fifteen judges of the supreme court from the North; eighteen from the South.

The office of Attorney-general has been four times filled by Northern men, fourteen times by men from the slave States. Out of thirty Congresses, eleven only have had a speaker from the North. These are significant facts, and plainly show the aptitude of Southern men to manage the political affairs of America. There are pilots for fair weather; pilots also only trusted in a storm.

VII.

SLAVERY CONSIDERED AS A WRONG.

I AM now to speak of slavery considered as a wrong, an offence against the natural and eternal laws of God. You all know it is wrong—a crime against humanity, a sin before Almighty God. The great men who call slavery—right and just;—do they not know better? The little and humble men who listen to their speech—do not we all know better? Yes, we all know that slavery is a sin before God;—is the union of many sins. On this theme I will say but a word.

The Roman code declares liberty the natural estate of man, but calls slavery an institution of positive law, by which one man is made subject to another, contrary to nature. By the Hebrew law it was a capital offence to steal a man and sell him, or hold him as a slave.

Now if that doctrine be true which the American people once solemnly declared self-evident—that all men are created with equal rights—then every slave in the United States is stolen. Then slavery is a continual and aggravated theft. It matters not that the slave's mother was stolen before. To take the child of a slave must be theft as much as to take the child of a freeman; it is stealing mankind. He that murders a child has no defence in the fact that he first murdered the sire.

When we hear that the Emperor of Russia or Austria, for some political opinion, shuts a man in the Spielberg, or sends him to Siberia, for life—we pity the victim of such despotic power, thinking his natural rights debarred.

But the defence is that the man had shown himself dangerous to the welfare of the State, and so had justly forfeited his rights. When we reduce a man to a slave, making him a thing—we can plead no extenuation of the offence. The slave is only "guilty of a skin not coloured like our own,"—guilty of the misfortune to be weak and unprotected. For this he is deprived of his liberty; he and his children.

Slavery is against nature. It has no foundation in the permanent nature of man, in the nature of things, none in the eternal law of God, as reason and conscience declare that law. Its foundation is the selfishness, the tyranny of strong men. We all know it is so—the little and the great. Better say it at once, and with Mr Rutledge declare that religion and humanity have nothing to do with the matter, than make the miserable pretence that it is consistent with reason and accordant with Christianity; even the boys know better.

In the last century your fathers cried out to God against the oppressions laid on them by England, justly cried out. Yet those oppressions were but little things—a tax on sugar, parchment, paper, tea; nothing but a tax, allowing no voice in the granting thereof or its spending. They went to war for an abstraction—the great doctrine of human rights. They declared themselves free, free by right of birth, free because born men and children of God. For the justice of their cause they made solemn appeal to God Most High. What was the oppression the fathers suffered, to this their sons commit? It is no longer a question about taxes and representatives, a duty on sugar, parchment, paper, tea, but the liberty, the persons, the lives of three millions of men are in question. You have taken their liberty, their persons, and render their lives bitter by oppression. Was it right in your fathers to draw the sword and slay the oppressor, who taxed them for his own purpose, taking but their money, nor much of that? Were your fathers noble men for their resistance? when they fell in battle did they fall "in the sacred cause of God and their country?" Do you build monuments to their memory and write thereon, "Sacred to liberty and the rights of mankind?" Do you speak of Lexington and Bunker-Hill as spots most dear in the soil of the New world, the Zion of freedom, the Thermopylæ of universal right? Do you honour the name of Washington far beyond all political names of conqueror or king? How then can you justify your oppression? how refuse to admit that the bondmen of the United States have the same right, and a far stronger inducement to draw the sword and smite at your very life? Surely you cannot do so, not in America; never till Lexington and Bunker-Hill are wiped out of the earth; never till the history of your own Revolution is forgot; never till the names of the Adamses, of Jefferson, of Washington, are expunged from the memory of men.

When the rude African who rules over Dahomey or the Gaboon country burns a village and plunders the shrieking children of his fellow-barbarians to sell them away into bondage for ever, far from their humble but happy homes and their luxuriant soil, their bread-fruit and their palms, far from father and mother, from child and lover, from all the human heart clings to with tenderest longing—you are filled with horror at the deed. "What! steal a man," say you; "Great God," you ask, "is the Gaboon chieftain a man, or but a taller beast, with mind more cunning and far-reaching claws?" That chieftain is a barbarian. He knows not your letters, your laws, the tenets of your religion. The nobler nature of the man sleeps in his savage breast. His only plea is—his degradation. His defence before the world and before God is this: He is a savage, he knows no law but force, no right but only might alone. For that plea and defence the civilized man must excuse him, perhaps God holds him guiltless.

But when a civilized nation comes, with all the art and science which mankind has learned in the whole lifetime of the race, and steals the children of the defenceless, stimulating the savage to plunder his brothers and make them slaves, the offence has no such excuse; it is a conscious crime; a wrong before the judgment of the nations; a sin before Go

In your case it is worse still; the autocrat of all the Russias may have no theory of man's unalienable rights adverse to the slavery he aims to abolish on his broad estates and wide-spread realm; the Bey of Tunis deals not in abstractions, in universal laws, knows nothing of unalienable rights and the inborn equality of man. But you, the people of the United States; you, a nation of freemen, who owe allegiance to none; you, a republic, one of the foremost nations of the earth; you with your theories of human, universal justice; you who earliest made national proclamation to mankind of human right, and those three political ideas whereon the great American commonwealth now stands and rests; you who profess to form a government not on force, but law, not on national traditions, but abstract justice—the nation's constant and perpetual will to give to every one his constant and perpetual right; you who would found a state not on cannon balls, but universal laws, thoughts of God,—what plea can you put forth in your defence?

You call yourselves Christians. It is your boast. "Christianity," say the courts, "is the common law of the land." You have a religion which tells that God is the Father, equal, just, and loving to all mankind,—the red man, whom you murdered, and the black man, whom you have laid in iron, hurting his feet with fetters. It tells you, all are brothers, African, American, red man, and black, and white. It tells you, as your highest duty, to love God with all your heart; to love his justice, love his mercy, love his love; to love that brother as yourself—the more he needs, to love him still the more; that without such love for men there is no love for God. The sacred books of the nation—read in all pulpits, sworn over in all courts of justice, borne even in your war-ships, and sheltered by the battle-flag of your armies—the sacred books of the nation tell, that Jesus, the highest, dearest revelation of God to men, who loved them all, that He laid down his life for them, for all; and bade you follow Him! What is a natural action in the savage, a mere mistake in the despot of Turkey or of Russia, with you becomes a conscious and fearful wrong. For you to hold your brothers in bondage, to keep them from all chance of culture, growth in mind, or heart, or soul; for you to breed them as swine, and beat them as oxen; to treat them as mere things, without soul, or rights,—why, what was a mistake in political economy, a wrong before your ideas of government, becomes a sin foul and heinous before your ideas of man, and Christ, and God.

When you remember the intelligence of this age, its accumulated stores of knowledge, science, art, and wealth of matter and of mind, its knowledge of justice and eternal right; when you consider that in political ideas you stand the first people in the vanguard of mankind, now moving towards new and peaceful conquests for the human race; when you reflect on the great doctrines of universal right set forth in so many forms amongst you by the senator and the school-boy; when you bring home to your bosoms the religion whose sacred words are taught in that Bible, laid up in your churches, reverently kept in your courts of justice, carried under the folds of your flag over land and sea—that Bible, by millions multiplied and spread throughout the peopled world in every barbarous and stammering tongue,—and then remember that slavery is here; that three million men are now by Christian Republican America held in bondage worse than Egyptian, hopeless as hell,—you must take this matter to heart, and confess that American slavery is the greatest, foulest wrong which man ever did to man; the most hideous and detested sin a nation has ever committed before the just, all-bounteous God—a wrong and a sin wholly without excuse.

CONCLUSION.

Fellow-Citizens of America,

You see some of the effects of slavery in your land. It costs you millions of dollars each year. If there had been no slaves in America for forty years, it is within bounds to say, your annual earnings would be three hundred million dollars more than now. It has cost you also millions of men. But for this curse, Virginia had been as populous as New York, as rich in wealth and intelligence; without this the freemen of the South must have increased as rapidly as in the North, and at this day, perhaps five-and-twenty million men would rejoice at their welfare in the United States. Slavery retards industry in all its forms; the education of the people in all its forms, intellectual, moral, and religious. It hinders the application of those great political ideas of America; hinders the development of mankind, the organization of the rights of man in a worthy state, society, or church. Such effects are the Divine sentence against the cause thereof.

It is not for me to point out the remedy for the evil, and show how it can be applied; that is work for those men you dignify with place and power. I pretend not to give counsel here, only to tell the warning truth. Will you say, that in the free States also there is oppression, ignorance, and want and crime? 'Tis true. But an excuse, specious and popular, for its continuance, is this: that the evils of slavery are so much worse, men will not meddle with the less till the greater is removed. Men are so wonted to this monstrous wrong, they cannot see the little wrongs with which modern society is full; evils, which are little only when compared to that. When this shame of the nation is wiped off, it will be easy, seeing more clearly, to redress the minor ills of ignorance and want and crime. But there is one bright thing connected with this wrong. I mean the heroism which wars against it with pure hands; historic times have seen no chivalry so heroic.

Not long ago Europe and the whole Christian world rung with indignation at the outrage said to be offered, by the Russian government, to some Polish nuns who were torn from their home, driven from place to place, brutally beaten, and vexed with continual torments. Be the story false or true, the ears of men tingled at the tale. But not one of the nuns was sold. Those wrongs committed against a few defenceless women are doubled, trebled in America, and here continually applied to thousands of American women. This is no fiction; a plain fact, and notorious; but whose ears tingle? Is it worse to abuse a few white women in Russia, than a nation of black women in America? Is that worse for a European than this for the democratic republicans of America? The truth must be spoken; the voice of the bondman's blood cries out to God against us; His justice shall make reply. How can America ask mercy, who has never shown it there?

Civilization extends everywhere: the Russian and the Hottentot feel its influence. Christian men send the Bible to every island in the Pacific sea. Plenty becomes general; famine but rare. The arts advance, the useful, the beautiful, with rapid steps. Machines begin to dispense with human drudgery. Comfort gets distributed through their influence, more widely than ancient benefactors dared to dream. What were luxuries to our fathers, attainable only by the rich, now find their way to the humble home. War—the old demon which once possessed each strong nation, making it deaf and blind, but yet exceeding fierce, so that no feebler one could pass near and be safe—war is losing his hold of the human race, the devil getting cast out by the finger of God. The day of peace begins to dawn upon mankind, wandering so long in darkness, and watching for that happy star. Science, letters, religion, break down the barriers betwixt man and man, 'twixt class and class. The obstacles which severed nations once now join them. Trade mediates between land and land—the gold entering where steel could never force its way. New powers are developed to hasten the humanizing work; they post o'er land and ocean without rest, or serve our bidding while they stand and wait. The very lightning comes down, is caught, and made the errand-boy of the nations. Steamships are shooting across the ocean, weaving East and West in one united web. The soldier yields to the merchant. The man-child of the old world, young but strong, carries bread to his father in the hour of need. The ambassadors of science, letters and the arts, come from the old world to reside near the court of the new, telling truth for the common welfare of all. The genius of America sends also its first-fruits and a scion of its own green tree, a token of future blessings, to the parent land. These things help the great synthesis of the human race, the reign of peace on earth, of good-will amongst all men.

Everywhere in the old world the poor, the ignorant, and the oppressed, get looked after as never before. The hero of force is falling behind the times; the hero of thought, of love, is felt to deserve the homage of mankind. The Pope of Rome himself essays the reformation of Italy; the King of Denmark sets free the slaves in his dominions, East and West; the Russian Emperor liberates his serfs from the milder bondage of the Sclavonian race; his brother monarch of Turkey will have no slave-market in the Mahometan metropolis, no shambles there for human flesh; the Bey of Tunis cannot bear a slave; it grieves his Islamitish heart, swarthy African though he be.

Yet amid all this continual advance, America, the first of the foremost nations to proclaim equality, and human rights inborn with all; the first confessedly to form a state on nature's law—America restores barbarism; will still hold slaves. More despotic than Russia, more barbarous than the chieftain of Barbary, she establishes ferocity by federal law. There is suffering enough amongst the weak and poor in the cities of the free laborious North. England has her misery patent to the eye, and Ireland her looped and windowed raggedness, her lean and brutal want. So it is everywhere; there is sadness amid all the splendours of modern science and civilization, though far less than ever before. But amidst the ills of Christendom, the saddest and most ghastly spectacle on earth is American slavery. The misery of the old world grows less and less; the monster-vice of America, to make itself more awful yet, must drag your cannon to invade new lands.

I have addressed you as citizens, members of the state. I cannot forget that you are men; are members of the great brotherhood of man, children of the one and blessed God, whose equal love has only made to bless us all, v o will not suffer wrong to pass without its due. Think of the nation's deed, done continually and afresh. God shall hear the voice of your brother's blood, long crying from the ground; His justice asks you even now, AMERICA, WHERE IS THY BROTHER? This is the answer which America must give: "Lo, he is there in the rice-swamps of the South, in her fields teeming with cotton and the luxuriant cane. He was weak and I seized him; naked and I bound him; ignorant, poor and savage, and I over-mastered him. I laid on his feebler shoulders my grievous yoke. I have chained him with my fetters; beat him with my whip. Other tyrants had dominion over him, but my finger was thicker than their loins. I have branded the mark of my power, with red-hot iron, upon his human flesh. I am fed with his toil; fat, voluptuous on his sweat, and tears, and blood. I stole the father, stole also the sons, and set them to toil; his wife and daughters are a pleasant spoil to me. Behold the children also of thy servant and his handmaidens—sons swarthier than their sire. Askest Thou for the African? I found him a barbarian. I have made him a beast. Lo, there Thou hast what is thine."

That voice shall speak again : "America, why dost thou use him thus—thine equal, born with rights the same as thine ?"

America may answer: "Lord, I knew not the negro had a right to freedom. I rejoiced to eat the labours of the slave; my great men, North and South, they told me slavery was no wrong; I knew no better, but believed their word, for they are great, O Lord, and excellent."

That same voice may answer yet again, quoting the nation's earliest and most patriotic words : "'All men are created equal, and endowed by their Creator with unalienable rights—the right to life, to liberty, and the pursuit of happiness.' America, what further falsehood wilt thou speak?"

The nation may reply again: "True, Lord, all that is written in the nation's creed, writ by my greatest spirits in their greatest hour. But since then, why, holy men have come and told me in Thy name that slavery was good; was right; that Thou thyself didst once establish it on earth, and He who spoke Thy words spoke nought against this thing. I have believed these men, for they are holy men, O Lord, and excellent."

Then may that Judge of all the earth take down the Gospel from the pulpit's desk, and read these few plain words : "Thou shalt love the Lord thy God with all thy heart; and thou shalt love thy neighbour as thyself. Whatsoever ye would that others should do to you, do also even so to them."

Further might He speak and say: "While the poor Mussulman, whom thou call'st pagan and shut'st out from heaven, sets free all men, how much more art thou thyself condemned; yea, by the Bible which thou sendest to the outcasts of the world?"

Across the stage of time the nations pass in the solemn pomp of their historical procession; what kingly forms sweep by, leading the nations of the past, the present age! Let them pass—their mingled good and ill. A great people now comes forth, the newest born of nations, the latest hope of mankind, the heir of sixty centuries—the bridegroom of the virgin West. First come those Pilgrims, few and far between, who knelt on the sands of a wilderness, whose depth they knew not, nor yet its prophecy, who meekly trusting in their God, in want and war, but wanting not in faith, laid with their prayers the deep foundations of the State and Church. Then follow more majestic men, bringing great truths for all mankind, seized from the heaven of thought, or caught, ground-lightning, rushing from the earth; and on their banners have they writ these words: EQUALITY AND INBORN RIGHTS. Then comes the one with venerable face, who ruled alike the senate and the camp, and at whose feet the attendant years spread garlands, laurel-wreaths, calling him first in war, and first in peace, and first in his country's heart, as it in his. Then follow men bearing the first-fruits of our toil, the wealth of the sea and land, the labours of the loom, the stores of commerce and the arts. A happy people comes, some with shut Bibles in their hands, some with the nation's laws, some uttering those mighty truths which God has writ on man, and men have copied into golden words. Then comes, to close this long historic pomp,—the panorama of the world—the NEGRO SLAVE, bought, branded, beat.

I remain your fellow-citizen and friend,

THEODORE PARKER.

Boston, December 22, 1847.

SPEECH

AT A MEETING OF

THE AMERICAN ANTI-SLAVERY SOCIETY,

TO CELEBRATE

THE ABOLITION OF SLAVERY BY THE FRENCH REPUBLIC, APRIL 6, 1848.

MR CHAIRMAN,—The gentleman before me* has made an allusion to Rome. Let me also turn to that same city. Underneath the Rome of the Emperors, there was another Rome; not seen by the sun, known only to a few men. Above, in the sunlight, stood Rome of the Cæsars, with her markets and her armies, her theatres, her temples, and her palaces, glorious and of marble. A million men went through her brazen gates. The imperial city, she stood there, beautiful and admired, the queen of nations. But underneath all that, in caverns of the earth, in the tombs of dead men, in quarries whence the upper city had been slowly hewn, there was another population, another Rome, with other thoughts; yes, a devout body of men, who swore not by the public altars; men whose prayers were forbidden; their worship disallowed, their ideas prohibited, their very lives illegal. Time passed on; and gradually Rome of the pagans disappeared, and Rome of the Christians sat there in her place, on the Seven Hills, and stretched out her sceptre over the nations.

So underneath the laws and the institutions of each modern nation, underneath the monarchy and the republic,

* Mr Wendell Phillips.

there is another and unseen state, with sentiments not yet become popular, and with ideas not yet confirmed in actions, not organized into institutions, ideas scarcely legal, certainly not respectable. Slowly from its depths comes up this ideal state, the state of the future; and slowly to the eternal deep sinks down the actual state, the state of the present. But sometimes an earthquake of the nations degrades of a sudden the actual; and speedily starts up the ideal kingdom of the future. Such a thing has just come to pass. In France, within five-and-forty days, a new state has arisen from underneath the old. Men, whose words were suppressed, and their ideas reckoned illegal but two months ago, now hold the sceptre of five-and-thirty millions of grateful citizens, hold it in clean and powerful hands. A great revolution has taken place; one which will produce effects that we cannot foresee. It is itself the greatest act of this century. God only knows what it will lead to. We are here to express the sympathy of republicans for a new republic. We are here to rejoice over the rising hopes of the new state, not to exult over the fallen fortunes of the Bourbons. Louis Philippe has done much which we may thank him for. He has kept mainly at peace the fiercest nation in the world; has kept the peace of Europe for seventeen years. Let us thank him for that. He has consolidated the French nation, helped to give them a new unity of thought and unity of action, which they had not before. Perhaps he did not intend all this. Since he has brought it about, let us thank him for it, even if his conduct transcended his intention. But, most of all, I would thank this "Citizen King" for another thing. His greatest lesson is his last. He has shown that five-and-thirty millions of Frenchmen, in this nineteenth century, are only to be ruled by justice and the eternal law of right. We have seen this crafty king, often wise and always cunning, driven from his throne. He was the richest man in Europe, and the embodiment of the idea of modern wealth. He had an army the best disciplined, probably, in the world, and, as he thought, completely in his power. He had a Chamber of Peers of his own appointment; a Chamber of Deputies almost of his own election. He ruled a nation that contained three hundred thousand office-holders, appointed by himself, and only two hundred and forty thousand voters! Who sat so safe as the citizen king on his throne, surrounded by republican institutions! So confident was he, as the journals tell, that he bade a friend stop a day or two, "and see how I will put down the people!" For once, this shrewd calculator reckoned without his host.

Well, we have seen this man, this citizen monarch, who married his children only to kings, rush from his place; his peers and his deputies were unavailing; his officeholders could not sustain him; his army "fraternized with the people;" and he, forgetful of his own children, ignominiously is hustled out of the kingdom, in a street cab, with nothing but a five-franc piece in his pocket. For the lesson thus taught, let us thank him most of all.

Men tell us it is too soon to rejoice; "perhaps the revolution will not hold;" "it will not last;" "the kings of Europe will put it down." When a sound, healthy child is born, the friends of the family congratulate the parents then; they do not wait till the child has grown up, and got a beard. Now this is a live child; it is well born in both senses, come of good parentage, and give signs of a good constitution. Let us rejoice at its birth, and not wait to see if it will grow up. Let us now baptize it in the crystal fountain of our own hope.

In a great revolution, there are always two things to be looked at, namely, the actions, and the ideas which produce the actions. The actions I will say little of; you have all read of them in the newspapers. Some of the actions were bad. It is not true that all at once the French have become angels. There are low and base men, who swarm in the lanes and alleys of Paris; for that great city also is like all capitals, girt about with a belt of misery, of vice, and of crime, eating into her painful loins. It was a bad thing to sack the Tuileries; to burn bridges, and chateaux, and railroad stations. Property is under the insurance of mankind, and the human race must pay in public for private depredations. It was a bad thing to kill men; the human race cannot make up that loss; only suffer and be penitent. I am sorry for these bad actions; but I am not surprised at them. You cannot burn down the poor dwelling of a widow in Boston, but some miserable man will steal pot or pan, in the confusion of the fire. How much more should we expect pillage and violence in the earthquake which throws down a king!

I have said enough of the actions; but there was one deed too symbolical to be passed by. In the garden of the Tuileries, before the great gate of the palace, there stands a statue of Spartacus, a colossal bronze, his broken chain in the left hand, his Roman sword in the right. Spartacus was a Roman gladiator. He broke his chains; gathered about him other gladiators, fugitive slaves, and assembled an army. He and his comrades fought for freedom; they cut off four consular armies sent against them; at last the hero fell amid a heap of men, slain by his own well-practised hand. When the people took the old and emblematic French throne, and burned it solemnly with emblematic fire, they stripped off some of the crimson trappings of the royal seat, made a tiara thereof, and bound it on the gladiator's brazen head! But red is the colour of revolution, the colour of blood; the unconscious gladiator was an image too savage for new France. So they hid the Roman sword in his hand, and wreathed it all over with a chaplet of flowers!

Let us say a word of the ideas. Three ideas filled the mind of the nation: the idea of liberty, equality, and fraternity. Three noble words. Liberty meant liberty of all. So, at one word, they set free the slaves, and, if my friend's ciphers are correct, at once three hundred thousand souls rise up from the ground disenthralled, freemen. That is a great act. A population as large as the whole family of our sober sister Connecticut, all at once find their chains drop off, and they are free: not beasts, but men. This may not hold. Our Declaration of Independence was not the Confederation of '78—still less was it the Constitution of '87. The French may be as false as the Americans to their idea of liberty. At any rate, it is a good beginning. Let us rejoice at that.

Equality means that all are equal before the law; equal in rights, however unequal in mights. So all titles of nobility came at once to the ground. The royal family is like the family of our Presidents. The Chamber of Peers is abolished. Universal suffrage is decreed; all men over twenty-one are voters. Men here in America say, " The French are not ready for that." No doubt the king thought so. At any rate, he was not ready for it. But it is not a thing altogether unknown in France. It has been tried several times before. The French constitution was accepted by the whole people in 1800; Napoleon was made Consul by the whole people; made Emperor by the whole people. Even in 1815, the "acte additionelle" to the "Charte" was accepted by the whole people. To decree universal suffrage was the most natural thing in the world. Those two ideas, liberty and equality, have long been American ideas; they were never American facts. America sought liberty only for the whites. Our fathers thought not of universal suffrage.

But France has not only attempted to make our ideas into facts; she has advanced an idea not hinted at in the American Declaration; the idea of fraternity. By this she means human brotherhood. This points not merely to a political, but to a social revolution. It is not easy for us to understand how a government can effect this. Here, all comes from the people, and the people have to take care of the government, meaning thereby the men in official power; have to furnish them with ideas, and tell them what application to make thereof. There all comes from the government. So the new provisional government of France must be one that can lead the nation; have ideas in advance of the nation. Accordingly, it proposes many plans which with us could never have come from any party in power. Here, the government is only the servant of the people. There, it aims to be the father and teacher thereof; a patriarchal government with Christian thoughts and feelings. But as an eloquent man is to come after me, whose special aim is to develope the idea of human brotherhood into social institutions, I will not dwell on this, save to mention an act of the provisional authorities. They have abolished the punishment of death for all political offences. You remember the guillotine, the massacres of September, the drowning in the Loire and the Seine, the dreadful butchery in the name of the law.

Put this new decree side by side with the old, and you see why Spartacus, though crowned by a revolution, bears peaceful blossoms in his hand.

But let us hasten on; time would fail me to speak of the cause or point out the effect of this movement of the people. Only a word concerning the objections made to it. Some say, "It is only an extempore affair. Men drunk with new power are telling their fancies, and trying in their heat to make laws thereof." It is not so. The ideas I have hinted at have been long known and deeply cherished by the best minds in France. Last autumn, M. Lamartine, in his own newspaper, for the deputy for Macon is an editor, published the "Programme and confession of his political faith."*

Others say, "The whole thing seems rash." Well, so it does; so does any good thing seem rash to all except the man who does it, and such as would do it if he did not. What is rash to one is not to another. It is dangerous for an old man to run, fatal for him to leap, while his grandson jumps over wall and ditch without hurt. The American Revolution was a rash act; the English Revolution a rash act; the Protestant Reformation was a rash act. Was it safe to wihtstand the Revolution? Did the king of the French find it so? Yet others say, "The leaders are unknown." "Lamartine, you might as well put any man in the street at the head of the nation." But when the American Revolution begun, who, in England, had ever heard of John Hancock, President of the Congress? To the men who knew him, John Hancock was a country trader, the richest man in a town of ten thousand inhabitants: that did not sound very great at London. Samuel Adams, and John Adams, and Thomas Jefferson, and all the other men, what did the world know of them? Only that they had been christened with Hebrew names. Why, George Washington was only, as Gen. Braddock called him, "A young Buckskin." But the world heard of these men afterwards. Let us leave the French statesmen to make to the future what report of themselves they can! Let me tell a story of Dupont de l'Eure, the head of the government at this moment. He was one of the movers of the Revolution of 1830. He dined with the citizen king, once, in some council. At the table, he and the king differed; the king affirmed, and Dupont denied. Said the king, "Do you tell me I lie?" Said Dupont, "When the king says yes, and Dupont de l'Eure replies no, France will know which to believe!" The king said, "Yes, we

* See the *Courier des Etats Unis*, for Nov. 24, 1847, which contains passages from M. Lamartine's programme, which set forth all the schemes that the provisional government had afterwards tried to carry out.

will put the people down;" Dupont said, "No, you shall not put the people down;" and now France knows which to believe.

Again, say others yet, "War may come; royalty may come back, despotism may come back. Other kings will interpose, and put down a republic." Other kings interpose to put down the French! Perhaps they will. They tried it in 1793, but did not like the experiment very well. They will be well off if they do not find it necessary to put down a republic a little nearer at hand; their anti-revolutionary work may begin at home. War followed the American Revolution. It cost money, it cost men. But if we calculate the value of American ideas, they are worth what they cost. Even the French Revolution, with all its carnage, robbery, and butchery, is worth what it cost. But it is possible that war will not come. From a foreign war, France has little to fear. There seems little danger that it will come at all. What monarchy will dare fight republican France? Internal trouble may indeed come. It is to be expected that the new republic will make many a misstep. But is it likely that all the old tragedies will be enacted again? Surely not; the burnt child dreads the fire. Besides, the France of '48 is not the France of '89. There is no triple despotism weighing on the nation's neck, a trinity of despotic powers—the throne, the nobility, the church. The king has fled; the nobles have ceased to be; the church seems republican. There is no hatred between class and class, as before. The men of '89 sought freedom for the middle class, not for all classes, neither for the high, nor for the low. Religion pervades the church and the people, as never before. Better ideas prevail. It is not the gospel of Jean Jaques, and the scoffing negations of Voltaire, that are now proclaimed to the people; but the broad maxims of Christian men; the words of human brotherhood. The men of terror knew no weapon but the sword; the provisional government casts the sword from its hands, and will not shed blood for political crimes.

Still, troubles may come; war may come from without, and, worse still, from within; the republic may end. But if it lasts only a day, let us rejoice in that day. Suppose it is only a dream of the nation; it is worth while to dream of liberty, of equality, of fraternity; and to dream that we are awake, and trying to make them all into institutions and common life. What is only a dream now, will be a fact at last.

Next Sunday is the election day of France; six millions of voters are to choose nine hundred representatives! Shall not the prayers of all Christian hearts go up with them on that day, a great deep prayer for their success? The other day, the birthday of Washington, the calm, noiseless spirit of death came to release the soul of the patriarch of American statesmen. While his sun was slowly sinking in the western sky, the life-star of a new nation was visibly rising there, far off in the east. A pagan might be pardoned for the thought, that the intrepid soul of that old man foresaw the peril, and, slowly quitting its hold of the worn-out body, went thither to kindle anew the flames of liberty he fanned so often here. That is but a pagan thought. This is a Christian thought: The same God who formed the world for man's abode, presides also in the movements of mankind, and directs their voluntary march. See how this earth has been brought to her present firm and settled state. By storm and earthquake, continent has been rent from continent; oceans have swept over the mountains, and the scars of ancient war still mark our parent's venerable face. So is it in the growth of human society: it is the child of pain; revolutions have rocked its cradle, war and violence rudely nursed it into hardy life. Good institutions, how painfully, how slowly have they come!

> "Slowly as spreads the green of earth
> O'er the receding ocean's bed,
> Dim as the distant stars come forth,
> Uncertain as a vision, slow,
> Has been the old world's toiling pace,
> Ere she can give fair freedom place."

Let us welcome the green spot, when it begins to spread; let us shout as the sterile sea of barbarism goes back; let us rejoice in the vision of good things to come; let us welcome the distant and rising orb, for it is the Bethlehem star of a great nation, and they who behold it may well say—"Peace on earth, and good-will to men."

SPEECH AT FANEUIL HALL,

BEFORE

THE NEW ENGLAND ANTI-SLAVERY CONVENTION, MAY 31, 1848.

THE design of the abolitionists is this,—to remove and destroy the institution of slavery. To accomplish this well, two things are needed, ideas and actions. Of the ideas first, and then a word of the actions.

What is the idea of the abolitionists? Only this, That all men are created free, endowed with unalienable rights; and in respect of those rights, that all men are equal. This is the idea of Christianity, of human nature. Of course, then, no man has a right to take away another's rights; of course, no man may use me for his good, and not my own good also; of course, there can be no ownership of man by man; of course, no slavery in any form. Such is the idea, and some of the most obvious doctrines that follow from it.

Now, the abolitionists aim to put this idea into the minds of the people, knowing that if it be there, actions will follow fast enough.

It seems a very easy matter to get it there. The idea is nothing new; all the world knows it. Talk with men, Democrats and Whigs, they will say they like freedom in the abstract, they hate slavery in the abstract. But you find that somehow they like slavery in the concrete, and dislike abolitionism when it tries to set free the slave. Slavery is the affair of the whole people; not Congress, but the nation, made slavery; made it national, constitutional. Not Congress, but the voters, must unmake slavery; make it un-constitutional, un-national. They say Congress cannot do it. Well, perhaps it is so; but they that make can break. If the people made slavery, they can unmake it.

You talk with the people; the idea of freedom is there. They tell you they believe the Declaration of Independence —that all men are created equal. But somehow they contrive to believe that negroes now in bondage are an exception to the rule, and so they tell us that slavery must not be meddled with, that we must respect the compromises of the Constitution. So we see that respect for the Constitution overrides respect for the inalienable rights of three millions of negro men.

Now, to move men, it is necessary to know two things —first, What they think, and next, Why they think it. Let us look a little at both.

In New England, men over twenty-one years old may be divided into two classes. First, the men that vote, and secondly, the men that choose the Governor. The voters in Massachusetts are some hundred and twenty thousand; the men that choose the Governor, who tell the people how to vote, whom to vote for, what laws to make, what to forbid, what policy to pursue—they are not very numerous. You may take one hundred men out of Boston, and fifty men from the other large towns in the State—and if you could get them to be silent till next December, and give no counsel on political affairs, the people would ιt know what to do. The Democrats would not know whι to do, nor the Whigs. We are a very democratic people, and suffrage is almost universal; but it is a very few men who tell us how to vote, who make all the most important laws. Do I err in estimating the number at one hundred and fifty? I do not like to exaggerate—suppose there are six hundred men, three hundred in each party; that six hundred manage the political action of the State, in ordinary times.

I need not stop to ask what the rest of the people think about freedom and slavery. What do the men who control our politics think thereof? I answer, They are not opposed to slavery; to the slavery of three milllions of men. They may not like slavery in the abstract, or they may like it, I do not pretend to judge; but slavery in the concrete, at the South, they do like; opposition to that slavery, in the mildest form, or the sternest, they do hate.

That is a serious charge to bring against the prominent rulers of the State. Let me call your attention to a few facts which prove it. Look at the men we send to Congress. There are thirty-one New England men in Congress. By the most liberal construction you can only make out five anti-slavery men in the whole number. Who ever heard of an anti-slavery Governor of Massachusetts in this century? Men know what they are about when they select candidates for election. Do the voters always know what they are about when they choose them?

Then these men always are in favour of a pro-slavery President. The President must be a slave-holder. There have been fifteen presidential elections. Men from the free States have filled the chair twelve years, or three terms; men from the slave States forty-four years, or eleven terms. During one term, the chair was filled by an amphibious presidency, by General Harrison, who was nothing but a concrete availability, and John Tyler, who was—John Tyler. They called him an accident; but there are no accidents in politics. A slave-holder presides over the United States forty-eight years out of sixty! Do those men who control the politics of New England not like it? It is no such thing. They love to have it so. We have just seen the Democratic party, or their leaders, nominate General Cass for their candidate—and General Cass is a Northern man; but on that account is he any the less a pro-slavery man? He did oppose the South once, but it was in pressing a war with England. Everybody knows General Cass, and I need say no more about him. But the Northern Whigs have their leaders—are they anti-slavery men? Not a whit more. Next week you will see them nominate, not the great Eastern Whig, though he is no opponent of slavery, only an expounder and defender of the Constitution; not the great Western Whig, the compromiser, though steeped to the lips in slavery; no, they will nominate General Taylor, a man who lives a little further South, and is at this moment dyed a little more scarlet with the sin of slavery.

But go a step further as to the proof. Those men who control the politics of Massachusetts, or New England, or the whole North, they have never opposed the aggressive movements of the slave power. The annexation of Texas, did they oppose that? No, they were glad of it. True, some earnest men came up here in Faneuil Hall, and passed resolutions, which did no good whatever, because it was well known that the real controllers of our politics thought the other way. Then followed the Mexican war. It was a war for slavery, and they knew it; they lik) it now—that is, if a man's likings can be found out by his doings, not his occasional and exceptional deeds, but his regular and constant actions. They knew that there would be a war against the currency, a war against the tariff, or a war against Mexico. They chose the latter. They knew what they were about.

The same thing is shown by the character of the press. No "respectable" paper is opposed to slavery; no Whig paper, no Democratic paper. You would as soon expect a Catholic newspaper to oppose the Pope and his church, for the slave power is the pope of America, though not exactly a pious pope. The churches show the same thing; they also are in the main pro-slavery, at least not anti-slavery. There are some forty denominations or sects in New England. Mr President, is one of these anti-slavery? Not one! The land is full of ministers, respectable men, educated men—are they opposed to slavery? I do not know a single man, eminent in any sect, who is also eminent in his opposition to slavery. There was one such man, Dr Channing; but just as he became eminent in the cause of freedom, he lost power in his own church, lost caste in his own little sect; and though men are now glad to make sectarian capital out of his reputation after he is dead, when he lived, they cursed him by their gods! Then, too, all the most prominent men of New England fraternize with slavery. Massachusetts received such an insult from South Carolina as no State ever before received from another State in this Union; an affront which no nation would dare offer another, without grinding its sword first. And what does Massachusetts do? She does—nothing. But her foremost man goes off there, "The schoolmaster that gives no lessons," * to accept the hospitality of the

* This was a sentiment offered at a public dinner given by the citizens of Charleston, S. C., to Hon. Daniel Webster.

South, to take the chivalry of South Carolina by the hand; the Defender of the Constitution fraternizes with the State which violates the Constitution, and imprisons his own constituents on account of the colour of their skin.

Put all these things together, and they show that the men who control the politics of Massachusetts, of all New England, do not oppose or dislike slavery.

So much for what they think; and now for the why they think so.

First, there is the general indifference to what is absolutely right. Men think little of it. The Anglo-Saxon race, on both sides of the water, have always felt the instinct of freedom, and often contended stoutly enough for their own rights. But they never cared much for the rights of other men. The slaves are at a distance from us, and so the wrong of this institution is not brought home to men's feelings as if it were our own wrong.

Then the pecuniary interests of the North are supposed to be connected with slavery, so that the North would lose dollars if the South lost slaves. No doubt this is a mistake; still, it is an opinion currently held. The North wants a market for its fabrics, freight for its ships. The South affords it; and, as men think, better than if she had manufactures and ships of her own, both of which she could have, were there no slaves. All this seems to be a mistake. Freedom, I think, can be shown to be the interest of both North and South.

Yet another reason is found in devotion to the interests of a party. Tell a Whig he could make Whig capital out of anti-slavery, he would turn abolitionist in a moment, if he believed you. Tell a Democrat that he can make capital out of abolition, and he also will come over to your side. But the fact is, each party knows it would gain nothing for its political purposes by standing out for the rights of man. The time will come, and sooner too than some men think, when it will be for the interest of a party to favour abolition, but that time is not yet. It does seem strange, that while you can find men who will practise a good deal of self-denial for their sect or their party, lending, and hoping nothing in return, you so rarely find a man who will compromise even his popularity for the sake of mankind.

Then, again, there is the fear of change. Men who control our politics seem to have little confidence in man, little in truth, little in justice, and the eternal right. Therefore, while it is never out of season to do something for the tariff, for the moneyed interests of men, they think it is never in time to do much for the great work of elevating mankind itself. They have no confidence in the people, and take little pains to make the people worthy f confidence. So any change which gives a more liberal government to a people, which gives freedom to the slave, they look on with distrust, if not alarm. In 1830, when the French expelled the despotic king who encumbered their throne, what said Massachusetts, what said New England, in honour of the deed? Nothing. Your old men? Nothing. Your young men? Not a word. What did they care for the freedom of thirty millions of men? They were looking at their imports and exports. In 1838, when England set free eight hundred thousand men in a day, what did Massachusetts say about that? What had New England to say? Not a word in its favour from these political leaders of the land. Nay, they thought the experiment was dangerous, and ever since that it is with great reluctance you can get them to confess that the scheme works well. In 1848, when France again expels her king, and all the royalty in the kingdom is carted off in a one horse cab—when the broadest principles of human government are laid down, and a great nation sets about the difficult task of moving out of her old political house, and into a new one, without tearing down the old, without butchering men in the process of removal,—why, what has Boston to say to that? What have the political leaders of Massachusetts, of New England, to say? They have nothing to say for liberty; they are sorry the experiment was made; they are afraid the French will not want so much cotton; they have no confidence in man, and fear every change.

Such are their opinions, to judge by what they do; such the reasons thereof, judging by what they say.

But how can we change this, and get the idea of freedom into men's minds? Something can be done by the gradual elevation of men, by schools and churches, by the press. The churches and colleges of New England have not directly aided us in the work of abolishing slavery. No doubt by their direct action they have retarded that work,

and that a good deal. But indirectly they have done much
to hasten the work. They have helped educate men;
helped make men moral, in a general way; and now this
moral power can be turned to this special business, though
the churches say, " No, you shall not." I see before me
a good and an earnest man,* who, not opening his mouth
in public against slavery, has yet done a great service in
this way: he has educated the teachers of the Commonwealth, has taught them to love freedom, to love justice,
to love man and God. That is what I call sowing the
seeds of anti-slavery. The honoured and excellent Secretary of Education,† who has just gone to stand in the place
of a famous man, and I hope to fill it nobly, has done
much in this way. I wish in his reports on education he
had exposed the wrong which is done here in Boston, by
putting all the coloured children in one school, by shutting
them out of the Latin school and the English high school.
I wish he had done that duty, which plainly belongs to
him to do. But without touching that, he has yet done,
indirectly, a great work towards the abolition of slavery.
He has sown the seeds of education wide spread over the
State. One day these seeds will come up; come up men,
men that will both vote and choose the Governor; men
that will love right and justice; will see the iniquity of
American slavery, and sweep it off the continent, cost
what it may cost, spite of all compromises of the Constitution, and all compromisers. I look on that as certain.
But that is slow work, this waiting for a general morality
to do a special act. It is going without dinner till the
wheat is grown for your bread.

So we want direct and immediate action upon the people
themselves. The idea must be set directly before them,
with all its sanctions displayed, and its obligations made
known. This can be done in part by the pulpit. Dr
Channing shows how much one man can do, standing on
that eminence. You all know how much he did do. I
am sorry that he came so late, sorry that he did not do
more, but thankful for what he did do. However, you cannot rely on the pulpit to do much. The pulpit represents
the average goodness and piety; not eminent goodness

* Rev. Cyrus Pierce, Teacher of the Normal School at Newton.
  † Hon. Horace Mann.

and piety. It is unfair to call ordinary men to do extraordinary works. I do not concur in all the hard things that are said about the clergy, perhaps it is because I am one of them; but I do not expect a great deal from them. It is hard to call a class of men all at once to rise above all other classes of men, and teach a degree of virtue which they do not understand. But you may call them to be true to their own consciences.

So the pulpit is not to be relied on for much aid. If all the ministers of New England were abolitionists, with the same zeal that they are Protestants, Universalists, Methodists, Calvinists, or Unitarians, no doubt the whole State would soon be an anti-slavery State, and the day of emancipation would be wonderfully hastened. But that we are not to look for.

Much can be done by lecturers, who shall go to the people and address them, not as Whigs or Democrats, not as sectarians, but as men, and in the name of man and God present the actual condition of the slaves, and show the duty of the North and South, of the nation, in regard to this matter. For this business, we want money and men, the two sinews of war; money to pay the men, men to earn the money. They must appeal to the people in their primary capacity, simply as men.

Much also may be done by the press. How much may be done by these two means, and that in a few years, these men * can tell; all the North and South can tell. Men of the most diverse modes of thought can work together in this cause. Here on my right is Mr Phillips, an old-fashioned Calvinist, who believes all the five points of Calvinism. I am rather a new-fashioned Unitarian, and believe only one of the five points, the one Mr Phillips has proved—the perseverance of the saints; but we get along without any quarrel by the way.

Some men will try political action. The action of the people, of the nation, must be political action. It may be constitutional, it may be unconstitutional. I see not why men need quarrel about that. Let not him that voteth condemn him that voteth not, nor let not him that voteth not condemn him that voteth, but let every man be faithful to his own convictions.

* Messrs Garrison, Phillips, and Quincy.

It is said, the abolitionists waste time and wind in denunciation. It is partly true. I make no doubt it inspires the slave-holder's heart to see division amongst his foes. I ought to say his friends, for such we are. He thinks the day of justice is deferred, while the ministers thereof contend. I do not believe a revolution is to be baptized with rose-water. I do not believe a great work is to be done without great passions. It is not to be supposed that the Leviathan of American slavery will allow himself to be drawn out of the mire in which he has made his nest, and grown fat and strong, without some violence and floundering. When we have caught him fairly, he will put his feet into the mud to hold on by; he will reach out and catch hold of everything that will hold him. He has caught hold of Mr Clay and Mr Webster. He will catch hold of General Cass and General Taylor. He will die, though slowly, and die hard. Still it is a pity that men who essay to pull him out, should waste their strength in bickerings with one another, or in needless denunciation of the leviathan's friends. Call slave-holding, slave-holding; let us tell all the evils which arise from it, if we can find language terrible enough; let us show up the duplicity of the nation, the folly of our wise men, the littleness of our great men, the baseness of our honourable men, if need be; but all that with no unkind feelings toward any one. Virtue never appears so lovely as when, destroying sin, she loves the sinner, and seeks to save him. Absence of love is absence of the strongest power. See how much Mr Adams lost of his influence, how much he wasted of his strength, by the violence with which he pursued persons. I am glad to acknowledge the great services he performed. He wished to have every man stand on the right side of the anti-slavery line; but I believe there were some men whom he would like to have put there with a pitchfork. On the other hand, Dr Channing never lost a moment by attacking a personal foe; and see what he gained by it! However, I must say this, that no great revolution of opinion and practice was ever brought about before with so little violence, waste of force, and denunciation. Consider the greatness of the work; it is to restore three millions to liberty; a work, in comparison with which the American Revolution was a little thing. Yet consider the violence, the denunciation, the persecution, and the long years of war, which that Revolution cost. I do not wonder that abolitionists are sometimes violent; I only deplore it. Remembering the provocation, I wonder they are not more so and more often. The prize is to be run for, "not without dust and heat."

Working in this way, we are sure to succeed. The idea is an eternal truth. It will find its way into the public mind, for there is that sympathy between man and the truth, that he cannot live without it and be blessed. What allies we have on our side! True, the cupidity, the tyranny, the fear, and the atheism of the land are against us. But all the nobleness, all the honour, all the morality, all the religion, are on our side. I was sorry to hear it said, that the religion of the land opposed us. It is not true. Religion never opposed any good work. I know what my friend meant, and I wish he had said it, calling things by their right names. It is the irreligion of the land that favours slavery; it is the idolatry of gold; it is our atheism. Of speculative atheism there is not much; you see how much of the practical!

We are certain of success; the spirit of the age is on our side. See how the old nations shake their tyrants out of the land. See how every steamer brings us good tidings of good things; and do you believe America can keep her slaves? It is idle to think so. So all we want is time. On our side are truth, justice, and the eternal right. Yes, on our side is religion, the religion of Christ; on our side are the hopes of mankind, and the great power of God.

SPEECH

AT THE

NEW ENGLAND ANTI-SLAVERY CONVENTION
IN BOSTON, MAY 29, 1850.

Mr. President,—If we look hastily at the present aspect of American affairs, there is much to discourage a man who believes in the progress of his race. In this republic, with the Declaration of Independence for its political creed, neither of the great political parties is hostile to the existence of slavery. That institution has the continual support of both the Whig and Democratic parties. There are now four eminent men in the Senate of the United States, all of them friends of slavery. Two of these are from the North, both natives of New England; but they surpass their Southern rivals in the zeal with which they defend that institution, and in the concessions which they demand of the friends of justice at the North. These four men are all competitors for the Presidency. Not one of them is the friend of freedom; he that is apparently least its foe, is Mr Benton, the senator from Missouri. Mr Clay, of Kentucky, is less effectually the advocate of slavery than Mr Webster, of Massachusetts. Mr Webster himself has said, "There is no North," and, to prove it experimentally, stands there as one mighty instance of his own rule.

In the Senate of the United States, only Seward and Chase and Hale can be relied on as hostile to slavery. In the House, there are Root and Giddings, and Wilmot and Mann, and a few others. "But what are these among so many?"

See "how it strikes a stranger." Here is an extract

from the letter of a distinguished and learned man,[*] sent out here by the king of Sweden to examine our public schools: "I have just returned from Washington, where I have been witnessing the singular spectacle of this free and enlightened nation being buried in sorrow, on account of the death of that great advocate of slavery, Mr Calhoun. Mr Webster's speech seems to have made a very strong impression upon the people of the South, as I have heard it repeated almost as a lesson of the catechism by every person I have met within the slave territory. It seems now to be an established belief, that slavery is not a *malum necessarium*, still less an evil difficult to get rid of, but desirable soon to get rid of. No, far from that; it seems to be considered as quite a natural, most happy, and essentially Christian institution!"

Not satisfied with keeping an institution which the more Christian religion of the Mohammedan Bey of Tunis has rejected as a "sin against God," we seek to extend it, to perpetuate it, even on soil which the half-civilized Mexicans made clear from its pollutions. The great organs of the party politics of the land are in favour of the extension; the great political men of the land seek to extend it; the leading men in the large mercantile towns of the North—in Boston, New York, and Philadelphia—are also in favour of extending slavery. All this is plain.

But, sir, as I come up here to this Convention year after year, I find some signs of encouragement. Even in the present state of things, the star of hope appears, and we may safely and reasonably say, "Now is our salvation nearer than when we first believed" in anti-slavery. Let us look a little at the condition of America at this moment, to see what there is to help or what to hinder us.

First, I will speak of the present crisis in our affairs; then of the political parties amongst us; then of the manner in which this crisis is met; next of the foes of freedom; and last, of its friends. I will speak with all coolness, and try to speak short. By the middle of the anniversary week, men get a little heated; I am sure I shall be cool, and I think I may also be dull.

There must be unity of action in a nation, as well as in a man, or there cannot be harmony and welfare. As a man "cannot serve two masters" antagonistic and dia-

[*] Mr Silgeström.

metrically opposed to one another, as God and Mammon, no more can a nation serve two opposite principles at the same time.

Now, there are two opposite and conflicting principles recognized in the political action of America: at this moment, they cor..end for the mastery, each striving to destroy the other.

There is what I call the American idea. I so name it, because it seems to me to lie at the basis of all our truly original, distinctive, and American institutions. It is itself a complex idea, composed of three subordinate and more simple ideas, namely: The idea that all men have unalienable rights; that in respect thereof, all men are created equal; and that government is to be established and sustained for the purpose of giving every man an opportunity for the enjoyment and development of all these unalienable rights. This idea demands, as the proximate organization thereof, a democracy, that is, a government of all the people, by all the people, for all the people; of course, a government after the principles of eternal justice, the unchanging law of God; for shortness' sake, I will call it the idea of freedom.

That is one idea; and the other is, that one man has a right to hold another man in thraldom, not for the slave's good, but for the master's convenience; not on account of any wrong the slave has done or intended, but solely for the benefit of the master. This idea is not peculiarly American. For shortness' sake, I will call this the idea of slavery. It demands for its proximate organization, an aristocracy, that is, a government of all the people by a part of the people—the masters; for a part of the people —the masters; against a part of the people—the slaves; a government contrary to the principles of eternal justice, contrary to the unchanging law of God. These two ideas are hostile, irreconcilably hostile, and can no more be compromised and made to coalesce in the life of this nation, than the worship of the real God and the worship of the imaginary devil can be combined and made to coalesce in the life of a single man. An attempt has been made to reconcile and unite the two. The slavery clauses of the Constitution of the United States is one monument of this attempt; the results of this attempt— you see what they are, not order, but confusion.

We cannot have any settled and lasting harmony until one or the other of these ideas is cast out of the councils of the nation: so there must be war between them before there can be peace. Hitherto, the nation has not been clearly aware of the existence of these two adverse principles; or, if aware of their existence, has thought little of their irreconcilable diversity. At the present time, this fact is brought home to our consciousness with great clearness. On the one hand, the friends of freedom set forth the idea of freedom, clearly and distinctly, demanding liberty for each man. This has been done as never before. Even in the Senate of the United States it has been done, and repeatedly during the present session of Congress. On the other hand, the enemies of freedom set forth the idea of slavery as this has not been done in other countries for a long time. Slavery has not been so lauded in any legislative body for many a year, as in the American Senate in 1850. Some of the discussions remind one of the spirit which prevailed in the Roman Senate, A. D. 62, when about four hundred slaves were crucified, because their master, Pedanius Secundus, a man of consular dignity, was found murdered in his bed. I mean to say, the same disregard of the welfare of the slaves, the same willingness to sacrifice them—if not their lives, which are not now at peril, at least their welfare, to the convenience of their masters. Anybody can read the story in Tacitus,* and it is worth reading, and instructive, too, at these times.

Here are some of the statements relative to slavery made in the thirty-first Congress of the United States. Hearken to the testimony of the Hon. Mr Badger, of North Carolina:

"It is clear that this institution [slavery] not only was not disapproved of, but was expressly recognized, approved, and its continuance sanctioned by the divine lawgiver of the Jews."

"Whether an evil or not, it is not a sin; it is not a violation of the divine law.

"What treatment did it receive from the founder of the gospel dispensation? It was approved, first negatively, because, in the whole New Testament, there is not to be found one single word, either spoken by the Saviour, or by any of the evangelists or apostles, in which that institution is either directly or indi-

* Annal. Lib. XIV. cap. 42, et seq.

rectly condemned; and also affirmatively." This he endeavours to show, by quoting the passages from St Paul, usually quoted for that purpose. " Nothing would be easier than for St Paul to have said—' Slaves, be obedient to your heathen masters; but I say to you, feeling masters, emancipate your slaves; the law of Christ is against that relation, and you are bound, therefore, to set them at liberty.' No such word is spoken."

Thus far goes the Hon. Senator Badger, of North Carolina.

Mr Brown, of Mississippi, goes further yet. He knows what some men think of slavery, and tells them, "Very well, think so; but keep your thoughts to yourselves." He is not content with bidding the "freest and most enlightened nation in the world," be silent on this matter: he is not content, with Mr Badger, to declare that if an evil, it is not a sin, and to find it upheld in the Old Testament, and allowed in the New Testament; he tells us that he "regards slavery as a great moral, social, political, and religious blessing—a blessing to the slave, and a blessing to the master."

Thus, the issue is fairly made between the two principles. The contradiction is plain. The battle between the two is open, and in sight of the world.

But this is not the first time there has been a quarrel between the idea of slavery and the idea of freedom in America. The quarrel has lasted, with an occasional truce, for more than sixty years. In six battles, slavery has been victorious over freedom.

1. In the adoption of the Constitution supporting slavery.
2. In the acquisition of Louisiana as slave territory.
3. In the acquisition of Florida as slave territory.
4. In making the Missouri Compromise.
5. In the annexation of Texas as a slave State.
6. In the Mexican war—a war mean and wicked, even amongst wars.

Since the Revolution, there have been three instances of great national importance, in which freedom has overcome slavery; there have been three victories:

1. In prohibiting slavery from the North-west territory, before the adoption of the Constitution.
2. In prohibiting the slave-trade in 1808. I mean, in

prohibiting the African slave-trade; the American slave-trade is still carried on in the capital of the United States.

3. The prohibition of slavery in Oregon may be regarded as a third victory, though not apparently of so much consequence as the others.

Now comes another battle, and it remains to be decided whether the idea of slavery or the idea of freedom is to prevail in the territory we have conquered and stolen from Mexico. The present strife is to settle that question. Now, as before, it is a battle between freedom and slavery; one on which the material and spiritual welfare of millions of men depends; but now the difference between freedom and slavery is more clearly seen than in 1787; the consequences of each are better understood, and the sin of slavery is felt and acknowledged by a class of persons who had few representatives sixty years ago. It is a much greater triumph for slavery to prevail now, and carry its institutions into New Mexico in 1850, than it was to pass the pro-slavery provisions of the Constitution in 1787. It will be a greater sin now to extend slavery, than it was to establish it in 1620, when slaves were first brought to Virginia.

Ever since the adoption of the Constitution, protected by that shield, mastering the energies of the nation, and fighting with that weapon, slavery has been continually aggressive. The slave-driver has coveted new soil; has claimed it; has had his claim allowed. Louisiana, Florida, Texas, California, and New Mexico are the results of Southern aggression. Now the slave-driver reaches out his hand towards Cuba, trying to clutch that emerald gem set in the tropic sea. How easy it was to surrender to Great Britian portions of the Oregon Territory in a high Northern latitude! Had it been South of 36° 30', it would not have been so easy to settle the Oregon question by a compromise. So when we make a compromise there, "the reciprocity must be all on one side."

Let us next look at the position of the political parties with respect to the present crisis. There are now four political parties in the land.

1. There is the Government party, represented by the President, and portions of his Cabinet, if not the whole of it. This party does not attempt to meet the question

which comes up, but to dodge and avoid it. Shall freedom or slavery prevail in the new territory? is the question. The Government has no opinion; it will leave the matter to be settled by the people of the territory. This party wishes California to come into the Union without slavery, for it is her own desire so to come; and does not wish a territorial government to be formed by Congress in New Mexico, but to leave the people there to form a State, excluding or establishing slavery as they see fit. The motto of this party is inaction, not intervention. King James I. once proposed a question to the judges of England. They declined to answer it, and the king said, "If ye give no counsel, then why be ye counsellors?" The people of the United States might ask the Government, "If ye give us no leading, then why be ye leaders?" This party is not hostile to slavery; not opposed to its extension.

2. Then there is the Whig party. This party has one distinctive idea; the idea of a tariff for protection; whether for the protection of American labour, or merely American capital, I will not now stop to inquire. The Whig party is no more opposed to slavery, or its extension, than the Government party itself.

However, there are two divisions of the Whigs, the Whig party South, and the Whig party North. The two agree in their ideas of protection, and their pro-slavery character. But the Whig party South advocates slavery and protection; the Whig party North, protection and slavery.

In the North there are many Whigs who are opposed to slavery, especially to the extension of slavery; there are also many other persons, not of the Whig party, opposed to the extension of slavery; therefore in the late electioneering campaign, to secure the votes of these persons, it was necessary for the Whig party North to make profession of anti-slavery. This was done accordingly, in a general form, and in special an attempt was made to show that the Whig party was opposed to the extension of slavery.

Hear what Senator Chase says on this point. I read from his speech in the Senate, on March 26, 1850:—

"On the Whig side it was urged, that the candidate of the Philadelphia Convention was, if not positively favourable to the Proviso, at least pledged to leave the matter to Congress free from executive influence, and ready to prove it when enacted by that body."

General Cass had written the celebrated "Nicholson Letter," in which he declared that Congress had no constitutional power to enact the Proviso. But so anxious were the Democrats of the North to assume an anti-slavery aspect,—continues Mr Chase,—that

"Notwithstanding this letter, many of his friends in the free States persisted in asserting that he would not, if elected, veto the Proviso; many also insisted that he regarded slavery as excluded from the territories by the Mexican laws still in force; while others maintained that he regarded slavery as an institution of positive law, and Congress as constitutionally incompetent to enact such law, and that therefore it was impossible for slavery to get into the territories, whether Mexican law was in force or not."

This, says Mr Chase, was the Whig argument :—

"Prohibition is essential to the certain exclusion of slavery from the territories. If the Democratic candidate shall be elected, prohibition is impossible, for the veto will be used: if the Whig candidate shall be elected, prohibition is certain, provided you elect a Congress who will carry out your will. Vote, therefore, for the Whigs."

Such was the general argument of the Whig party. Let us see what it was in Massachusetts in special. Here I have documentary evidence. This is the statement of the Whig Convention at Worcester in 1848, published shortly before the election ;—

"We understand the Whig party to be committed in favour of the principles contained in the ordinance of 1787, the prohibition of slavery in territory now free, and of its abolition wherever it can be constitutionally effected."

They professed to aim at the same thing which the free soil party aimed at, only the work must be done by the old Whig organization. Free soil cloth must be manufactured, but it must be woven in the old Whig mill, with the old Whig machinery, and by the Whig weavers. See what the Convention says of the Democratic party :—

"We understand the Democratic party to be pledged to decline any legislation upon the subject of slavery, with a view either to its prohibition or restriction in places where it does not exist, or to its abolition in any of the territories of the United States."

There is no ambiguity in that language. Men can talk very plain when they will. Still there were some that doubted; so the great and famous men of the party came out to convince the doubters that the Whigs were the men to save the country from the disgrace of slavery.

Here let me introduce the testimony of Mr Choate. This which follows is from his speech at Salem. He tells us the great work is, "The passage of a law to-day that California and New Mexico shall remain for ever free. That is . . . an object of great and transcendent importance : . . . we should go up to the very limits of the Constitution itself . . . to defeat the always detested and forever-to-be detested object of the dark ambition of that candidate of the Baltimore Convention, who has consented to pledge himself in advance, that he will veto the future law of freedom!" "Is there a Whig upon this floor who doubts that the strength of the Whig party next March will extend freedom to California and New Mexico, if by the Constitution they are entitled to freedom at all? Is there a member of Congress that would not vote for freedom?" [*Sancta simplicitas! Ora pro nobis!*] "Is there a single Whig constituency, in any free State in this country, that would return any man that would not vote for freedom? Do you believe that Daniel Webster himself could be returned, if there was the least doubt upon this question?"

That is plain speech. But, to pass from the special to the particular, hear Mr Webster himself. What follows is from his famous speech at Marshfield, September, 1848.

"General Cass (he says) will have the Senate; and with the patronage of the Government, with the interest that he, as a Northern man, can bring to bear, co-operating with every interest that the South can bring to bear, we cry *safety* before we are out of the woods, if we feel that there is no danger as to these new territories!" "In my judgment, the interests of the country and the feelings of a vast majority of the people require that a President of these United States shall be . ected, who will neither use his official influence to promote, nor who feels any disposition in his heart to promote, the further extension of slavery in this country, and the further influence of it in the public councils."

Speaking of the free soil party and the Buffalo platform, he says—"I hold myself to be as good a free soil man as any of the Buffalo convention." Of the platform, he says —" I can stand upon it pretty well." "I beg to know who is to inspire into my breast a more resolute and fixed determination to resist, unyieldingly, the encroachments and advances of the slave power in this country, than has inspired it, ever since the day that I first opened my mouth in the councils of the country."

If such language as this would not "deceive the very elect," what was more to the point, it was quite enough to deceive the electors. But now this language is forgotten; forgotten in general by the Whig party North; forgotten in special by those who seemed to be the exponents of the Whig party in Massachusetts ; forgotten at any rate by the nine hundred and eighty-seven men who signed the letter to Mr Webster; and in particular it is forgotten by Mr Webster himself, who now says that it would disgrace his own understanding to vote for the extension of the Wilmot Proviso over the new territory !

There were some men in New England who did not believe the statements of the Whig party North in 1848, because they knew the men that uttered the sentiments of the Whig party South. The leaders put their thumbs in the eyes of the people, and then said, "Do you see any dough in our faces ?" "No!" said the people, "not a speck." "Then vote our ticket, and never say we are not hostile to slavery so long as you live."

At the South, the Whig party used language somewhat different. Here is a sample from the New Orleans Bee :—

" General Taylor is from birth, association, and conviction, identified with the South and her institutions ; being one of the most extensive slave-holders in Louisiana—and supported by the slave-holding interest, as opposed to the Wilmot Proviso, and in favour of securing the privilege to the owners of slaves to remove with them to newly acquired territory."

3. Then there is the Democratic party. The distinctive

idea of the Democrats is represented by the word anti-protection, or revenue tariff. This party, as such, is still less opposed to slavery than the Whigs; however, there are connected with it, at the North, many men who oppose the extension of slavery. This party is divided into two divisions, the Democratic party South, and the Democratic party North. They agree in their idea of anti-protection and slavery, differing only in the emphasis which they give to the two words. The Democrats of the South say Slavery and anti-protection; the Democrats North, Anti-protection and slavery. Thus you see, that while there is a specific difference between Democrats and Whigs, there is also a generic agreement in the matter of slavery. According to the doctrine of elective affinities, both drop what they have a feeble affinity for, and hold on with what their stronger affinity demands. The Whigs and Democrats of the South are united in their attachment to slavery, not only mechanically, but by a sort of chemical union.

Mr Cass's Nicholson letter is well known. He says, Congress has no constitutional right to restrict slavery in the territories. Here is the difference between him and General Taylor. General Taylor does not interfere at all in the matter. If Congress puts slavery in, he says, Very well! If Congress puts slavery out, he says the same, Very well! But if Congress puts slavery out, General Cass would say, No. You shall not put it out. One has the policy of King Log, the other that of King Serpent. So far as that goes Log is the better king.

So much for the Democratic party.

4. The free soil party opposes slavery so far as it is possible to do, and yet comply with the Constitution of the United States. Its idea is declared by its words,—No more slave territory. It does not profess to be an anti-slavery party in general, only an anti-slavery party subject to the Constitution. In the present crisis in the Congress of the United States, it seems to me the men who represent this idea, though not always professing allegiance to the party, have yet done the nation good and substantial service. I refer more particularly to Messrs Chase, Seward, and Hale in the Senate, to Messrs Root, Giddings, and Mann in the House. Those gentlemen swear to keep the Constitution; in what sense and with what limitations

I know not. It is for them to settle that matter with their own consciences. I do know this, that these men have spoken very noble words against slavery; heroic words in behalf of freedom. It is not to be supposed that the free soil party, as such, has attained the same convictions as to the sin of slavery, which the anti-slavery party has long arrived at. Still they may be as faithful to their convictions as any of the men about this platform. If they have less light to walk by, they have less to be accountable for. For my own part, spite of their short-comings, and of some things which to me seem wrong in the late elections in New England, I cannot help thinking they have done good as individuals, and as a party; it seems to me they have done good both ways. I will honour all manly opposition to slavery, whether it come up to my mark, or does not come near it. I will ask every man to be true to his conscience, and his reason, not to mine.

In speaking of the parties, I ought not to omit to say a word or two respecting some of the most prominent men, and their position in reference to this slavery question. It is a little curious, that of all the candidates for the Presidency, Mr Benton, of Missouri, should be the least inclined to support the pretensions of the slave power. But so it is.

Of Mr Cass, nothing more need be said at present; his position is defined and well known. But a word must be said of Mr Clay. He comes forward, as usual, with a "Compromise." Here it is, in the famous "Omnibus Bill." In one point it is not so good as the Government scheme. General Taylor, as the organ of the party, recommends the admission of California, as an independent measure. He does not huddle and lump it together with any other matters; and in this respect, his scheme is more favourable to freedom than the other; for Mr Clay couples the admission of California with other things. But in two points Mr Clay's bill has the superiority over the General's scheme.

1. It limits the Western and Northern boundaries of Texas, and so reduces the territory of that State, where slavery is now established by law. Yet, as I understand it, he takes off from New Mexico about seventy thousand square miles, enough to make eight or ten States like

Massachusetts, and delivers it over to Texas to be slave soil; as Mr Webster says, out of the power of Congress to redeem from that scourge.

2. It does not maintain that Congress has no power to exclude slavery in admitting a new State; whereas, if I understand the President in his message, he considers such an act " An invasion of their rights." *

Let us pass by Mr Clay, and come to the other aspirant for the Presidency.

At the Philadelphia Convention, Mr Webster, at the most, could only get one half the votes of New England; several of these not given in earnest, but only as a compliment to the great man from the North. Now, finding his presidential wares not likely to be bought by New England, he takes them to a wider market; with what success we shall one day see.

Something has already been said in the newspapers and elsewhere, about Mr Webster's speech. No speech ever delivered in America has excited such deep and righteous indignation. I know there are influential men in Boston, and in all large towns, who must always have somebody to sustain and applaud. They some time since applauded Mr Webster, for reasons very well known, and now continue their applause of him. His late speech pleases them; its worst parts please them most. All that is as was to be expected; men like what they must like. But, in the country, among the sober men of Massachusetts and New England, who prize right above the political expediency of to-day, I think Mr Webster's speech is read with indignation. I believe no one political act in America, since the treachery of Benedict Arnold, has excited so much moral indignation, as the conduct of Daniel Webster.

But I pass by his speech, to speak of other things connected with that famous man. One of the most influential pro-slavery newspapers of Boston, calls the gentlemen who signed the letter to him, the " Retainers " of Mr Webster. The word is well chosen and quite descriptive. This word is used in a common, a feudal, and a legal sense. In the common sense, it means one who has complete possession of the thing retained; in the feudal sense, it means a

* Executive Documents: House of Representatives, No. 17, p. 3.

dependent or vassal, who is bound to support his liege lord; in the legal sense, it means the person who hires an attorney to do his business; and the sum given to secure his services, or prevent him from acting for the opposite party, is called a retaining fee. I take it the word "Retainers" is used in the legal sense; certainly it is not in the feudal sense, for these gentlemen do not owe allegiance to Mr Webster. Nor is it in its common sense, for events have shown that they have not a "complete possession" of Mr Webster.

Now a word about this letter to him. Mr Webster's retainers—nine hundred and eighty-seven in number—tell him, "You have pointed out to a whole people the path of duty, have convinced the understanding, and touched the conscience of a nation." "We desire, therefore, to express to you our entire concurrence in the sentiments of your speech, and our heartfelt thanks for the inestimable aid it has afforded towards the preservation and perpetuation of the Union."

They express their entire concurrence in the sentiments of his speech. In the speech, as published in the edition "revised and corrected by himself," Mr Webster declares his intention to support the famous fugitive slave bill, and the amendments thereto, "with all its provisions, to the fullest extent." When the retainers express their "entire concurrence in the sentiments of the speech," they express their entire concurrence in that intention. There is no ambiguity in the language; they make a universal affirmation—(*affirmatio de omni*). Now Mr Webster comes out, by two agents, and recants this declaration. Let me do him no injustice. He shall be heard by his next friend, who wishes to amend the record, a correspondent of the Boston Courier, of May 6th :—

"The speech now reads thus :—'My friend at the head of the Judiciary Committee has a bill on the subject, now before the Senate, with some amendments to it, which I propose to support, with all its provisions, to the fullest extent.' Change the position of the word which, and the sentence would read thus :—' My friend at the head of the Judiciary Committee has a bill on the subject, now before the Senate, which, with some amendments to it, I propose to support, with all its provisions, to the fullest extent.'"

"Call you that backing your friends?" Really, it is too bad, after his retainers have expressed their "entire concurrence in the sentiments of the speech," for him to back out, to deny that he entertained one of the sentiments already approved of and concurred in! Can it be possible, we ask, that Mr Webster can resort to this device to defend himself, leaving his retainers in the lurch? It does not look like him to do such a thing. But the correspondent of the Courier goes on as follows:—

"We are authorized to state, first—That Mr Webster did not revise this portion of his speech, with any view to examine its exact accuracy of phrase; and second—That Mr Webster at the time of the delivery of the speech, had in his desk three emendatory sections, ... and one of which provides expressly for the right of trial by jury."

But who is the person "authorized to state" such a thing? Professor Stuart informs the public that it "comes from the hand of a man who might claim a near place to Mr Webster, in respect to talent, integrity, and patriotism."

Still, this recantation is so unlike Mr Webster, that one would almost doubt the testimony of so great an unknown as is the writer in the Courier. But Mr Stuart removes all doubt, and says—"I merely add that Mr Webster himself has personally assured me that his speech was in accordance with the correction here made, and that he has now in his desk the amendments to which the corrector refers." So the retainers must bear the honour, or the shame, whichsoever it may be, of volunteering the advocacy of that remarkable bill.

When Paul was persecuted for righteousness' sake, how easily might "the offence of the cross" have been made to cease, by a mere transposition! Had he pursued that plan, he need not have been let down from the wall in a basket: he might have had a dinner given him by forty scribes, at the first hotel in Jerusalem, and a doctor of the law to defend him in a pamphlet.

But, alas! in Mr Webster's case, admitting the transposition is real, the transubstantiation is not thereby effected; the transfer of the *which* does not alter the character of the sentence to the requisite degree. The bill, which he volunteers to advocate, contains provisions to this effect:

That the owner of a fugitive slave may seize his fugitive, and, on the warrant of any "judge, commissioner, clerk, marshal, post-master, or collector," "residing or being" within the State where the seizure is made, the fugitive, without any trial by jury, shall be delivered up to his master, and carried out of the State. Now, this is the bill which Mr Webster proposes "to support, with all its provisions, to the fullest extent." Let him transfer his *which*, it does not transubstantiate his statement so that he can consistently introduce a section which "provides expressly for the right of trial by jury." This attempt to evade the plain meaning of a plain statement, is too small a thing for a great man.

I make no doubt that Mr Webster had in his desk, at the time alleged, a bill designed to secure the trial by jury to fugitive slaves, prepared as it is set forth. But how do you think it came there, and for what purpose? Last February Mr Webster was intending to make a very different speech; and then, I make no doubt, it was that this bill was prepared, with the design of introducing it! But I see no reason for supposing, that when he made his celebrated speech, he intended to introduce it as an amendment to Mr Mason's or Butler's bill. It is said that he will present it to the Senate. Let us wait and see.*

But, since the speech at Washington, Mr Webster has said things at Boston almost as bad. Here they are; extracts from his speech at the Revere House. I quote from the report in the Daily Advertiser. "Neither you nor I shall see the legislation of the country proceed in the old harmonious way, until the discussions in Congress and out of Congress upon the subject, to which you have alluded [the subject of slavery], shall be, in some way, suppressed. Take that truth home with you—and take it as truth." A very pretty truth that is to take home with us, that "discussion" must be "suppressed!"

* Since the delivery of the above, Mr Webster has introduced his bill, providing a trial by jury for fugitive slaves. If I understand it, Mr Webster does not offer it as a substitute for the Judiciary Bill on the subject, does not introduce it as an amendment to that or to anything else. Nay, he does not formally introduce it—only lays it before the Senate, with the desire that it may be printed! The effect it is designed to produce, it is very easy to see. The retainers can now say—See! Mr Webster himself wishes to provide a trial by jury for fugitives! Some of the provisions of the bill are remarkable, but they need not be dwelt on here.

Again, he says :—

"Sir, the question is, whether Massachusetts will stand to the truth against temptation [that is the question]! whether she will be just against temptation! whether she will defend herself against her own prejudices! She has conquered everything else in her time; she has conquered this ocean which washes her shore; she has conquered her own sterile soil; she has conquered her stern and inflexible climate; she has fought her way to the universal respect of the world; she has conquered every one's prejudices but her own. The question is, whether she will conquer her own prejudices!"

The trumpet gives no uncertain sound; but before we prepare ourselves for battle, let us see who is the foe. What are the "prejudices" Massachusetts is to conquer? The prejudice in favour of the American idea; the prejudice in favour of what our fathers called self-evident truths; that all men "are endowed with certain unalienable rights;" that "all men are created equal," and that "to secure these rights, governments are instituted amongst men." These are the prejudices Massachusetts is called on to conquer. There are some men who will do this "with alacrity;" but will Massachusetts conquer her prejudices in favour of the "unalienable rights of man"? I think, Mr President, she will first have to forget two hundred years of history. She must efface Lexington and Bunker Hill from her memory, and tear the old rock of Plymouth out from her bosom. These are prejudices which Massachusetts will not conquer till the ocean ceases to wash her shore, and granite to harden her hills. Massachusetts has conquered a good many things, as Mr Webster tells us. I think there are several other things we shall try our hand upon, before we conquer our prejudice in favour of the unalienable rights of man.

There is one pleasant thing about this position of Mr Webster. He is alarmed at the fire which has been kindled in his rear. He finds " considerable differences of opinion prevail . . . . on the subject of that speech," and is "grateful to receive . . . . opinions so decidedly concurring with " his own,—so he tells the citizens of Newburyport. He feels obliged to do something to escape the obloquy which naturally comes upon him. So he revises his speech; now supplying an omission, now altering a little; authorizes another great man to transpose his relative pronoun, and anchor it fast to another antecedent; appeals to amendments in the senatorial desk, designed to secure a jury trial for fugitive slaves; derides his opponents, and compares them with the patriots of ancient times. Here is his letter to the citizens of Newburyport—a very remarkable document. It contains some surprising legal doctrines, which I leave others to pass upon. But in it he explains the fugitive slave law of 1793, which does not "provide for the trial of any question whatever by jury, in the State in which the arrest is made." "At that time," nobody regarded any of the provisions of that bill as "repugnant to religion, liberty, the constitution, or humanity;" and he has "no more objections to the provisions of this law, than was seen to them" by the framers of the law itself. If he sees therein nothing "repugnant to religion, liberty, the constitution, or humanity," then why transpose that relative pronoun, and have an amendment "which provides expressly for the right of trial by jury?"

"In order to allay excitement," he answers, "and remove objections." "There are many difficulties, however, attending any such provision [of a jury trial]; and a main one, and perhaps the only insuperable one, has been created by the States themselves, by making it a penal offence in their own officers, to render any aid in apprehending or securing such fugitives, and absolutely refusing the use of their jails for keeping them in custody, till a jury could be impanelled, witnesses summoned, and a regular trial be had."

Think of that! It is Massachusetts, Pennsylvania, Ohio, and New York, which prohibit the fugitive from getting a trial for his freedom, before a jury of twelve good men and true! But Mr Webster goes on: "It is not too much to say, that to these State laws is to be attributed the actual and practical denial of trial by jury in these cases." Generally, the cause is thought to precede the effect, but here is a case in which, according to Mr Webster, the effect has got the start of the cause, by more than fifty years. The fugitive slave law of Congress, which allowed the master to capture the runaway, was passed in 1793; but the State laws he refers to, to which "is to be attributed the actual and practical denial of trial by jury in these cases," were not passed till after 1840. "To what base uses may we come at last!" Mr Webster would never have made such a defence of his pro-slavery conduct, had he not been afraid of the fire in his rear, and thought his retainers not able to put it out. He seems to think this fire is set in the name of religion: so, to help us "conquer our prejudices," he cautions us against the use of religion, and quotes from the private letter of "one of the most distinguished men in England," dated as late as the 29th of January—"Religion is an excellent thing in every matter except in politics: there it seems to make men mad." In this respect, it seems religion is inferior to money, for the Proverbs tell us that money "answereth all things;" religion, it seems, "answereth all things," except politics. Poor Mr Webster! If religion is not good in politics, I suppose irreligion is good there; and, really, it is often enough introduced there. So, if religion "seems to make men mad" in politics, I suppose irreligion makes them sober in politics. But Mr Webster, fresh from his transposition of his own relative, explains this: His friend ascribes the evils not to "true and genuine religion," but to "that fantastic notion of religion." So, making the transposition, it would read thus: "That fantastical notion of religion," "is an excellent thing in any matter except politics." Alas! Mr Webster does not expound his friend's letter, nor his own language, so well as he used to expound the Constitution. But he says, "The religion of the New Testament is as sure a guide to duty in politics, as in any other concern of life." So, in the name of "conscience and the Constitution," Professor Stuart comes forward to defend Mr Webster, "by the religion of the New Testament; that religion which is founded on the teachings of Jesus and his apostles." How are the mighty fallen!

Mr Webster makes a "great speech," lending his mighty influence to the support and extension of slavery, with all its attendant consequences, which paralyze the hand of industry, enfeeble the thinking mind, and brutify the conscience which should discern between right and wrong; nine hundred and eighty-seven of his retainers in Boston thank him for reminding them of their duty. But still the fire in his rear is so hot, that he must come on to Boston, talk about having discussion suppressed, and ask Massachusetts to conquer her prejudices. That is not enough.

He must go up to Andover, and get a minister to defend him, in the name of "conscience and the Constitution," supporting slavery out of the Old Testament and New Testament. "To what mean uses may we not descend!"

There is a "short and easy method" with Professor Stuart, and all other men who defend slavery out of the Bible. If the Bible defends slavery, it is not so much the better for slavery, but so much the worse for the Bible. If Mr Stuart and Mr Webster do not see that, there are plenty of obscurer men that do. Of all the attacks ever made on the Bible, by "deists" and "infidels," none would do so much to bring it into disrepute, as to show that it sanctioned American slavery.

It is rather a remarkable fact, that an orthodox minister should be on Mr Webster's paper, endorsing for the Christianity of slavery.

Let me say a word respecting the position of the Representative from Boston. I speak only of his position, not of his personal character. Let him, and all men, have the benefit of the distinction between their personal character and official conduct. Mr Winthrop is a consistent Whig; a representative of the idea of the Whig party North, protection and slavery. When he first went into Congress, it was distinctly understood that he was not going to meddle with the matter of slavery; the tariff was the thing. All this was consistent. It is to be supposed that a Northern Whig will put the mills of the North before the black men of the South: and "Property before persons," might safely be writ on the banner of the Whig party, North or South.

Mr Winthrop seems a little uneasy in his position. Some time ago he complained of a "nest of vipers" in Boston, who had broken their own teeth in gnawing a file; meaning the "vipers" in the free soil party, I suppose, whose teeth, however, have a little edge still left on them. He finds it necessary to define his position, and show that he has kept up his communication with the base line of operations from which he started. This circumstance is a little suspicious.

Unlike Mr Webster, Mr Winthrop seems to think religion is a good thing in politics, for in his speech of May

7th, he says—"I acknowledge my allegiance to the whole Constitution of the United States... And whenever I perceive a plain conflict of jurisdiction and authority between the Constitution of my country and the laws of my God, my course is clear. I shall resign my office, whatever it may be, and renounce all connection with public service of any sort." That is fair and manly. He will not hold a position under the Constitution of the United States which is inconsistent with the Constitution of the Universe. But he says—"There are provisions in the Constitution [of the United States, he means, not of the universe], which involve us in painful obligations, and from which some of us would rejoice to be relieved; and this [the restoration of fugitive slaves] is one of them. But there is none, none, in my judgment, which involves any conscientious or religious difficulty." So he has no "conscientious or religious" objection to return a fugitive slave. He thinks the Constitution of the United States "avoids the idea that there can be property in man," but recognizes "that there may be property in the service or labour of man." But when it is property in the service of man without value received by the servant, and a claim which continues to attach to a man and his children for ever, it looks very like the idea of property in man. At any rate, there is only a distinction in the words, no difference in the things. To claim the sum of the accidents, all and several of a thing, is practically to claim the thing.

Mr Winthrop once voted for the Wilmot Proviso, in its application to the Oregon Territory. Some persons have honoured him for it, and even contended that he also was a free soiler. He wipes off that calumny by declaring, that he attached that proviso to the Oregon bill for the purpose of defeating the bill itself. "This proviso was one of the means upon which I mainly relied for the purpose." "There can be little doubt," he says, "that this clause had its influence in arresting the bill in the other end of the capitol," where it was "finally lost." That is his apology for appearing to desire to prevent the extension of slavery. It is worth while to remember this.

Unlike Mr Webster, he thinks slavery may go into New Mexico. "We may hesitate to admit that nature has everywhere [in the new territory] settled the question against slavery." Still he would not now pass the proviso to exclude slavery. It "would . . . unite the South as one man, and if it did not actually rend the Union asunder, would create an alienation and irritation in that quarter of the country, which would render the Union hardly worth preserving." "Is there not ample reason for an abatement of the Northern tone, for a forbearance of Northern urgency upon this subject, without the imputation of tergiversation and treachery?"

Here I am reminded of a remarkable sentence in Mr Webster's speech at Marshfield, in relation to the Northern men who helped to annex Texas. Here it is:—

"For my part, I think that Dough-faces is an epithet not sufficiently reproachful. Now, I think such persons are dough-faces, dough-heads, and dough-souls, that they are all dough; that the coarsest potter may mould them at pleasure to vessels of honour or dishonour, but most readily to vessels of dishonour."

The Representative from Boston, in the year 1850, has small objection to the extension of slave soil. Hearken to his words:—

"I can never put the question of extending slave soil on the same footing with one of directly increasing slavery and multiplying slaves. If a positive issue could ever again be made up for our decision, whether human beings, few or many, of whatever race, complexion, or condition, should be freshly subjected to a system of hereditary bondage, and be changed from freemen into slaves, I can conceive that no bonds of union, no ties of interest, no cords of sympathy, no consideration of past glory, present welfare, or future grandeur, should be suffered to interfere, for an instant, with our resolute and unceasing resistance to a measure so iniquitous and abominable. There would be a clear, unquestionable moral element in such an issue, which would admit of no compromise, no concession, no forbearance whatever. . . . A million of swords would leap from their scabbards to assert it, and the Union itself would be shivered like a Prince Rupert's dress in the shock.

"But, Sir, the question whether the institution of slavery, as it already exists, shall be permitted to extend itself over a hundred or a hundred thousand more square miles than it now occupies, is a different question. . . It is not, in my judgment, such an issue that conscientious and religious men may not be free to acquiesce in whatever decision may be arrived at by the constituted authorities of the country. ... It is not with a view of cooping up slavery ... within limits too narrow for its natural growth; ... it is not for the purpose of girding it round with lines of fire, till its sting, like that of the scorpion, shall be turned upon itself, ... that I have ever advocated the principles of the Ordinance of 1787."

Mr Mann, I think, is still called a Whig, but no member of the free soil party has more readily or more ably stood up against the extension of slavery. His noble words stand in marvellous contrast to the discourse of the Representative from Boston. Mr Mann represents the country, and not the "metropolis." His speech last February, and his recent letter to his constituents, are too well known, and too justly prized, to require any commendation here. But I cannot fail to make a remark on a passage in the letter. He says, if we allow Mr Clay's compromise to be accepted, "Were it not for the horrible consequences which it would involve, a roar of laughter, like a *feu de joie*, would run down the course of the ages." He afterwards says—"Should the South succeed in their present attempt upon the territories, they will impatiently await the retirement of General Taylor from the executive chair to add the 'State of Cuba' ... to this noble triumph." One is a little inclined to start such a laugh himself at the idea of the South waiting for that event before they undertake that plan!

Mr Mann says: "If no moral or religious obligation existed against holding slaves, would not many of those opulent and respectable gentlemen who signed the letter of thanks to Mr Webster, and hundreds of others, indeed, instead of applying to intelligence offices for domestics, go at once to the auction room, and buy a man or a woman with as little hesitancy or compunction as they now send to Brighton for beeves?" This remark has drawn on him some censures not at all merited. There are men enough in Boston, who have no objection to slavery. I know such men, who would have been glad if slavery had been continued here. Are Boston merchants unwilling to take mortgages on plantations and negroes? Do Northern men not acquire negroes by marrying wealthy women at the South, and keep the negroes as slaves? If the truth could be known, I think it would appear that Dr Palfrey had lost more reputation in Boston than he gained, by emancipating the human beings which fell to his lot. But here is a story which I take from the Boston Republican. It is worth preserving as a monument of the morals of Boston in 1850, and may be worth preserving at the end of the century :—

"A year or two since, a bright-looking mulatto youth, about twenty years of age, and whose complexion was not much, if any, darker than that of the great 'Expounder of the Constitution,' entered the counting-room, on some errand for his master, a Kentuckian, who was making a visit here. A merchant on one of our principal wharves, who came in and spoke to him, remarked to the writer that he once owned this "boy" and his mother, and sold them for several hundred dollars. Upon my expressing astonishment to him that he could thus deal in human flesh, he remarked that 'When you are among the Romans, you must do as the Romans do.' I know of others of my Northern acquaintances, and good Whigs too, who have owned slaves at the South, and who, if public opinion warranted it, would be as likely, I presume, to buy and sell them at the North."

I have yet to learn that the controlling men of this city have any considerable aversion to domestic slavery.*

Mr Mann's zeal in behalf of freedom, and against the extension of slavery, has drawn upon him the indignation of Mr Webster, who is grieved to see him so ignorant of American law. But Mr Mann is able to do his own fighting.

So much for the political parties and their relation to the matters at issue at this moment. Still, there is some reason to hope that the attempt to extend slavery, made in the face of the world, and supported by such talent, will yet fail; that it will bring only shame on the men who aim to extend and perpetuate so foul a blight. The fact that Mr Webster's retainers must come to the rescue of their attorney; that himself must write letters to defend himself, and must even obtain the services of a clergyman to help him—this shows the fear that is felt from the anti-slavery spirit of the North. Depend upon it, a politician

* While this is passing through the press, I learn that several worthy citizens of Boston are at this moment owners of several hundreds of slaves. I think they would lose reputation among their fellows if they should set them free.

is pretty far gone when he sends for the minister, and he thinks his credit failing when he gets a clergyman on his paper to indorse for the Christian character of American slavery.

Here I ought to speak of the party not politicians, who contend against slavery not only beyond the limits of the Constitution, but within those limits; who are opposed not only to the extension, but to the continuance of slavery; who declare that they will keep no compromises which conflict with the eternal laws of God,—of the anti-slavery party. Mr President, if I were speaking to Whigs, to Democrats, or to free soil men, perhaps I might say what I think of this party, of their conduct, and their motives; but, Sir, I pass it by, with the single remark, that I think the future will find this party where they have always been found. I have before now attempted to point out the faults of this party, and before these men; that work I will not now attempt a second time, and this is not the audience before which I choose to chant its praises.

There are several forces which oppose the anti-slavery movement at this day. Here are some of the most important.

The demagogues of the parties are all, or nearly all, against it. By demagogue I mean the man who undertakes to lead the people for his own advantage, to the harm and loss of the people themselves. All of this class of men, or most of them, now support slavery—not, as I suppose, because they have any special friendship for it, but because they think it will serve their turn. Some noble men in politics are still friends of the slave.

The demagogues of the churches must come next. I am not inclined to attribute so much original power to the churches as some men do. I look on them as indications of public opinion, and not sources thereof—not the wind, but only the vane which shows which way it blows. Once the clergy were the masters of the people, and the authors of public opinion to a great degree; now they are chiefly the servants of the people, and follow public opinion, and but seldom aspire to lead it, except in matters of their own craft, such as the technicalities of a sect, or the form of a ritual. They may lead public opinion in regard to the " posture in prayer," to the " form of baptism," and the like. In important matters which concern the welfare of the nation, the clergy have none or very little weight. Still, as representatives of public opinion, we really find most of the clergy of all denominations, arrayed against the cause of eternal justice. I pass over this matter briefly, because it is hardly necessary for me to give any opinion on the subject. But I am glad to add, that in all denominations here in New England, and perhaps in all the North, there are noble men, who apply the principles of justice to this question of the nation, and bear a manly testimony in the midst of bad examples. Some of the theological newspapers have shown a hostility to slavery and an attachment to the cause of liberty which few men expected; which were quite unknown in those quarters before. To do full justice to men in the sects who speak against this great and popular sin of the nation, we ought to remember that it is harder for a minister than for almost any other man to become a reformer. It is very plain that it is not thought to belong to the calling of a minister, especially in a large town, to oppose the actual and popular sins of his time. So when I see a minister yielding to the public opinion which favours unrighteousness, and passing by, in silence and on the other side, causes which need and deserve his labours and his prayers, I remember what he is hired for, and paid for,—to represent the popular form of religion; if that be idolatry, to represent that. But when I see a minister oppose a real sin which is popular, I cannot but feel a great admiration for the man. We have lately seen some examples of this.

Yet, on the other side, there are some very sad examples of the opposite. Here comes forward a man of high standing in the New England churches, a man who has done real service in promoting a liberal study of matters connected with religion, and defends slavery out of what he deems the "Infallible word of God,"—the Old Testament and the New Testament. Well, if Christianity supports American slavery, so much the worse for Christianity, that is all. Perhaps I ought not to say, *if* Christianity supports slavery. We all know it does not, never did, and never can. But if Paul was an apologist for slavery, so much the worse for Paul. If Calvinism or Catholicism supports slavery, so much the worse for them, not so much the better for slavery! I can easily understand the conduct of the leaders of the New York mob: considering the character of the men, their ignorance and general position, I can easily suppose they may have thought they were doing right in disturbing the meetings there. Considering the apathy of the public authorities, and the attempt, openly made by some men,—unluckily of influence in that city,—to excite others to violence, I have a good deal of charity for Rynders and his gang. But it is not so easy to excuse the conspicuous ecclesiastical defenders of slavery. They cannot plead their ignorance. Let them alone, to make the best defence they can.

The Toryism of America is also against us. I call that man a Tory, who prefers the accidents of man to the substance of manhood. I mean one who prefers the possessions and property of mankind to man himself, to reason and to justice. Of this Toryism we have much in America, much in New England, much in Boston. In this town, I cannot but think the prevailing influence is still a Tory influence. It is this which is the support of the demagogues of the State and the Church.

Toryism exists in all lands. In some, there is a good deal of excuse to be made for it. I can understand the Toryism of the Duke of Medina Sidonia, and of such men. If a man has been born to great wealth and power, derived from ancestors for many centuries held in admiration and in awe; if he has been bred to account himself a superior being, and to be treated accordingly, I can easily understand the Toryism of such a man, and find some excuse for it. I can understand the Tory literature of other nations. The Toryism of the "London Quarterly," of "Blackwood," is easily accounted for, and forgiven. It is, besides, sometimes adorned with wit, and often set off by much learning. It is respectable Toryism. But the Toryism of men who only know they had a grandfather by inference, not by positive testimony; who inherited nothing but their bare limbs; who began their career as tradesmen or mechanics, —mechanics in divinity or law as well as in trade,—and get their bread by any of the useful and honourable callings of life—that such men, getting rich, or lifting their heads out of the obscurity they were once in, should become Tories, in a land, too, where institutions are founded on the idea of freedom and equity and natural justice—that is another thing. The Toryism of American journals, with little scholarship, with no wit, and wisdom in homœopathic doses; the Toryism of a man who started from nothing, the architect of his own fortune; the Toryism of a republican, of a Yankee, the Toryism of a snob,—it is Toryism reduced to its lowest denomination, made vulgar and contemptible; it is the little end of the tail of Toryism. Let us loathe the unclean thing in the depth of our soul, but let us pity the poor Tory; for he, also, in common with the negro slave, is "A man and a brother."

Then the spirit of trade is often against us. Mr Mann, in his letter, speaks of the opposition made to Wilberforce by the " Guinea merchants " of Liverpool, in his attempts to put an end to the slave-trade. The Corporation of Liverpool spent over ten thousand pounds in defence of a traffic, "the worst the sun ever shone upon." This would seem to be a reflection upon some of the merchants of Boston. It seems, from a statement in the Atlas, that Mr Mann did not intend his remarks to apply to Boston, but to New York and Philadelphia, where mass meetings of merchants had been held, to sustain Mr Clay's compromise resolutions. Although Mr Mann did not apply his remarks to Boston, I fear they will apply here as well as to our sister cities. I have yet to learn that the letter of Mr Webster's retainers was any less well adapted to continue and extend slavery, than the resolutions passed at New York and Philadelphia. I wish the insinuations of Mr Mann did not apply here.

One of the signers of the letter to Mr Webster incautiously betrayed, I think, the open secret of the retainers when he said—"I don't care a damn how many slave States they annex !" This is a secret, because not avowed; open, because generally known, or at least believed, to be the sentiment of a strong party in Massachusetts. I am glad to have it also expressed; now the issue is joined, and we do not fight in the dark.

It has long been suspected that some inhabitants of Boston were engaged in the slave-trade. Not long since, the brig "Lucy Anne," of Boston, was captured on the coast of Africa, with five hundred and forty-seven slaves on board. This vessel was built at Thomaston in 1839;

repaired at Boston in 1848, and now hails from this port. She was commanded by one "Captain Otis," and is owned by one "Salem Charles." This, I suppose, is a fictitious name, for certainly it would not be respectable in Boston to extend slavery in this way. Even Mr Winthrop is opposed to that, and thinks "a million swords would leap from their scabbards to oppose it." But it may be that there are men in Boston who do not think it any worse to steal men who were born free, and have grown up free in Africa, and make slaves of them, than to steal such as are born free in America, before they are grown up. If we have the Old Testament decidedly sustaining slavery, and the New Testament never forbidding it; if, as we are often told, neither Jesus nor his early followers ever said a word against slavery; if scarcely a Christian minister in Boston ever preaches against this national sin; if the Representative from Boston has no religious scruples against returning a fugitive slave, or extending slavery over a " hundred or a hundred thousand square miles." of new territory; if the great senator from Massachusetts refuses to vote for the Wilmot Proviso, or re-affirm an ordinance of nature, and re-enact the will of God; if he calls on us to return fugitive slaves " with alacrity," and demands of Massachusetts that she shall conquer her prejudices; if nine hundred and eighty-seven men in this vicinity, of lawful age,* are thankful to him for enlightening them as to their duty, and a professor of theology comes forward to sanction American slavery in the name of religion—why, I think Mr " Salem Charles," with his " Captain Otis," may not be the worst man in the world, after all ! Let us pity him also, as " A man and a brother."

Such is the crisis in our affairs ; such the special issue in the general question between freedom and slavery ; such the position of parties and of great men in relation to this question; such the foes to freedom in America.

On our side, there are great and powerful allies. The American idea is with us ; the spirit of the majority of men in the North, when they are not blindfolded and muzzled by the demagogues of State and Chr h. The religion of the land, also, is on our side ; the irreligion, the

* It has since appeared that several of those persons were at the time, and still are, holders of slaves. Their conduct need excite no surprise.

idolatry, the infidelity thereof, all of that is opposed to us. Religion is love of God and love of man: surely, all of that, under any form, Catholic or Quaker, is in favour of the unalienable rights of man. We know that we are right; we are sure to prevail. But in times present and future, as in times past, we need heroism, self-denial, a continual watchfulness, and an industry which never tires.

Let us not be deceived about the real question at issue. It is not merely whether we shall return fugitive slaves without trial by jury. We will not return them with trial by jury! neither "with alacrity," nor "with the solemnity of judicial proceedings!" It is not merely whether slavery shall be extended or not. By and by there will be a political party with a wider basis than the free soil party, who will declare that the nation itself must put an end to slavery in the nation; and if the Constitution of the United States will not allow it, there is another Constitution that will. Then the title, Defender and expounder of the Constitution of the United States, will give way to this,—"Defender and expounder of the Constitution of the Universe," and we shall re-affirm the ordinance of nature, and re-enact the will of God. You may not live to see it, Mr President, nor I live to see it; but it is written on the iron leaf that it must come; come, too, before long. Then the speech of Mr Webster, and the defence thereof by Mr Stuart, the letter of the retainers and the letters of the retained, will be a curiosity,; the conduct of the Whigs and Democrats an amazement, and the peculiar institution a proverb amongst all the nations of the earth. In the turmoil of party politics, and of personal controversy, let us not forget continually to move the previous question, whether freedom or slavery is to prevail in America. There is no attribute of God which is not on our side; because, in this matter, we are on the side of God.

Mr President: I began by congratulating you on the favourable signs of the times. One of the most favourable is the determination of the South to use the powers of Government to extend slavery. At this day, we exhibit a fact worse than Christendom has elsewhere to disclose; the fact that one-sixth part of our population are mere property; not men, but things. England has a proletary population, the lowest in Europe; we have three million of proletaries lower than the "pauper labourers" of England, which the Whig protectionists hold up to us in terror. The South wishes to increase the number of slaves, to spread this blot, this blight and baneful scourge of civilization, over new territory. Hot-headed men of the South declare that, unless it is done, they will divide the Union; famous men of the North "cave in," and verify their own statements about "dough-faces" and "dough-souls." All this is preaching anti-slavery to the thinking men of the North; to the sober men of all parties, who prefer conscience to cotton. The present session of Congress has done much to overturn slavery. "Whom the gods destroy they first make mad."

THE FUNCTION AND PLACE OF CONSCIENCE, IN RELATION TO THE LAWS OF MEN:

A SERMON FOR THE TIMES.

PREACHED AT THE MELODEON, ON SUNDAY, SEPT. 22, 1850.

Herein do I exercise myself to have always a conscience void of offence toward God and toward men.—ACTS xxiv. 16.

THERE are some things which are true, independent of all human opinions. Such things we call facts. Thus it is true that one and one are equal to two, that the earth moves round the sun, that all men have certain natural unalienable rights, rights which a man can alienate only for himself, and not for another. No man made these things true; no man can make them false. If all the men in Jerusalem and ever so many more, if all the men in the world, were to pass a unanimous vote that one and one were not equal to two, that the earth did not move round the sun, that all men had not natural and unalienable rights, the opinion would not alter the fact, nor make truth false and falsehood true.

So there are likewise some things which are right, independent of all human opinions. Thus it is right to love a man and not to hate him, to do him justice and not injustice, to allow him the natural rights which he has not alienated. No man made these things right; no man can make them wrong. If all the men in Jerusalem and ever so many more, if all the men in the world, were to pass a unanimous vote that it was right to hate a man and not love him, right to do him injustice and not justice, right to deprive him of his natural rights not alienated by himself, the opinion would not alter the fact, nor make right wrong and wrong right.

There are certain constant and general facts which occur in the material world, the world of external perception, which represent what are called the laws of matter, in virtue of which things take place so and not otherwise. These laws are the same everywhere and always; they never change. They are not made by men, but only discovered by men, are inherent in the constitution of matter, and seem designed to secure the welfare of the material world. These natural laws of matter, inherent in its constitution, are never violated, nor can be, for material nature is passive, or at least contains no element or will that is adverse to the will of God, the ultimate Cause of these laws as of matter itself. The observance of these laws is a constant fact of the universe; "the most ancient heavens thereby are fresh and strong." These laws represent the infinity of God in the world of matter, His infinite power, wisdom, justice, love, and holiness.

So there are likewise certain constant and general facts which occur in what may be called the spiritual world, the world of internal consciousness. They represent the laws of spirit—that is, of the human spirit—in virtue of which things are designed to take place so and not otherwise. These laws are the same everywhere and always; they never change. They are not made by men, but only discovered by men. They are inherent in the constitution of man, and as you cannot conceive of a particle of matter without extension, impenetrability, figure, and so on, no more can you conceive of man without these laws inhering in him. They seem designed to secure the welfare of the spiritual world. They represent the infinity of God in the world of man, His infinite power, wisdom, justice, love, and holiness. But while matter is stationary, bound by necessity, and man is progressive and partially free, to the extent of a certain tether, so it is plain that there may be a will in the world of man adverse to the will of God, and thus the laws of man's spirit may be violated to a certain extent. The laws of matter depend for their execution only on the infinite will of God, and so cannot be violated.

The laws of man depend for their execution also on the finite will of man, and so may be broken.*

Let us select a portion of these laws of the human spirit; such as relate to a man's conduct in dealing with his fellow-men, a portion of what are commonly called moral laws, and examine them. They partake of the general character-istics mentioned above; they are universal and unchange-able, are only discovered and not made by man, are in-herent in man, designed to secure his welfare, and represent the infinity of God. These laws are absolutely right; to obey them is to be and do absolutely right. So being and doing, a man answers the moral purpose of his existence, and attains moral manhood. If I and all men keep all the laws of man's spirit, I have peace in my own heart, peace with my brother, peace with my God; I have my delight in myself, in my brother, in my God, they theirs and God His in me.

What is absolutely right is commonly called justice. It is the point in morals common to me and all mankind, common to me and God, to mankind and God; the point where all duties unite—to myself, my brethren, and my God; the point where all interests meet and balance—my interests, those of mankind, and the interests of God. When justice is done, all is harmony and peaceful pro-gress in the world of man; but when justice is not done, the reverse follows, discord and confusion; for injustice is not the point where all duties and all interests meet and balance, not the point of morals common to mankind and me, or to us and God.

We may observe and study the constant facts of the material world, thus learn the laws they represent, and so get at a theory of the world which is founded on the facts thereof. Such a theory is true; it represents the thought of God, the infinity of God. Then for every point of theory we have a point of fact. Instead of pursuing this course we may neglect these constant facts, with the laws they represent, and forge a theory which shall not rest on these facts. Such a theory will be false and will represent the

* The terms *laws of the human spirit, spiritual laws*, &c., are sometimes used to denote exclusively those laws which man *must* keep, not merely what he *ought* to keep, laws in relation to which man has no more freedom than a mass of marble. The words are used above in a different sense.

imperfection of men, and not the facts of the universe and the infinity of God.

In like manner we may study the constant facts of the spiritual world, and, in special, of man's moral nature, and thereby obtain a rule to regulate our conduct. If this rule is founded on the constant facts of man's moral nature, then it will be absolutely right, and represent justice, the thought of God, the infinity of God, and for every point of moral theory we shall have a moral fact. Instead of pursuing that course, we may forge a rule for our conduct, and so get a theory which shall not rest on those facts. Such a rule will be wrong, representing only the imperfection of men.

In striving to learn the laws of the universe, the wisest men often go astray, propound theories which do not rest upon facts, and lay down human rules for the conduct of the universe, which do not agree with its nature. But the universe is not responsible for that; material nature takes no notice thereof. The opinion of an astronomer, of the American academy, does not alter a law of the material universe, or a fact therein. The philosophers once thought that the sun went round the earth, and framed laws on that assumption; but that did not make it a fact; the sun did not go out of his way to verify the theory, but kept to the law of God, and swung the earth round him once a year, say the philosophers what they might say, leaving them to learn the fact and thereby correct their theory.

In the same way, before men attain the knowledge of the absolute right, they often make theories which do not rest upon the fact of man's moral nature, and enact human rules for the conduct of men which do not agree with the moral nature of man. These are rules which men make and do not find made. They are not a part of man's moral nature, writ therein, and so obligatory thereon, no more than the false rules for the conduct of matter are writ therein, and so obligatory thereon. You and I are no more morally bound to keep such rules of conduct, because King Pharaoh or King People say we shall, than the sun is materially bound to go round the earth every day, because Hipparchus and Ptolemy say it does. The opinion or command of a king, or a people, can no more change a fact and alter a law of man's nature, than the opinion of a philosopher can do this in material nature.

We learn the laws of matter slowly, by observation, experiment, and induction, and only get an outside knowledge thereof, as objects of thought. In the same way we might study the facts of man's moral nature, and arrive at rules of conduct, and get a merely outside acquaintance with the moral law as something wholly external. The law might appear curious, useful, even beautiful, moral gravitation as wonderful as material attraction. But no sense of duty would attach us to it. In addition to the purely intellectual powers, we have a faculty whose special function it is to discover the rules for a man's moral conduct. This is conscience, called also by many names. As the mind has for its object absolute truth, so conscience has for its object absolute justice. Conscience enables us not merely to learn the right by experiment and induction, but intuitively, and in advance of experiment; so, in addition to the experimental way, whereby we learn justice from the facts of human history, we have a transcendental way, and learn it from the facts of human nature, from immediate consciousness.

It is the function of conscience to discover to men the moral law of God. It will not do this with infallible certainty, for, at its best estate, neither conscience nor any other faculty of man is absolutely perfect, so as never to mistake. Absolute perfection belongs only to the faculties of God. But conscience, like each other faculty, is relatively perfect,—is adequate to the purpose God meant it for. It is often immature in the young, who have not had time for the growth and ripening of the faculty, and in the old, who have checked and hindered its development. Here it is feeble from neglect, there from abuse. It may give an imperfect answer to the question, What is absolutely right?

Now, though the conscience of a man lacks the absolute perfection of that of God, in all that relates to my dealing with men, it is still the last standard of appeal. I will hear what my friends have to say, what public opinion has to offer, what the best men can advise me to, then I am to ask my own conscience, and follow its decision; not that of my next friend, the public, or the best of men. I will not say that my conscience will always disclose to me the absolutely right, according to the conscience of God, but it will disclose the relatively right, what is my conviction of right to-day, with all the light I can get on the matter; and as all I can know of the absolute right, is my conviction thereof, so I must be true to that conviction. Then I am faithful to my own conscience, and faithful to my God. If I do the best thing I can know to-day, and to-morrow find a better one and do that, I am not to be blamed, nor to be called a sinner against God, because not so just to-day as I shall be to-morrow. I am to do God's will soon as I know it, not before, and to take all possible pains to find it out; but am not to blame for acting childish when a child, nor to be ashamed of it when grown up to be a man. Such is the function of conscience.

Having determined what is absolutely right, by the conscience of God, or at least relatively right, according to my conscience to-day, then it becomes my duty to keep it. I owe it to God to obey His law, or what I deem His law; that is my duty. It may be uncomfortable to keep it, unpopular, contrary to my present desires, to my passions, to my immediate interests; it may conflict with my plans in life; that makes no difference. I owe entire allegiance to my God. It is a duty to keep His law, a personal duty, my duty as a man. I owe it to myself, for I am to keep the integrity of my own consciousness; I owe it to my brother, and to my God. Nothing can absolve me from this duty, neither the fact that it is uncomfortable or unpopular, nor that it conflicts with my desires, my passions, my immediate interests, and my plans in life. Such is the place of conscience amongst other faculties of my nature.

I believe all this is perfectly plain, but now see what it leads to. In the complicated relations of human life, various rules for the moral conduct of men have been devised, some of them in the form of statute laws, some in the form of customs; and, in virtue of these rules, certain artificial demands are made of men, which have no foundation in the moral nature of man; these demands are thought to represent duties. We have the same word to describe what I ought to do as subject to the law of God, and what is demanded of me by custom, or the statute. We call each a duty. Hence comes no small confusion: the conventional and official obligation is thought to rest on the same foundation as the natural and personal duty. As the natural duty is at first sight a little vague, and not written out in the law-book, or defined by custom, while the conventional obligation is well understood, men think that in case of any collision between the two, the natural duty must give way to the official obligation.

For clearness' sake, the natural and personal obligation to keep the law of God as my conscience declares it, I will call Duty; the conventional and official obligation to comply with some custom, keep some statute, or serve some special interest, I will call Business. Here then are two things—my natural and personal duty, my conventional and official business. Which of the two shall give way to the other,—personal duty or official business? Let it be remembered that I am a man first of all, and all else that I am is but a modification of my manhood, which makes me a clergyman, a fisherman, or a statesman; but the clergy, the fish, and the state, are not to strip me of my manhood. They are valuable in so far as they serve my manhood, not as it serves them. My official business as clergyman, fisherman, or statesman, is always beneath my personal duty as man. In case of any conflict between the two, the natural duty ought to prevail and carry the day before the official business; for the natural duty represents the permanent law of God, the absolute right, justice, the balance-point of all interests; while the official business represents only the transient conventions of men, some partial interest; and besides, the man who owes the personal duty is immortal, while the officer who performs the official business is but for a time. At death, the man is to be tried by the justice of God, for the deeds done, and character attained, for his natural duty, but he does not enter the next life as a clergyman, with his surplice and prayer-book, or a fisherman, with his angles and net, nor yet as a statesman, with his franking privilege, and title of honourable and member of Congress. The officer dies, of a vote or a fever. The man lives for ever. From the relation between a man and his occupation, it is plain, in general, that all conventional and official business is to be overruled by natural personal duty. This is the great circle, drawn by God, and discovered by conscience, which girdles my sphere, including all the smaller circles, and itself included by none of them. The law of God has eminent domain everywhere, over the private passions of Oliver and Charles, the special interests of Carthage and of Rome, over all customs, all official business, all precedents, all human statutes, all treaties between Judas and Pilate, or England and France, over all the conventional affairs of one man or of mankind. My own conscience is to declare that law for me, yours for you, and is before all private passions, or public interests, the decision of majorities, and a world full of precedents. You may resign your office, and escape its obligations, forsake your country, and owe it no allegiance, but you cannot move out of the dominions of God, nor escape where conscience has not eminent domain.

See some examples of a conflict between the personal duty and the official business. A man may be a clergyman, and it may be his official business to expound and defend the creed which is set up for him by his employers, his bishop, his association, or his parish, to defend and hold it good against all comers ; it may be, also, in a certain solemn sort, to please the audience, who come to be soothed, caressed, and comforted,—to represent the average of religion in his society, and so to bless popular virtues and ban unpopular vices, but never to shake off or even jostle with one of his fingers the load of sin, beloved and popular, which crushes his hearers down till they are bowed together and can in nowise lift themselves up; unpopular excellence he is to call fanaticism, if not infidelity. But his natural duty as a man, standing in this position, overrides his official business, and commands him to tell men of the false things in their creed, of great truths not in it; commands him to inform his audience with new virtue, to represent all of religion he can attain, to undo the heavy burden of popular sin, private or national, and let the men oppressed therewith go free. Excellence, popular or odious, he is to commend by its own name, to stimulate men to all nobleness of character and life, whether it please or offend. This is his duty, however uncomfortable, unpopular, against his desires, and conflicting with his immediate interests and plans of life. Which shall he do? His official business, and pimp and pander to the public lust, with base compliance serving the popular idols, which here are money and respectability, or shall he serve his God? That is the question. If the man considers himself substantially a man, and accidentally a clergyman, he will perform his natural duty; if he counts the priesthood his substance, and manhood an accident of that, he will do only his official business.

I may be a merchant, and my official business may be to buy, and sell, and get gain; I may see that the traffic in ardent spirits is the readiest way to accomplish this. So it becomes my official business to make rum, sell rum, and by all means to induce men to drink it. But presently I see that the common use of it makes the thriving unthrifty, the rich less wealthy, the poor miserable, the sound sick, and the sane mad; that it brings hundreds to the jail, thousands to the alms-house, and millions to poverty and shame, producing an amount of suffering, wretchedness, and sin, beyond the power of man to picture or conceive. Then my natural duty as man is very clear, very imperative. Shall I sacrifice my manhood to money?—the integrity of my consciousness to my gains by rum-selling? That is the question. And my answer will depend on the fact, whether I am more a man or more a rum-seller. Suppose I compromise the matter, and draw a line somewhere between my natural duty as man, and my official business as rum-seller, and for every three cents that I make by iniquity, give one cent to the American Tract Society, or the Board for Foreign Missions, or the Unitarian Association, or the excellent Society for promoting the Gospel among the Indians (and others) in North America. That does not help the matter; business is not satisfied, though I draw the line never so near to money; nor conscience, unless the line comes up to my duty.

I am a citizen, and the State says, "You must obey all the statutes made by the proper authorities; that is your official business!" Suppose there is a statute adverse to the natural law of God, and the convictions of my own conscience, and I plead that fact in abatement of. my obligation to keep the statute, the State says, "Obey it none the less, or we will hang you. Religion is an excellent thing in every matter except politics; there it seems to make men mad." Shall I keep the commandment of men, or the law of my God?

A statute was once enacted by King Pharaoh for the destruction of the Israelites in Egypt; it was made the official business of all citizens to aid in their destruction: "Pharaoh charged all his people saying, Every son that is born ye shall cast into the river, and every daughter ye shall save alive." It was the official business of every Egyptian who found a Hebrew boy to throw him into the Nile,—if he refused, he offended against the peace and dignity of the kingdom of Egypt, and the form of law in such case made and provided. But if he obeyed, he murdered a man. Which should he obey, the Lord Pharaoh, or the Lord God? That was the question. I make no doubt that the priests of Osiris, Orus, Apis, Isis, and the judges, and the justices of the peace and quorum, and the members of Congress of that time, said, "Keep the king's commandment, O ye that worship the crocodile and fear the cat, or ye shall not sleep in a whole skin any longer!" So said everything that loveth and maketh a lie.

King Charles II. made a statute some one hundred and ninety years ago, to punish with death the remnant of the nine-and-fifty judges who had brought his father's head to the block, teaching kings "that they also had a joint in their necks." He called on all his subjects to aid in the capture of these judges. It was made their official business as citizens to do so; a reward was offered for the apprehension of some of them "alive or dead;" punishment hung over the head of any who should harbour or conceal them. Three of these regicides, who had adjudged a king for his felony, came to New England. Many Americans knew where they were, and thought the condemnation of Charles I. was the best thing these judges ever did. With that conviction ought they to have delivered up these fugitives, or afforded them shelter? In time of peril, when officers of the English government were on the look-out for some of these men, a clergyman in the town where one of them was concealed, preached, it is said, on the text "Bewray not him that wandereth," an occasional sermon, and put the duty of a man far before the business of a citizen. When Sir Edmund Andros was at New Haven looking after one of the judges, and attended public worship in the same meeting-house with the fugitive, the congregation sung an awful hymn in his very ears.*

Would the men of Connecticut have done right, bewraying him that wandered, and exposing the outcast, to give up the man who had defended the liberties of the world and the rights of mankind against a tyrant,—give him up because a wanton king, and his loose men and loose women, made such a commandment? One of the regicides dwelt in peace eight-and-twenty years in New England, a monument of the virtue of the people.

Of old time the Roman statute commanded the Christians to sacrifice to Jupiter; they deemed it the highest sin to

* Why dost thou, Tyrant, boast abroad
  thy wicked works to praise?
Dost thou not know there is a God,
  whose mercies last alwaies?
    *   *   *   *   *

On mischiefe why sett'st thou thy minde,
  and wilt not walke upright?
Thou hast more lust false tales to find,
  than bring the truth to light.
Thou dost delight in fraud and guile,
  in mischiefe, bloud and wrong.
Thy lips have learned the flattering stile,
  oh false deceitful tongue.

Therefore shall God for aye confound,
  and pluck thee from thy place;
Thy seed root out from off the ground,
  and so shall thee deface.
The just, when they behold thy fall,
  with feare shall praise the Lord;
And in reproach of thee withall,
  crie out with one accord:—

"Behold the man that woulde not take
  the Lord for his defence;
But of his goods his God did make,
  and trust his corrupt sense.
But I, as olive, fresh and green,
  shall spring and spread abroad;
For why? my trust all times hath been,
  upon the living God!

"For this therefore will I give praise
  to Thee with heart and voyce;
I will set forth Thy name alwayes,
  wherein Thy saints rejoyce."

Psalm lii. *in Sternhold and Hopkins.*

do so, but it was their official business as Roman citizens. Some of them were true to their natural duty as men, and took the same cross Jesus had borne before them; Peter and John had said at their outset to the authorities—"Whether it be right in the sight of God to hearken unto you more than unto God, judge ye." The Emperor once made it the official business of every citizen to deliver up the Christians. But God made it no man's duty. Nay, it was each man's duty to help them. In such cases what shall a man do? You know what we think of men who comply basely, and save their life with the loss of their soul. You know how the Christian world honours the saints and martyrs, who laid down their lives for the sake of truth and right; a handful of their dust, which was quieted of its trouble by the headsman's axe seventeen hundred years ago, and is now gathered from the catacombs of Saint Agnes at Rome—why it is enough to consecrate half of the Catholic churches in New England. As I have stood among their graves, have handled the instruments with which they tasted of bitter death, and crumbled their bones in my hands,—I keep their relics still with reverent awe,—I have thought there was a little difference between their religion, and the pale decency that haunts the churches of our time, and is afraid lest it lose its dividends, or its respectability, or hurt its usefulness, which is in no danger.

Do I speak of martyrs for conscience' sake? To-day is St Maurice's day, consecrated to him and the "Thebæan legion." Maurice appears to have been a military tribune in the Christian legion, levied in the Thebais, a part of Egypt. In the latter part of the third century this legion was at Octodurum, near the little village of Martigni, in Valais, a Swiss Canton, under the command of Maximian, the associate emperor, just then named Herculeus, going to fight the Bagaudæ. The legion was ordered to sacrifice to the gods after the heathen fashion. The soldiers refused; every tenth man was hewn down by Maximian's command. They would not submit, and so the whole legion, as the Catholic story tells us, perished there on the 22nd of September, fifteen hundred and fifty-three years ago this day. Perhaps the account is not true; it is probable that the number of martyrs is much exaggerated, for six hundred soldiers would not stand still and be slaughtered without striking a blow. But the fact that the Catholic church sets apart one day in the calendar to honour this alleged heroism, shows the value men put on fidelity to conscience in such cases.

Last winter a bill for the capture of fugitive slaves was introduced into the Senate of the United States of America; the senator who so ably represented the opinions and wishes of the controlling men of this city, proposed to support that bill, "with all its provisions to the fullest extent;" that bill, with various alterations, some for the better, others for the worse, has become a law—it received the vote of the Representative from Boston, who was not sent there, I hope, for the purpose of voting for it. That statute allows the slave-holder, or his agent, to come here, and by summary process seize a fugitive slave, and, without the formality of a trial by jury, to carry him back to eternal bondage. The statute makes it the official business of certain magistrates to aid in enslaving a man; it empowers them to call out force enough to overcome any resistance which may be offered, to summon the bystanders to aid in that work. It provides a punishment for any one who shall aid and abet, directly or indirectly, and harbour or conceal the man who is seeking to maintain his natural and unalienable right to life, liberty, and the pursuit of happiness. He may be fined a thousand dollars, imprisoned six months, and be liable to a civil action for a thousand dollars more!

This statute is not to be laid to the charge of the slave-holders of the South alone; its most effective supporters are Northern men; Boston is more to be blamed for it than Charleston or Savannah, for nearly a thousand persons of this city and neighbourhood, most of them men of influence through money if by no other means, addressed a letter of thanks to the distinguished man who had volunteered to support that infamous bill, telling him that he had "convinced the understanding and touched the conscience of the nation." A man falls low when he consents to be a slave, and is spurned for his lack of manhood; to consent to be a catcher of fugitive slaves is to fall lower yet; but to consent to be the defender of a slave-catcher—it is seldom that human nature is base enough for that.

But such examples are found in this city! This is now the law of the land. It is the official business of judges, commissioners, and marshals, as magistrates, to execute the statute and deliver a fugitive up to slavery; it is your official business and mine, as citizens, when legally summoned, to aid in capturing the man. Does the command make it any man's duty? The natural duty to keep the law of God overrides the obligation to observe any human statute, and continually commands us to love a man and not hate him, to do him justice, and not injustice, to allow him his natural rights not alienated by himself; yes, to defend him in them, not only by all means legal, but by all means moral.

Let us look a little at our duty under this statute. If a man falls into the water and is in danger of drowning, it is the natural duty of the bystanders to aid in pulling him out, even at the risk of wetting their garments. We should think a man a coward who could swim, and would not save a drowning girl for fear of spoiling his coat. He would be indictable at common law. If a troop of wolves or tigers were about to seize a man, and devour him, and you and I could help him, it would be our duty to do so, even to peril our own limbs and life for that purpose. If a man undertakes to murder or steal a man, it is the duty of the bystanders to help their brother, who is in peril, against wrong from the two-legged man, as much as against the four-legged beast. But suppose the invader who seizes the man is an officer of the United States, has a commission in his pocket, a warrant for his deed in his hand, and seizes as a slave a man who has done nothing to alienate his natural rights—does that give him any more natural right to enslave a man than he had before? Can any piece of parchment make right wrong, and wrong right?

The fugitive has been a slave before? does the wrong you committed yesterday, give you a natural right to commit wrong afresh and continually? Because you enslaved this man's father, have you a natural right to enslave his child? The same right you would have to murder a man because you butchered his father first. The right to murder is as much transmissible by inheritance as the right to enslave! It is plain to me that it is the natural duty of citizens to rescue every fugitive slave from the hands of the marshal who essays to return him to bondage; to do it peaceably if they can, forcibly if they must, but by all means to do it. Will you stand by and see your countrymen, your fellow-citizens of Boston, sent off to slavery by some commissioner? Shall I see my own parishioners taken from under my eyes and carried back to bondage, by a man whose constitutional business it is to work wickedness by statute? Shall I never lift an arm to protect him? When I consent to that, you may call me a hireling shepherd, an infidel, a wolf in sheep's clothing, even a defender of slave-catching if you will; and I will confess I was a poor dumb dog, barking always at the moon, but silent as the moon when the murderer came near.

I am not a man who loves violence. I respect the sacredness of human life. But this I say, solemnly, that I will do all in my power to rescue any fugitive slave from the hands of any officer who attempts to return him to bondage. I will resist him as gently as I know how, but with such strength as I can command; I will ring the bells, and alarm the town; I will serve as head, as foot, or as hand to any body of serious and earnest men, who will go with me, with no weapons but their hands, in this work. I will do it as readily as I would lift a man out of the water, or pluck him from the teeth of a wolf, or snatch him from the hands of a murderer. What is a fine of a thousand dollars, and jailing for six months, to the liberty of a man? My money perish with me, if it stand between me and the eternal law of God. I trust there are manly men enough in this house to secure the freedom of every fugitive slave in Boston, without breaking a limb or rending a garment.

One thing more I think is very plain, that the fugitive has the same natural right to defend himself against the slave-catcher, or his constitutional tool, that he has against a murderer or a wolf. The man who attacks me to reduce me to slavery, in that moment of attack alienates his right to life, and if I were the fugitive, and could escape in no other way, I would kill him with as little compunction as I would drive a mosquito from my face. It is high time this was said. What grasshoppers we are before the statute of men! what Goliaths against the law of God! What capitalist heeds your statute of usury when he can get illegal interest? How many banks are content with six per cent. when money is scarce? Did you never hear of a merchant evading the duties of the custom-house? When a man's liberty is concerned, we must keep the law, must we? betray the wanderer, and expose the outcast?*

* It has been said that the fugitive slave law cannot be executed in Boston. Let us not be deceived. Who would have thought a year ago, that the Senator of Boston would make such a speech as that of last March, that so many of the leading citizens of Boston would write such a letter of approval, that such a bill could pass the Congress, and a man be found in this city (Mr Samuel A. Eliot) to vote for it and get no rebuke from the people! Yet a single man should not endure the shame alone, which belongs in general to the leading men of the city. The member for Boston faithfully represented the public opinion of his most eminent constituents, lay and clerical. Here is an account of what took place in New York since the delivery of the sermon.

[From the New York Tribune.]

"SLAVE-CATCHING IN NEW YORK—FIRST CASE UNDER THE LAW.

"The following case, which occurred yesterday, is one of peculiar interest from the fact of its being the first case under the new Fugitive Slave Law. It will be noticed that there is very little of the 'law's delay' here; the proceedings were as summary as an Arkansas court audience could desire.

"U. S. COMMISSIONER'S OFFICE—Before Commissioner Gardiner.—*Examination as to James Hamlet, charged to be a fugitive slave, the property of Mary Brown, of Baltimore.*—No person was present as counsel for accused, and only one coloured man. He is a light mulatto. The marshal said Mr Wood had been there. The commissioner said they would go on, and if counsel came in, he would read proceedings.

"*Thomas J. Clare* (a man with dark eyes and hair), sworn.—Am thirty years of age; clerk for Merchant's Shot Manufacturing Company in Baltimore; know James Hamlet; he is slave of Mary Brown, a mother-in-law of mine, residing in Baltimore; have known Hamlet about twenty years; he left my mother-in-law about two years ago this season, by absenting himself from the premises, the dwelling where he resided in Baltimore; she is entitled to his services; he is a slave for life; she never parted with him voluntarily; she came into possession of him by will from John G. Brown, her deceased husband; the written paper shown is an extract from his will; she held him under that from the time she inherited him till he escaped, as I have testified; this is the man (pointing to Hamlet, a light mulatto man, about twenty-four or twenty-five years of age, looking exceedingly pensive).

"*Gustavus Brown*, sworn.—Am twenty-five years of age; reside in New York; clerk with A. M. Fenday, 25 Front-street; resided before coming here in Baltimore; I know James Hamlet; I have known him since a boy; he is a slave to my mother; he is a slave for life; my mother inherited him under the will of my father; he left her service by running away, I suppose; absenting himself from the house in the city of Baltimore, about two years since; I have seen him several times, within the last six months, in the city; first time I saw him was in April last; my mother is still entitled to possession of him; she never has parted with him; the man sitting here (Hamlet) is the man.

"Mr Asa Child, Counsellor at Law, here came into the room, and took his seat; he said he had been sent to this morning, through another, by a gentleman with whom Hamlet had lived in this city (Mr S. N. Wood), but he had

In the same manner the natural duty of a man overrides all the special obligations which a man takes on him-

no directions in the matter; he merely came to see that the law is properly administered, and supposed it would be without him.

"Mr Child was then shown the law, the power of attorney to Mr Clare, the affidavit of Mr Clare on which Hamlet was arrested—and the testimony thus far.

"*Mr Clare*, cross-examined by Mr Child.—I married Mrs Brown's daughter about seventeen years ago ; Hamlet has always lived with us in the family : I am in her family now, and was at the time he went away; think he is about twenty-eight years of age (he looks much younger than that—his features are very even, as those of a white person of the kind); he occasionally worked at the shot tower where I worked; he was hired there as a labourer, and Mrs Brown got the benefit of him—that is, when I had no other use for him; he had formerly been employed as a dray-man; after I married into the family some year or two, we lived together, I furnishing the house; such wages as I got for the man it was returned to Mrs Brown, to be used as she saw fit; I was her agent to get employment for him as I could ; I had him in various occupations; I have a power of attorney; I have no further interest in him than he is her property, and we wish to get him back to Maryland again, where he left.

"*Mr Brown*, cross-examined.—Left home 27th March last. Was home when Hamlet went away. At the time he was engaged at the shot tower business.

"Mr Child said he had no further questions to ask. He supposed the rules of the law had been complied with.

"Mr Gardiner, the commissioner, then said, I will deliver the fugitive over to the marshal, to be delivered over to the claimant.

"Mr Child suggested if that was the law. The commissioner then said he would hand him, as the law said, to the claimant, and if there should be any danger of rescue, he would deliver him to the United States marshal.

"The United States marshal said he had performed his duty in bringing him in.

"Mr Clare said he would demand such aid from the United States marshal as would secure the delivery of the man to his owner in Baltimore.

"Mr Child suggested that it must be an affidavit that he apprehends a rescue. Mr Clare said that he did so apprehend.

"Mr Talmadge, the marshal, said he would have to perform his duty, if called upon.

"Mr Child replied he supposed he would, but there were doubts as to the form.

"The necessary papers were made out by the commissioner, Mr Clare swearing he feared a rescue, and Hamlet was delivered to him, thence to the United States marshal, and probably was conveyed with all possible despatch to Baltimore, a coach being in waiting at the door; and he was taken off in irons, an officer accompanying the party."

Here is the charge of Judge McLean in a similar case.

"No earthly power has a right to interpose between a man's conscience and his Maker. He has a right, an inalienable and absolute right, to worship God, according to the dictates of his own conscience. For this he alone must answer, and he is entirely free from all human restraint to think and act for himself.

"But this is not the case when his acts affect the rights of others. Society has a claim upon all citizens. General rules have been adopted in the form of laws, for the protection of the rights of persons and things. These laws lie at the foundation of the social compact, and their observance is essential to the maintenance of civilization. In these matters the law, and not conscience,

self as a magistrate by his official oath. Our theory of office is this: The man is sunk in the magistrate; he constitutes the rule of action. You are sworn to decide this case according to the law and testimony; and you become unfaithful to the solemn injunctions you have taken upon yourselves, when you yield to an influence which you call conscience, that places you above the law and the testimony.

"Such a rule can only apply to individuals; and when assumed as a basis of action on the rights of others, it is utterly destructive of all law. What may be deem ' a conscientious act by one individual, may he held criminal by another. In view of one, the act is meritorious; in the view of the other, it should be punished as a crime. And each has the same right, acting under the dictates of his conscience, to carry out his own view. This would overturn the basis of society. We must stand by the law. We have sworn to maintain it. It is expected that the citizens of the free States should be opposed to slavery. But with the abstract principles of slavery we have nothing to do. As a political question there could be no difference of opinion among us on the subject. But our duty is found in the Constitution of the Union, as construed by the Supreme Court. The fugitives from labour we are bound, by the highest obligations, to deliver up on claim of the master being made; and there is no State power which can release the slave from the legal custody of his master.

"In regard to the arrest of fugitives from labour, the law does not impose active duties on our citizens generally. They are not prohibited from exercising the ordinary charities of life towards the fugitive. To secrete him or convey him from the reach of his master, or to rescue him when in legal custody, is forbidden; and for doing this a liability is incurred. This gives to no one a just ground of complaint. He has only to refrain from an express violation of the law, which operates to the injury of his neighbour."

He seems to think the right to hold slaves as much a natural right as the absolute right to worship God according to the "dictates of conscience." One man has an unalienable right to liberty, other men an unalienable right to alienate and take it from him!

Here is something in a different spirit from a Boston newspaper.

"THE FUGITIVE SLAVE BILL.

"This infamous bill has finally passed both branches of Congress.* My opinion on this subject may have little weight with those who voted for it, but may help sustain the sinking spirit of some poor disconsolate one, who, having fled from the land of oppressors, is anxiously looking to see if there is any one who will give him a cheering look, or a kind reception, or who dares to give him a crust of bread, or a cup of water, and help him on his way.

"Allow me to say to such an one, that if pursued by the merciless slave-holder, and every other door in Boston is shut against him, there is a door that will be open at No. 2, Beach-street, and that the fear of fines and imprisonment will be ineffectual when the pursuer shall demand his victim. If he enters before the fleeing captive is safe, it will be at his peril. I am opposed to war, and all the spirit of war; even to all preparations for what is called self-defence in times of peace; yet I should resist the pursuer, and not allow him to enter my dwelling until he was able to tread me under his feet. I will not trample upon any

---

* I call this bill *infamous*, because by it the man or woman who is charged with being a slave is deprived of all the means of self-defence allowed to those who are charged with crimes, and to be delivered up summarily, without the right of trial by jury, or any other proper means of proving the charge groundless. Is it a worse crime to be a slave than a thief or a murderer?

is un homme couvert; his individual manhood is covered up and extinguished by his official cap; he is no longer a law, oi her of my own State, or of the nation, that does not conflict with my conscientious duty to my God; but Jesus has commanded, saying, 'All things whatsoever yo would that men should do to you, do ye even so to them.'

"If, for no crime, I had been taken and sold, and deprived of all the rights of my manhood, and degraded to the rank of a beast of burden; not only deprived of the opportunity to labour for the support of my wife and children, but even deprived of their kind sympathy and companionship, whenever the interest or will of my oppressors should require it; and I should, at the peril of my life, flee from my oppressors, and they should pursue me to the dwelling of some poor disciple of Jesus, it may be that of a coloured man, and I should beg of him to protect me, and help me to escape from the pursuer's grasp, should I not hope, if he was a Christian, he would give me bread and water, and help me on my way, regardless of the fines and imprisonment that such a kind act might render him liable to? Could I expect to meet the approbation of my Lord, if I did not do as much for the fleeing slave? Can there be a Christian, in this land of the Pilgrims, who will not do it, and besides, do all in his power to prevent any one of those Senators or Representatives in Congress who voted for that infamous bill from ever again misrepresenting any portion of the friends of freedom, in Boston or elsewhere? It is said, this is a law of the land, and must be obeyed: to such I would say, 'Whether it be right in the sight of God to hearken unto men more than unto God, judge ye.'

"I prefer to obey God, if in so doing I must break the laws of men and be punished, rather than violate the laws of God and obey the laws of men, to escape fines and imprisonments, or even death.

"Boston, Sept. 23, 1850.   T. GILBERT."

Here is yet more:

"THE FUGITIVE SLAVE BILL.

"MESSRS EDITORS:—The bold and manly avowal of your correspondent, Mr T. Gilbert, in last evening's Traveller, in commenting upon what he very justly denominates the 'infamous fugitive slave bill,' is but the very echoing of thousands of hearts equally true to the cause of freedom, and who seek the elevation of the down-trodden sons and daughters of American slavery. That gentleman, acting upon the dictates of an enlightened patriotism, and in deep sympathy with the fleeing captive, has the courage to avow his determination to throw wide open his door, and offers to make his house—even though he should stand alone among his fellow-citizens—an asylum to the fugitive slave, in his retreat from the prison-house of bondage. The paramount claims which he awards to the Divine law over that which is but human, and therefore necessarily imperfect, commend his spirited letter to the consideration of all those that have in any way aided in the passage of a bill at variance with the first principles of civil freedom, and in direct hostility to the instruction of that great Teacher who hath commanded us to 'Do unto others as we would that they should do unto us.' That the determination of your correspondent may be true and unfaltering, is the hearty prayer of one, at least, of his fellow-citizens, who is ready at all times to co-operate in making an asylum for the fugitive slave, even though bonds and imprisonments should prove the penalty.

"Boston, Sept. 26, 1850.   GEORGE W. CARNES."

Here follow some characteristic remarks on the terror which the fugitives here in Boston feel in apprehension of being torn from their families and their freedom.

"THE FUGITIVE SLAVE LAW.

"The coloured people had a grand time last evening, at Zion's Chapel in

man, but a mere president, general, governor, representative, sheriff, juror, or constable; he is absolved from all allegiance to God's law of the universe when it conflicts with man's law of the land; his official business as a magistrate supersedes his natural duty as a man. In virtue of this theory, President Polk, and his coadjutors in Congress and out of it, with malice, afore-thought, and intent to rob and to kill, did officially invade Mexico, and therein "slay, kill, and murder" some thousands of men, as well Americans as Mexicans. This is thought right because he did it officially. But the fact that he and they were magistrates, doing official business, did not make the killing any the less a wrong than if he and they had been private men, with General Lopez and not General Taylor to head or back them. The official killing of a man who has not alienated his right to live, is just as much violation of the law of God, and the natural duty of man, as the unofficial killing of such a person. Because you and I and some other foolish people put a man in a high office, and get him to take an oath, does that, all at once, invest him with a natural right to kill anybody he sees fit; to kill an innocent Mexican? All his natural rights he had before,

Church-street. Their object was to denounce the fugitive slave law; and this was done with hearty good-will, or, we should say, malediction.

"The steam would have been well up, without any extraneous elements of excitement; but what added a special interest to the occasion, and raised the temperament to blood-heat, was the announcement, made by Mr Downing, that the wife of James Hamlet (the fugitive slave who was returned to his owner in Baltimore, a few days since, under a process of law) had died yesterday, of grief and convulsions.

"This filled the measure of indignation which burned in the bosoms of all present, against a law which, besides its other abominations, could produce such fatal effects. In the fever of the moment, a contribution was called for, to defray the expense of her funeral, and about twenty dollars was collected.

"Shortly after, information was received that it was all a mistake about her dying of convulsions, or in any other way; and that she was as well as ever. This was a damper upon the enthusiasm of the occasion, but the money was already collected, and seeing it could not be applied just now to defray her funeral expenses, it was very properly decided to apply it to her living expenses. The meeting adjourned.

"Mrs Hamlet was in our office yesterday, accompanied by her mother and a coloured man. She appeared to be in good health (though of course distressed at the misfortune of her husband), and we hope she will live a thousand years. She certainly shall, if his return will have that effect."—*N. Y. Journal of Commerce.*

I print these passages, hoping that some hundred years hence they may be found in some old library, and valued as monuments of the state of Christianity in the free States in the year 1850.

and it would be difficult to ascertain where the people could find the right to authorize him to do a wrong. A man does not escape from the jurisdiction of natural law and the dominion of God by enlisting in the army, or by taking the oath of the President; for justice, the law paramount of the universe, extends over armies and ₁ations.

A little while ago a murderer was hanged in Boston, by the Sheriff of Suffolk county, at the command of the Governor and Council of Massachusetts, by the aid of certain persons called grand and petit jurors, all of them acting in their official capacity, and doing the official business they had sworn to do. If it be a wrong thing to hang a man, or to take his life except in self-defence, and while in imminent peril, then it is not any less a wrong because men do it in their official character, in compliance with their oath. I am speaking of absolute wrong, not merely what is wrong relatively to the man's own judgment, for I doubt not that all those officers were entirely conscientious in what they did, and therefore no blame rests on them. But if a man believes it wrong to take human life deliberately, except in the cases named, then I do not see how, with a good conscience, he can be partaker in the death of any man, notwithstanding his official oath.

Let me suppose a case which may happen here, and before long. A woman flies from South Carolina to Massachusetts to escape from bondage. Mr Greatheart aids her in her escape, harbours and conceals her, and is brought to trial for it. The punishment is a fine of one thousand dollars and imprisonment for six months. I am drawn to serve as a juror, and pass upon this offence. I may refuse to serve, and be punished for that, leaving men with no scruples to take my place, or I may take the juror's oath to give a verdict according to the law and the testimony. The law is plain, let us suppose, and the testimony conclusive. Greatheart himself confesses that he did the deed alleged, saving one ready to perish. The judge charges, that if the jurors are satisfied of that fact, then they must return that he is guilty. This is a nice matter. Here are two questions. The one, put to me in my official capacity as juror, is this: "Did Greatheart aid the woman?" The other, put to me in my natural character as man, is this: "Will you help punish Greatheart with fine and imprisonment for helping a woman obtain her unalienable rights?" I am to answer both. If I have extinguished my manhood by my juror's oath, then I shall do my official business and find Greatheart guilty, and I shall seem to be a true man; but if I value my manhood, I shall answer after my natural duty to love a man and not hate him, to do him justice, not injustice, to allow him the natural rights he has not alienated, and shall say "Not guilty." Then foolish men, blinded by the dust of courts, may call me forsworn and a liar; but I think human nature will justify the verdict.*

* THE FUNCTION OF THE JURY.

There are two theories of the function of the jury in criminal trials. One I will call the theory of the government; the other the theory of the people. The first has of late been insisted on in certain courts, and laid down by some judges in their charges to the jury. The second lies, perhaps dimly, in the consciousness of the people, and may be gathered from the conduct of juries in trials where the judges' law would do obvious injustice to the prisoner.

I. According to the theory of the government. The judge is to settle the law for the jury. This involves two things:

1. He is to declare the law denouncing punishment on the alleged crime.
2. To declare what constitutes the crime. Then the jury are only to determine whether the prisoner did the deed which the judge says constitutes the crime. He, exclusively, is to decide what is the law, and what deed constitutes the crime; they only to decide if the prisoner did the deed. For example, to take a case which has not happened yet, to my knowledge: John Doe is accused of having eaten a Medford cracker; and thereupon, by direction of the government, has been indicted by a grand jury for the capital offence of treason, and is brought before a traverse jury for trial. The judge tells the jury, 1. That eating a Medford cracker constitutes the crime of treason. 2. That there is a law denouncing death on that crime. Then the jury are to hearken to the evidence, and if it is proved to their satisfaction that John Doe ate the Medford cracker, they are to return a verdict of guilty. They are only to judge of the matter of fact, and take the law on the judge's authority.

II. According to the theory of the people, in order to render their verdict, the jury are to determine three things:

1. Did the man do the deed alleged?
2. If so, Is there a legal and constitutional statute denouncing punishment upon the crime? Here the question is twofold: (a) as to the deed which constitutes the crime, and (b) as to the statute which denounces the crime.
3. If all this is settled affirmatively, then, Shall this man suffer the punishment thus legally and constitutionally denounced?

For example: John Doe is accused of having eaten a Medford cracker, is indicted for treason, and brought to trial; the judge charges as above. Then the jury are to determine:

1. Did John Doe eat the Medford cracker in the manner alleged?
2. If so: (a) Does that deed constitute the crime of treason? and (b) Is there a legal and constitutional statute denouncing the punishment of death on that crime?
3. If so likewise, Shall John Doe suffer the punishment of death?

The first question, as to the fact, they are to settle by the evidence presented in open court, according to the usual forms, and before the face of the prisoner;

In cases of this kind, when justice is on one side and the court on the other, it seems to me a conscientious man the testimony of each witness forms one element of that evidence. The jury alone are to determine whether the testimony of the witnesses proves the fact.

The second question, (a) as to the deed which constitutes the crime, and (b) as to the law which denounces the crime, they are to settle by evidence; the testimony of the judge, of the States' Attorney, of the prisoner's counsel, each forms an element of that evidence. The jury alone are to determine whether that testimony proves that the deed constitutes the crime, and that there is a law denouncing death against it; and the jury are to remember that the judge and the attorney who are the creatures of the government, and often paid to serve its passions, may be, and often have been, quite as partial, quite as unjust, as the prisoner's counsel.

The third question, as to punishing the prisoner, after the other questions are decided against him, is to be settled solely by the mind and conscience of the jury. If they know that John Doe did eat the Medford cracker, that the deed legally constitutes the crime of treason, and that there is a legal and constitutional statute denouncing death on that crime, they are still to determine, on their oath as jurors, on their manhood as men, whether John Doe shall suffer the punishment of death. They are jurors to do justice, not injustice; what they think is justice, not what they think injustice.

The government theory, though often laid down in the charge, is seldom if ever practically carried out by a judge in its full extent. For he does not declare on his own authority what is the law and what constitutes the crime, but gives the statutes, precedents, decisions, and the like; clearly implying by this very course that the jury are not to take his authority barely, but his reasons if reasonable.

In the majority of cases, the statute and the ruling of the court come as near to real justice as the opinion of the jury does; then if they are satisfied that the prisoner did the deed alleged, they return a verdict of guilty with a clear conscience, and subject the man to what they deem a just punishment for an unjust act. Their conduct then seems to confirm the government theory of the jurors' function. Lawyers and others sometimes reason exclusively from such cases, and conclude such is the true and actual theory thereof. But when a case occurs, wherein the ruling of the judge appears wrong to the jury; when he declares legal and constitutional what they think is not so; when he declares that a trifling offence constitutes a great crime; when the statute is manifestly unjust, forbidding what is not wrong, or when the punishment denounced for a real wrong is excessive, or any punishment is provided for a deed not wrong, though there is no doubt of the facts, the jury will not convict. Sometimes they will acquit the prisoner; sometimes fail to agree. The history of criminal trials in England and America proves this. In such cases the jury are not false to their function and jurors' oath, but faithful to both, for the jurors are the "country" —the justice and humanity of men.

Suppose some one should invent a machine to be used in criminal trials for determining the testimony given in court. Let me call it a Martyrion. This instrument receives the evidence and determines and reports the fact that the prisoner did, or did not, do the deed alleged. According to the government theory, the Martyrion would perfectly perform all the functions of the jury in a criminal case; but would any community substitute the machine for the jury of "twelve good men and true?" If the jury is to be merely the judge's machine, it had better be of iron and gutta-percha than of human beings.

In Philadelphia, some years ago, a man went deliberately and shot a person who had seduced his sister under circumstances of great atrocity. He was indicted for wilful murder. There was no doubt as to the fact, none as to the law,

must either refuse to serve as a juror, or else return a verdict at variance with the facts and what courts declare to be his official business as juror; but the eyes of some men have been so long blinded by what the court declares is the law, and by its notion of the juror's function, that they will help inflict such a punishment on their brother, and the judge decree the sentence, in a case where the arrest, the verdict, and the sentence are the only wrong in which the prisoner is concerned. It seems to me it is time this matter should be understood, and that it should be known that no official oath can take a man out of the jurisdiction of God's natural law of the universe.

A case may be brought before a commissioner or judge of the United States, to determine whether Daniel is a slave, and therefore to be surrendered up. His official business, sanctioned by his oath, enforced by the law of the land, demands the surrender; his natural duty, sanctioned by his conscience, enforced by absolute justice, forbids the surrender. What shall he do? There is no serving of God and Mammon both. He may abandon his commission and refuse to remain thus halting between two opposites. But if he keeps his office, I see not how he can renounce his nature and send back a fugitive slave, and do as great a wrong as to make a freeman a slave!

Suppose the Constitution had been altered, and Congress had made a law, making it the business of the United States' commissioners to enslave and sell at public outcry all the red-haired men in the nation, and forbid us to aid and abet their escape, to harbour and conceal them, under

none as to the deed which constituted that crime. The jury returned, "Not guilty"—and were justified in their verdict. In 1850, in New Jersey, a man seduced the wife of another, under circumstances even more atrocious. The husband, in open day, coolly and deliberately shot the seducer; was tried for wilful murder. Here, too, there was no doubt of the fact, of the law, or the deed which constituted the crime of murder; but the jury, perfectly in accordance with their official function, returned "Not guilty."

The case of William Penn in 1670, who was tried under the Conventicle Act, is well known. The conduct of many English juries who would not condemn a fellow-creature to death for stealing a few pounds of money, is also well known, and shows the value of this form of trial to protect a man from a wicked law. I think most men will declare the verdict of "Not guilty" in the case of J. P. Zenger, tried for high treason in New York in 1735, a righteous judgment, made in strict accordance with the official function of the jurors; but it was plainly contrary to the evidence as well as to the ruling of the court.

See Mr Parker's Defence, p. 76, *et seq.*, for further remarks on the function of the Jury (Boston, 1855).

the same penalties just now mentioned; do you think any commissioner would be justified before God by his oath in kidnapping the red-haired men, or any person in punishing such as harboured or concealed them, such as forcibly took the victims out of the hand of officials who would work mischief by statute ? Will the colour of a hair make right wrong, and wrong right?

Suppose a man has sworn to keep the Constitution of the United States, and the Constitution is found to be wrong in certain particulars : then his oath is not morally binding, for before his oath, by his very existence, he is morally bound to keep the law of God as fast as learns it. No oath can absolve him from his natural ;iance to God. Yet I see not how a man can knowingly, ..d with a good conscience, swear to keep what he deems wrong to keep, and will not keep, and does not intend to keep.

It seems to me very strange that men so misunderstand the rights of conscience and their obligations to obey their country. Not long ago, an eminent man taunted one of his opponents, telling him he had better adhere to the "higher law." The newspapers echoed the sneer, as if there were no law higher than the Constitution. Latterly, the Democratic party, even more completely than the Whig party, seems to have forgotten that there is any law higher than the Constitution, any rights above vested rights.*

An eminent theologian of New England, who has hitherto done good and great service in his profession, grinding off the barb of Calvinism, wrote a book in defence of slave-catching, on "Conscience and the Constitution," a book which not only sins against the sense of the righteous in being wicked, but against the worldliness of the world in being weak,—and he puts the official business of keeping "a compact" far before the natural duty of keeping a conscience void of offence, and serving God. But suppose forty thieves assemble on Fire Island, and make a compact to rob very vessel wrecked on their coast, and reduce the survivors to bondage. Suppose I am born amongst that brotherhood of pirates, am I morally bound to keep that compact, or to perform any function which grows out of it? Nay, I am morally bound to violate the compact, to keep

* So it appeared in September, 1851 ; but since then the Whig party has vindicated its claim to the same bad eminence as the Democratic party.

the pirates from their plunder and their prey. Instead of forty thieves on Fire Island, suppose twenty millions of men in the United States make a compact to enslave every sixth man—the dark men—am . morally bound to heed that compact, or to perform any function which grows out of it? Nay, I am morally bound to violate the compact, in every way that is just and wise. The very men who make such a compact are morally discharged from it as soon as they see it is wrong. The forty Jews who bound themselves by wicked oath to kill Paul before they broke their fast,— were they morally bound to keep their word? Nay, morally bound to break it.

I will tell you a portion of the story of a fugitive slave whom I have known. I will call his name Joseph, though he was in worse than Egyptian bondage. He was "owned" by a notorious gambler, and once ran away, but was retaken. His master proceeded to punish him for that crime, took him to a chamber, locked the door, and lighted a fire; he then beat the slave severely. After that he put the branding-iron in the fire, took a knife,—I am not telling of what took place in Algiers, but in Alabama,—and proceeded to cut off the ears of his victim! The owner's wife, alarmed at the shrieks of the sufferer, beat down the door with a sledge-hammer, and prevented that catastrophe. Afterwards, two slaves of this gambler, for stealing their master's sheep, were beaten so that they died of the stripes. The "minister" came to the funeral, told the others that those were wicked slaves, who deserved their fate; that they would never "rise" in the general resurrection, and were not fit to be buried! Accordingly their bodies were thrown into a hole and left there. Joseph ran away again; he came to Boston; was sheltered by a man whose charity never fails; he has been in my house, and often has worshipped here with us. Shall I take that man and deliver him up?—do it "with alacrity"? Shall I suffer that gambler to carry his prey from this city? Will you allow it—though all the laws and constitutions of men give the commandment? God do so unto us if we suffer it.*

This we need continually to remember: that nothing in

---

* The person referred to fled away from Boston, and in one of the British provinces found the protection for his unalienable rights which could not be allowed him in New England.

the world without is so sacred as the eternal law of God; of the world within nothing is more venerable than our own conscience, the permanent, everlasting oracle of God. The Urim and Thummim were but Jewish or Egyptian toys on the breastplate of the Hebrew priest; the Delphic oracle was only a subtle cheat; but this is the true Shekinah and presence of God in your heart: as this

—"pronounces lastly on each deed,
Of so much fame in heaven expect your meed."

If I am consciously and continually false to this, it is of no avail that I seem loyal to all besides; I make the light that is in me darkness, and how great is that darkness! The centre of my manhood is gone, and I am rotten at my heart. Men may respect me, honour me, but I am not respectable, I am a base, dishonourable man, and like a tree, broad-branched, and leafed with green, but all its heart gnawed out by secret worms; at some slight touch one day, my rotten trunk will fall with horrid squelch, bringing my leafy honours to dishonoured dust, and men will wonder that bark could hide such rottenness and ruin.

But if I am true to this legate of God, holding his court within my soul, then my power to discover the just and right will enlarge continually; the axis of my little life will coincide with the life of the infinite God, His conscience and my own be one. Then my character and my work will lie in the plane of his Almighty action; no other will in me, His infinite wisdom, justice, holiness, and love, will flow into me, a ceaseless tide, filling with life divine and new the little creeklets of my humble soul. I shall be one with God, feel His delight in me and mine in Him, and all my mortal life run o'er with life divine and bless mankind. Let men abhor me, yea, scourge and crucify, angels are at hand; yes, the Father is with me!

How we mistake. Men think if they can but get wickedness dignified into a statute, enrolled in the capitol, signed by the magistrates, and popular with the people, that all is secure. Then they rejoice, and at their " Thanksgiving dinner," say with the short-lived tyrant in the play, after he had slain the rightful heirs of England's throne, and set his murderous hoof on justice at every step to power,—

"Now is the winter of our discontent
Made glorious summer" . . . .

and think th᷁ ↓ sin sits fast and rides secure.* But no
statute of men is ever fixed on man till it be first the
absolute, the right, the law of God. All else lasts but its
day, for ever this, for ever still the same. By "previous
questions," men may stop debate, vote down minorities
with hideous grin, but the still small voice of justice will
whisper in the human heart, will be trumpet-tongued in
history to teach you that you cannot vote down God.

In your private character, if you would build securely,
you must build on the natural law of God, inherent in your
nature and in his; if the nation would build securely, it
must build so. Out of their caprice, their selfishness, and
their sin, may men make statutes, to last for a day, built
up with joyous huzzas, and the chiming of a hundred guns,
to come down with the curses of the multitude, and smitten by the thunder of God; but to build secure, you must
build on the justice of the Almighty. The beatitudes of
Jesus will outlast the codes of all the tyrants of the old
world and the new. So I have seen gamblers hurry and
huddle up their booths at a country muster, on the un-
smoothed surface of a stubble-field, foundation good enough
for such a structure, not a post plumb, to endure a single
day of riot, drunkenness, and sin; but to build a pyramid
which shall outlast empires, men lay bare the bosom of the
primeval rock, and out of primeval rock they build thereon
their well-joined work, outlasting Syria, Greece, Carthage,
Rome, venerable to time, and underneath its steadfast foot
the earthquakes pass all harmlessly away.

All things conspire to overturn a wrong. Every advance of man is hostile to it. Reason is hostile; religion
is its deadly foe; the new-born generation will assail it,
and it must fall. Of old it was written, "Though hand
join in hand, the wicked shall not prosper," and the world's
wide walls, from the remotest bounds of peopled space,
laugh out their loud and long "Amen!" Let Iniquity be
never so old and respectable, get all the most eminent
votes, have the newspapers on her side, guns fired at her
success, it all avails nothing; for this is God's world, not
a devil's, and His eternal word has gone forth that right
alone shall last for ever and for ever.

* This refers to a speech of Mr Webster, occasioned by the passage of the
Fugitive Slave Law.

O young man, now in the period of the passions, reverence your conscience. Defer that to no appetite, to no passion, to no foolish compliance with other men's ways, to no ungodly custom, even if become a law. Ask always "Is it right for me?" Be brave and self-denying for conscience' sake. Fear not to differ from men; keeping your modesty, keep your integrity also. Let not even your discretion consume your valour. Fear not to be scrupulously upright and pure; be afraid neither of men's hate, nor even of their laugh and haughty scorn, but shudder at the thought of tampering with your sense of right, even in the smallest matters. The flesh will come up with deceitful counsels—the Spirit teaching the commandments of God; give both their due. Be not the senses' slave, but the soul's freeman.

O brother man, who once wert young, in the period of ambition, or beyond it, if such a time there be, can you trust the selfishness, the caprice, the passions, and the sin of men, before your own conscience, renounce the law of God for the customs of men? When your volcanic mountain has been capped with snow, Interest, subtler than all the passions of the flesh, comes up to give her insidious counsel. "On our side," says she, "is the applause of men; feasting is with us; the wise and prudent are here also, yea, the ancient and honourable, men much older than thy father; and with gray hairs mottling thy once auburn head, wilt thou forsake official business, its solid praise, and certain gain, for the phantom of natural duty, renounce allegiance to warm human lies for the cold truth of God remote and far!" Say, "Get thee behind me," to such counsellors; "I will not stain my age by listening to your subterranean talk."

O brother man, or old or young, how will you dare come up before your God and say: "O Lord, I heard, I heard thy voice in my soul, at times still and small, at times a trumpet talking with me of the right, the eternal right, but I preferred the low counsels of the flesh; the commands of interest I kept; I feared the rich man's decorous rage; I trembled at the public roar, and I scorned alike my native duty and thy natural law. Lo, here is the talent Thou gavest me, my sense of right. I have used each other sense, this only have I hid; it is eaten up with rust, but thus I bring it back to Thee. Take what is Thine!" Who would dare thus to sin against infinite justice? Who would wish to sin against it when it is also infinite love, and the law of right is but the highway on which the almightiness of the Father comes out to meet his prodigal, a great way off, penitent and returning home, or unrepentant still, refusing to be comforted, and famishing on draff and husks, while there is bread of heavenly life enough and yet to spare, comes out to meet us, to take us home, and to bless us for ever and for ever?

SPEECH

AT THE

MINISTERIAL CONFERENCE IN BOSTON,

MAY 29, 1851.

OCCASION OF THE SPEECH.

THE subject of debate was "The Duty of Ministers under the Fugitive Slave Law." This had been brought up, by Rev. Mr May of Syracuse, at a "Business Meeting" of the American Unitarian Association, and was refused a hearing. It was again brought forward at the meeting of the Ministerial Conference on Wednesday. The Conference adjourned to Thursday morning, at nine o'clock.

On Tuesday and Wednesday afternoons, a good deal was done to prevent the matter from being discussed at all; and done, as it seemed to me, in a disingenuous and unfair manner. And on Thursday morning much time was consumed in mere trifles, apparently with the intention of wearing away the few hours which would otherwise be occupied in discussing the matter at issue, before the Conference. At length the question was reached, and the debate began.

Several persons spoke. Mr Pierpont made a speech, able and characteristic, in which he declared that the Fugitive Slave Bill lacked all the essentials of a law; that it had no claim to obedience; and that it could not be administered with a pure heart or unsullied ermine.

Several others made addresses. Rev. Mr Osgood of New York defended his ministerial predecessor, Rev. Dr Dewey,—making two points.

1. Dr Dewey's conduct had been misrepresented; he had never said that he would send his own *mother* into slavery to preserve the Union; it was only his *son*, or *brother*. [Mr Parker remarked that the principle was the same in all three cases, there was only a diversity of measure.]

2. Dr Dewey's motives had been misrepresented. He had conversed with Dr Dewey; and Dr Dewey felt very bad; was much afflicted—even to weeping, at the misrepresentations made of him. He had not been understood. Dr Dewey met Dr Furness in the street, [Dr Furness had most manfully preached against the Fugitive Slave Act, and thereby drawn upon himself much odium in Philadelphia, and the indignation of some of his clerical brethren elsewhere,] and said, "Brother Furness—you have taken the easy road to duty. It is for me to take the hard and difficult way! I wish it could be otherwise. But I feared the dissolution of the Union!" &c., &c.

Mr Osgood then proceeded to censure "one of this Conference," [Mr Parker,] for the manner in which he had preached on this matter of the fugitive slave law. "It was very bad; it was unjust!" &c.

Rev. Dr Gannett spoke at some length.

1. He said the brethren had laughed, and shown an indecorum that was painful; it was unpardonable. [The chairman, Rev. Dr Farley of Brooklyn, N. Y., thought otherwise.]

2. He criticized severely the statement of Rev. Mr Pierpont that the fugitive slave law "could not be administered with a pure heart or unsullied ermine." [Mr Pierpont affirmed it anew, and briefly defended the statement. Mr Gannett still appeared dissatisfied.] His parishioner, Mr George T. Curtis, had the most honourable motives for attempting to execute the law.

3. He (Dr Gannett) was in a minority, and the majority had no right to think that he was not as honest in his opinion as the rest.

4. Here Dr Gannett made two points in defence of the fugitive slave bill, of making and obeying it.

(1.) If we did not obey it the disobedience would lead to the violation of *all law*. There were two things—law without liberty; and liberty without law. Law without liberty was only despotism; liberty without law only license. Law without liberty was the better of the two. If we began by disobeying any one law, we should come to violating all laws.

(2.) We must obey it to preserve the Union: without the fugitive slave law, the Union would have been dissolved; if it were not obeyed it would also be dissolved, and then he did not know what would become of the cause of human freedom and human rights.

Then Rev. George E. Ellis of Charlestown spoke. He would not have the Conference pass any resolutions; he stood on the first principles of Congregationalism,—that the minister was not responsible to his brothers, but to himself and his God. So the brethren have no right to come here and discuss and condemn the opinions or the conduct of a fellow-minister. We cannot bind one another; we have no right to criticize and condemn.

Next he declared his hatred of the fugitive slave bill. If we must either keep it or lose the Union, he said, "Perish the Union." He had always said so, and preached so.

After Mr Ellis, Mr Parker also spoke as follows:—

MR. CHAIRMAN AND GENTLEMEN,—I am one of those that laughed with the rest, and incurred the displeasure of Dr Gannett. It was not from lightness however; I think no one will accuse me of that. I am earnest enough; so much so as to be grim. Still it is natural even for a grim man to laugh sometimes; and in times like these I am glad we can laugh.

I am glad my friend, Mr Ellis, said the brethren had no right here to criticize and condemn the opinions of one of their members; but I wish he and they had come to this opinion ten years ago. I should have been a gainer by it; for this is the first time for nine years that I have attended this Conference without hearing something which seemed said with the intention of insulting me. I will not say I should have been in general a happier man if Mr Ellis's advice had been followed; nay, if he had always followed it himself; but I should have sat with a little more comfort in this body if they had thought I was not responsible to them for my opinions.

I am glad also to hear Dr Gannett say we have no right to attribute improper motives to any one who differs from us in opinion. It was rather gratuitous, however; no man has done it here to-day. But it is true, no man has a right thus to "judge another." But I will remind Dr Gannett that, a few years ago, he and I differed in opinion on a certain matter of considerable importance, and after clearly expressing our difference, I said, "Well, there is an honest difference of opinion between us," and he said, "Not an *honest* difference of opinion, brother Parker," for he called me "brother" then, and not "Mr" as since, and now, when he has publicly said he cannot take my hand *fraternally*. Still there was an honest difference of opinion on his part as well as mine.

Mr Osgood apologizes for Dr Dewey;—that is, he defends his motives. I am glad he does not undertake to defend his conduct, only to deny that he [Dr Dewey] uttered the words alleged. But I am sorry to say that I cannot agree with Mr Osgood in his defence. I do not believe a word of it to be true: I have evidence enough that he said so.

Mr Gannett in demanding obedience to the fugitive slave law made two points, namely ; if it be not obeyed, first, we shall violate all human laws; and next, there will be a dissolution of the Union.

Let me say a word of each. But first let me say that I attribute no unmanly motive to Mr Gannett. I thought him honest when he denied that I was; I think him honest now. I know him to be conscientious, laborious, and self-denying. I think he would sacrifice himself for another's good. I wish he could now sink through the floor for two or three minutes, that I might say of him absent yet more of honourable praise, which I will not insult him with or address to him while before my face. Let me only say this, that if there be any men in this Conference who honour and esteem Dr Gannett, I trust I am second to none of them. But I do not share his opinions nor partake of his fears. His arguments for obeying the fugitive slave law (*ab inconvenienti*) I think are of no value.

If we do not obey this law, he says, we shall disobey all laws. It is not so. There is not a country in the world where there is more respect for human laws than in New England; nowhere more than in Massachusetts. Even if a law is unpopular, it is not popular to disobey it. Our courts of justice are popular bodies, nowhere are judges more respected than in New England. No officer, constable or sheriff, hangman or jail-keeper, is unpopular on account of his office. Nay, it is popular to inform against your neighbour when he violates the law of the land. This is not so in any other country of the Christian world; but the informer is infamous everywhere else.

Why are we thus loyal to law? First, because we make the laws ourselves, and for ourselves; and next, because the laws actually represent the conscience of the people, and help them keep the laws of God. The value of human laws is only this—to conserve the great eternal law of God; to enable us to keep that; to hinder us from disobeying that. So long as laws do this we should obey them: New England will be loyal to such laws.

But the fugitive slave law is one which contradicts the acknowledged precepts of the Christian religion, universally acknowledged. It violates the noblest instincts of humanity; it asks us to trample on the law of God. It commands what nature, religion, and God alike forbid; it forbids what nature, religion, and God alike command. It tends to defeat the object of all just human law; it tends to annihilate the observance of the law of God. So faithful to God, to religion, to human nature, and in the name of law itself, we protest against this particular statute, and trample it under our feet.

Who is it that oppose the fugitive slave law? Men that have always been on the side of "law and order," and do not violate the statutes of men for their own advantage. This disobedience to the fugitive slave law is one of the strongest guarantees for the observance of any *just* law. You cannot trust a people who will keep law, *because it is law;* nor need we distrust a people that will only keep a law when it is just. The fugitive slave law itself, if obeyed, will do more to overturn the power of human law, than all disobedience to it—the most complete.

Then as to dissolution of the Union. I [have] thought if any State wished to go, she had a natural right to do so. But what States wished to go? Certainly not New England: by no means. Massachusetts has always been attached to the Union,—has made sacrifices for it. In 1775, if she had said, "There shall be no Revolution," there would have been none. But she furnished nearly half the soldiers for the war, and more than half of the money. In '87, if Massachusetts had said, "Let there be no Union!" there would have been none. It was with difficulty that Massachusetts assented to the Constitution. But that once formed, she has adhered to it; faithfully adhered to the Union. When has Massachusetts failed in allegiance to it? No man can say. There is no danger of a dissolution of the Union; the men who make the cry know that it is vain and deceitful. You cannot drive us asunder;—just yet.

But suppose that was the alternative: that we must have the fugitive slave law, or dissolution. Which were the worst; which comes nearest to the law of God which we all are to keep. It is very plain. Now for the first time since '87, many men of Massachusetts calculate the value of the Union. What is it worth? Is it worth so much to us as conscience; so much as freedom; so much as allegiance to the law of God? let any man lay his hand on his heart and say, "I will sacrifice all these for the union of the thirty States! For my own part, I would rather see my own house burnt to the ground, and my family thrown, one by one, amid the blazing rafters of my own roof, and I myself be thrown in last of all, rather than have a single fugitive slave sent back as Thomas Sims was sent back. Nay, I should rather see this Union "dissolved" till there was not a territory so large as the county of Suffolk! Let us lose everything but fidelity to God.

Mr Osgood reflects on me for my sermons; they are poor enough. You know it if you try to read such as are in print. I know it better than you. But I am not going to speak honeyed words and prophesy smooth things in times like these, and say, "Peace! Peace! when there is no peace!"

A little while ago we were told we must not preach on this matter of slavery, because it was "an abstraction;" then because the "North was all right on that subject;" and then because "we had nothing to do with it," "we must go to Charleston or New Orleans to see it." But now it is a most concrete thing. We see what public opinion is on the matter of slavery; what it is in Boston; nay, what it is with members of this Conference. It favours slavery and this wicked law! We need not go to Charleston and New Orleans to see slavery; our own Court House was a barracoon; our officers of this city were slave-hunters, and members of Unitarian churches in Boston are kidnappers.

I have in my church black men, fugitive slaves. They are the crown of my apostleship, the seal of my ministry. It becomes me to look after their bodies in order to "save their souls." This law has brought us into the most intimate connection with the sin of slavery. I have been obliged to take my own parishioners into my house to keep them out of the clutches of the kidnapper. Yes, gentlemen, I have been obliged to do that; and then to keep my doors guarded by day as well as by night. Yes, I have had to arm myself. I have written my sermons with a pistol in my desk,—loaded, a cap on the nipple, and ready for action. Yea, with a drawn sword within reach of my right hand. This I have done in Boston; in the middle of the nineteenth century; been obliged to do it to defend the [innocent] members of my own church, women as well as men!

You know that I do not like fighting. I am no non-resistant, "that nonsense* never went down with me." But it is no small matter which will compel me to shed human blood. But what could I do? I was born in the little town where the fight and bloodshed of the Revolution began. The bones of the men who first fell in that war are covered by the monument at Lexington, it is "sacred to liberty and the rights of mankind:" those men fell "in the sacred cause of God and their country." This is the first inscription that I ever read. These men were my kindred. My grandfather drew the first sword in the Revolution; my fathers fired the first shot; the blood which flowed there was kindred to this which courses in my veins to-day. Besides that, when I write in my library at home, on the one side of me is the Bible which my fathers prayed over, their morning and evening prayer, for nearly a hundred years. On the other side there hangs the firelock my grandfather fought with in the old French war, which he carried at the taking of Quebec, which he zealously

---

* Mr May of Syracuse afterwards objected to the word *nonsense* as applied to non-resistance. The phrase was quoted from another member of the Conference, whose eye caught mine while speaking, and suggested his own language.

used at the battle of Lexington, and beside it is another, a trophy of that war, the first gun taken in the Revolution, taken also by my grandfather. With these things before me, these symbols; with these memories in me, when a parishioner, a fugitive from slavery, a woman, pursued by the kidnappers, came to my house, what could I do less than take her in and defend her to the last? But who sought her life—or liberty? A parishioner of my brother Gannett came to kidnap a member of my church; Mr Gannett preaches a sermon to justify the fugitive slave law, demanding that it should be obeyed; yes, calling on his church members to kidnap mine, and sell them into bondage for ever. Yet all this while Mr Gannett calls himself "a Christian," and me an "Infidel;" his doctrine is "Christianity," mine only "Infidelity," "Deism, at the best!"

O my brothers, I am not afraid of men, I can offend them. I care nothing for their hate, or their esteem. I am not very careful of my reputation. But I should not dare to violate the eternal law of God. You have called me "Infidel." Surely I differ widely enough from you in my theology. But there is one thing I cannot fail to trust; that is the infinite God, Father of the white man, Father also of the white man's slave. I should not dare violate His laws come what may come;—should you? Nay, I can love nothing so well as I love my God.

THE BOSTON KIDNAPPING.

A DISCOURSE

TO COMMEMORATE

THE RENDITION OF THOMAS SIMS,

DELIVERED

ON THE FIRST ANNIVERSARY THEREOF, APRIL 12, 1852, BEFORE THE COMMITTEE OF VIGILANCE, AT THE MELODEON, IN BOSTON.*

THERE are times of private, personal joy and delight, when some good deed has been done, or some extraordinary blessing welcomed to the arms. Then a man stops, and pours out the expression of his heightened consciousness; gives gladness words; or else, in manly quietness, exhales to heaven his joy, too deep for speech. Thus the lover rejoices in his young heart of hearts, when another breast beats in conscious unison with his own, and two souls are first made one; so a father rejoices, so a mother is filled with delight, her hour of anguish over, when their gladdened eyes behold the new-born daughter

---

* REV. THEODORE PARKER :—
Dear Sir,—We know that we express the earnest and unanimous wish of all who listened to your appropriate and eloquent address last Monday, in asking a copy of it for the press.
Yours respectfully,
WENDELL PHILLIPS,
HENRY I. BOWDITCH,
TIMOTHY GILBERT,   } Committee
JOHN P. JEWETT,   of
M. P. HANSON,   Arrangements.
JOHN M. SPEAR,

Boston, April 15, 1852.

or the new-born son. Henceforth the day of newly welcomed love, the day of newly welcomed life, is an epoch of delight, marked for thanksgiving with a white stone in their calends of time,—their day of Annunciation or of Advent, a gladsome anniversary in their lives for many a year.

When these married mates are grown maturely wed, they rejoice to live over again their early loves, a second time removing the hindrances which once strewed all the way, dreaming anew the sweet prophetic dream of early hope, and bringing back the crimson mornings and the purple nights of golden days gone by, which still keep "trailing clouds of glory" as they pass. At their silver wedding, they are proud to see their children's manlifying face, and remember how, one by one, these olive-plants came up about their ever-widening hearth.

When old and full of memories of earth, their hopes chiefly of heaven now, they love to keep the golden wedding of their youthful joy, children and children's children round their venerable board.

Thus the individual man seeks to commemorate his private personal joy, and build up a monument of his domestic bliss.

So, in the life of a nation, there are proud days, when the people joined itself to some great idea of justice, truth, and love; took some step forward in its destiny, or welcomed to national baptism some institution born of its great idea. The anniversaries of such events become red-letter days in the almanac of the nation; days of rejoicing, till that people, old and gray with manifold experience, goes the way of all the nations, as of all its men.

Thus, on the twenty-second of December, all New England thanks God for those poor pilgrims whose wearied feet first found repose in this great wilderness of woods, not broken then. Each year, their children love to gather on the spot made famous now, and bring to mind the ancient deed; to honour it with speech and song, not without prayers to God. That day there is a springing of New England blood, a beating of New England hearts; not only here, but wherever two or three are gathered together in the name of New England, there is the memory of the pilgrims in the midst of them; and among the prairies of the West, along the rivers of the South, far off where the

Pacific waits to bring gold to our shores of rock and sand, —even there the annual song of gladness bursts from New England lips.

So America honours the birth of the nation with a holiday for all the people. Then we look anew at the national idea, reading for the six and seventieth time the programme of our progress,—its first part a revolution; we study our history before and since, bringing back the day of small things, when our fathers went from one kingdom to another people; we rejoice at the wealthy harvest gathered from the unalienable rights of men, sown in new soil. On that day the American flag goes topmost high; and men in ships, far off in the silent wilderness of the ocean, celebrate the nation's joyous day. In all the great cities of the Eastern world, American hearts beat quicker then, and thank their God.

But a few days ago, the Hebrew nation commemorated its escape out of Egypt, celebrating its Passover. Though three and thirty hundred years have since passed by, yet the Israelite remembers that his fathers were slaves in the land of the stranger; that the Pyramids, even then a fact accomplished and representing an obsolete idea, were witnesses to the thraldom of his race; and the joy of Jacob triumphant over the gods of Egypt lights up the Hebrew countenance in the melancholy Ghetto of Rome, as the recollection of the hundred and one pilgrims deepens the joy of the Californian New Englanders delighting in the glory of their nation, and their own abundant gain. The pillar of fire still goes before the Hebrew, in the long night of Israel's wandering; and still the Passover is a day of joy and of proud remembrance.

Every ancient nation has thus its calendar filled with joyful days. The worshippers of Jesus delight in their Christmas and their Easter; the Mahometans, in the Hegira of the Prophet. The year-book of mankind is thus marked all the way through with the red-letter days of history. And most beautifully do those days illuminate the human year, commemorating the victories of the race, the days of triumph which have marked the course of man in his long and varied, but yet triumphant, march of many a thousand years. Thereby Hebrews, Buddhists, Christians, Mahometans, men of every form of religion; English, French, Americans, men of all nations,—are reminded of the great facts in their peculiar story; and mankind learns the lesson they were meant to teach, writ in the great events of the cosmic life of man.

These things should, indeed, be so. It were wrong to miss a single bright day from the story of a man, a nation, or mankind. Let us mark these days, and be glad.

But there are periods of sorrow, not less than joy. There comes a shipwreck to the man; and though he tread the waters under him, and come alive to land, yet his memory drips with sorrow for many a year to come. The widow marks her time by dating from the day which shore off the better portion of herself, counting her life by years of widowhood. Marius, exiled, hunted after, denied fire and water, a price set on his head, just escaping the murderers and the sea, " sitting a fugitive on the ruins of Carthage " which he once destroyed, himself a sadder ruin now, folds his arms and bows his head in manly grief.

These days also are remembered. It takes long to efface what is written in tears. For ever the father bears the annual wound that rent his child away: fifty years do not fill up the tomb which let a mortal through the earth to heaven. The anniversaries of grief return. At St Helena, on the eighteenth of every June, how Napoleon remembered the morning and the evening of the day at Waterloo, the beginning and the ending of his great despair!

So the nations mourn at some great defeat, and hate the day thereof. How the Frenchman detests the very name of Waterloo, and wishes to wipe off from that battle-field the monument of earth the allies piled thereon, commemorative of his nation's loss! Old mythologies are true to this feeling of mankind, when they relate that the spirit of some great man who died defeated comes and relates that he is sad: they tell that—

"Great Pompey's shade complains that we are slow,
And Scipio's ghost walks unrevenged amongst us."

An antique nation, with deep faith in God, looks on these defeats as correction from the hand of Heaven. In sorrow the Jew counts from the day of his exile, mourning that the city sitteth solitary that was full of people; that among all her lovers she hath none to comfort her; that she dwelleth among the heathen and hath no rest. But, he adds, the Lord afflicted her, because of the multitude of her transgressions; for Jerusalem had greatly sinned. How, in the day of her miseries, the Jew remembers her pleasant things that she had in the days of old; how her children have swooned from their wounds in the streets of their city, and have poured out their soul into their mother's bosom; Jerusalem is ruined, and Judah is forsaken, because their tongue and their doings were against the Lord, to provoke the eyes of his glory!

It is well that mother and Marius should mourn their loss; that Napoleon and the Hebrew should remember each his own defeat. Poets say, that, on the vigil of a fight, the old soldier's wounds smart afresh, bleeding anew. The poets fancy should be a nation's fact.

But sometimes a man commits a wrong. He is false to himself, and stains the integrity of his soul. He comes to consciousness thereof, and the shame of the consequence is embittered by remorse for the cause. Thus Peter weeps at his own denial, and Judas hangs himself at the recollection of his treachery; so David bows his penitent forehead and lies prostrate in the dust. The anniversary of doing wrong is writ with fire on the dark tablets of memory. How a murderer convicted, yet spared in jail,—or, not convicted, still at large,—must remember the day when he first reddened his hand at his brother's heart! As the remorseless year brings back the day, the hour, the moment, and the memory of the deed, what recollections of ghastly visages come back to him!

I once knew a New England man who had dealt in slaves; I now know several such; but this man stole his brothers in Guinea to sell in America. He was a hard, cruel man, and had grown rich by the crime. But, hard and cruel as he was, at the mention of the slave-trade, the poor wretch felt a torture at his iron heart which it was piteous to behold. His soul wrought within him like the tossings of the tropic sea about his ship, deep fraught with human wretchedness. He illustrated the torments of that other "middle passage," not often named.

Benedict Arnold, successful in his treason, safe,—only André hanged, not he, the guilty man,—pensioned, feasted, rich, yet hated by all ingenuous souls not great enough to pity, hateful to himself; how this great public shame of

New England must have remembered the twenty-fifth September, and have lived over again each year the annual treason of his heart!

It is well for men to pause on such days, the anniversary of their crime, and see the letters which sin has branded in their consciousness come out anew, and burn, even in the scars they left behind. In sadness, in penitence, in prayers of resolution, should a man mark these days in his own sad calendar. They are times for a man to retire within himself, to seek communion with his God, and cleanse him of the elephantine leprosy his sin has brought upon his soul.

There are such days in the life of a nation, when it stains its own integrity, commits treason against mankind, and sin against the most high God; when a proud king, or wicked minister,—his rare power consorting with a vulgar aim,—misled the people's heart, abused the nation's strength, organized iniquity as law, condensing a world of wicked will into a single wicked deed, and wrought some hideous Bartholomew massacre in the face of the sun. The anniversary of such events is a day of horror and of shivering to mankind; a day of sorrow to the guilty State which pricks with shame at the anniversary of the deed.

The twelfth of April is such a day for Boston and this State. It is the first anniversary of a great crime,—a crime against the majesty of Massachusetts law, and the dignity of the Constitution of the United States: of a great wrong, —a wrong against you and me, and all of us, against the babe not born, against the nature of mankind; of a great sin,—a sin against the law God wrote in human nature, a sin against the Infinite God. It was a great crime, a great wrong, a great sin, on the side of American Government, which did the deed: on the people's part it was a great defeat; your defeat and mine.

Out of the iron house of bondage, a man, guilty of no crime but love of liberty, fled to the people of Massachusetts. He came to us a wanderer, and Boston took him in to an unlawful jail; hungry, and she fed him with a felon's meat; thirsty, she gave him the gall and vinegar of a slave to drink; naked, she clothed him with chains; sick and in prison, he cried for a helper, and Boston sent him a marshal and a commissioner; she set him between kid-

gave him their curse; he asked of us the sacrament of freedom, in the name of our God; and in the name of *their* Trinity, the Trinity of money,—Boston standing as godmother at the ceremony,—in the name of their God they baptized him a slave. The New England church of commerce said, "Thy name is Slave. I baptize thee in the name of the golden eagle, and of the silver dollar, and of the copper cent."

This is holy ground that we stand on: godly men laid here the foundation of a Christian church; laid it with prayers, laid it with tears, laid it in blood. Noble men laid here the foundation of a Christian state, with all the self-denial of New England men; laid that with prayers, with tears, laid that in blood. They sought a church without a bishop, a state without a king, a community without a lord, and a family without a slave. Yet even here in Massachusetts, which first of American colonies sent forth the idea of "inherent and unalienable rights," and first offered the conscious sacrament of her blood; here, in Boston, which was full of manly men who rocked the Cradle of Liberty,—even here the rights of man were of no value and of no avail. Massachusetts took a man from the horns of her altar—he had fled to her for protection,—and voluntarily gave him up to bondage without end; did it with her eyes wide open; did it on purpose; did it in notorious violation of her own law, in consciousness of the sin; did it after "fasting and prayer." *

It is well for us to come together, and consider the defeat which you and I have suffered when the rights of man were thus cloven down, and look at the crime committed by those whom posterity will rank among infidels to Christianity, among the enemies of man; it is well to commemorate the event, the disgrace of Boston, the perpetual shame and blot of Massachusetts. Yet it was not the people of Massachusetts who did the deed: it was only

---

* The annual day of "fasting and prayer" came between the seizure of Mr Sims and his rendition! Boston fasted and made long prayers, and devoured a man's liberty!

there would have been a "day of fasting and prayer," and next a muster of soldiers: one day the people would have thought of their trust in God, and the next looked to it that their powder was dry. Now nobody fasts, save to the eye; he prays best who, not asking God to do man's work, prays penitence, prays resolutions, and then prays deeds, thus supplicating with heart and head and hands. This is a day for such a prayer. The twelfth of last April issued the proclamation which brings us here to-day.

We have historical precedent for this commemoration, if men need such an argument. After the Boston Massacre of the fifth of March, 1770, the people had annually a solemn commemoration of the event. They had their great and honoured men to the pulpit on that occasion: Lovell, child of a Tory father,—the son's patriotism brought him to a British jail; Tudor and Dawes, honourable and honoured names; Thacher, "the young Elijah" of his times; Warren, twice called to that post, but destined soon to perish by a British hand; John Hancock,—his very name was once the pride and glory of the town. They stood here, and, mindful of their brothers slain in the street not long to bear the name of "King," taught the lesson of liberty to their fellow-men. The menace of British officers, their presence in the aisles of the church, the sight of their weapons on the pulpit-stairs, did not frighten Joseph Warren,—not a hireling shepherd, though he came in by the pulpit-window, while soldiers crammed the porch. Did they threaten to stop his mouth? It took bullet and bayonet both to silence his lips. John Hancock was of eyes too pure to fear the government of Britain. Once, when Boston was in the hands of the enemy of freedom,—I mean the foreign enemy,—the discourse could not be delivered here; Boston adjourned to Watertown to hear "the young Elijah" ask whether "the rising empire of America shall be an empire of slaves or of freemen." But on that day there was another commemoration held hard by; "one George Washington" discoursed from the "Heights of Dorchester;" and, soon after, Israel Putnam marched over the Neck,—and there was not a "Red-coat" south of the North End. The March of '76 was not far from the July of '76, when yet another discourse got spoken.

For twelve years did our fathers commemorate the first blood shed here by soldiers "quartered among us without our consent;" yes, until there was not a "Red-coat" left in the land; and the gloom of the Boston Massacre was forgot in the blaze of American independence; the murder of five men, in the freedom of two millions.

The first slave Boston has officially sent back since 1770 was returned a year ago. Let us commemorate the act, till there is not a kidnapper left in all the North; not a kidnapper lurking in a lawyer's office in all Boston, or in a merchant's counting-room; not a priest who profanes his function by flouting at the higher law of God; till there is not a slave in America; and sorrow at the rendition of Thomas Sims shall be forgotten in the freedom of three million men. Let us remember the Boston Kidnapping, as our fathers kept the memory of the Boston Massacre.

It is a fitting time to come together. There was once a "dark day" in New England, when the visible heavens were hung with night, and men's faces gathered blackness, less from the sky above than from the fears within. But New England never saw a day so black as the twelfth of April, 1851; a day whose Egyptian darkness will be felt for many a year to come.

New England has had days of misfortune before this, and of mourning at the sin of her magistrates. In 1761, a mean man in a high place in the British Island, thinking that "discussion must be suppressed," declared that citizens "are not to demand the reasons of measures; they must, and they easily may, be taught better manners." The British Ministry decided to tax the colonies without their consent. Massachusetts decided to be taxed only with her own consent. The Board of Trade determined to collect duties against the will of the people. The Government insisted; the mercenaries of the custom-house in Boston applied for "Writs of Assistance," authorizing them to search for smuggled goods where and when they pleased, and to call on the people to help in the matter. The mercenary who filled the governor's chair favoured the outrage. The court, obedient to power, and usually on the side of prerogative and against the right, seemed ready to pervert the law against justice. Massachusetts felt her liberty in peril, and began the war of ideas. James Otis, an irregular but brilliant and powerful man from Barnstable, and an acute lawyer, resigned his post of Advocate to the Admiralty; threw up his chance of preferment, and was determined "to sacrifice estate, ease, health, applause, and even life, to the sacred calls of my country," and in opposition to that kind of power " which cost one King of England his head, another his throne."

It was a dark day in Massachusetts when the Writs of Assistance were called for; when the talents, the fame, the riches, and the avarice of Chief-justice Hutchinson, the respectability of venerable men, the power of the Crown and its officers, were all against the right; but that brave lawyer stood up, his words "a flame of fire," to demonstrate "that all arbitrary authority was unconstitutional and against the law." His voice rung through the land like a war-psalm of the Hebrew muse. Hutchinson, rich, false, and in power, cowered before the " great incendiary" of New England. John Adams, a young lawyer from Quincy, who stood by, touched by the same inspiration, declared that afterwards he could never read the Acts of Trade without anger, nor " any portion of them without a curse." If the court was not convinced, the people were. It was a dark day when the Writs of Assistance were called for; but the birthplace of Franklin took the lightning out of that thundering cloud, and the storm broke into rain which brought forth the green glories of Liberty-tree, that soon blossomed all over in the radiance of the bow of promise set on the departing cloud. The seed from that day of bloom shall sow with blessings all the whole wide world of man.

There was another dark time when the Stamp Act passed, and the day came for the use of the Stamps, Nov. 1st, 1765. The people of Boston closed their shops; they muffled and tolled the bells of the churches; they hung on Liberty-tree the effigy of Mr Huské, a New Hampshire traitor of that time, who had removed to London, got a seat in Parliament, and was said to have proposed the Stamp Act to the British minister. Beside him they hung the image of Grenville, the ministerial author of the Act. In the afternoon, the public cut down the images; carried them in a cart, thousands following, to the town-house, where the governor and council were in session; carried the effigies solemnly through the building, and thence to the gallows, where, after hanging a while, they were cut down and torn to pieces. All was done quietly, orderly, and with no violence. It was All-Saints Day: two hundred and forty-eight years before, Martin Luther had pilloried the papacy on a church-door at Wittenberg, not knowing what would fall at the sound of his hammer nailing up the Ninety-five Theses.

Nobody would touch the hated stamps. Mr Oliver, the secretary of the province, and "distributor of stamps," had been hanged in effigy before. His stamp-office had already given a name to the sea, "Oliver's Dock" long commemorating the fate of the building. Dismayed by the voice of the people, he resigned his office. Not satisfied with that, the people had him before an immense meeting at Liberty-tree; and at noonday, under the very limb where he had been hung in effigy, before a justice of the peace he took an oath that he never would take any measures .... for enforcing the Stamp Act in America. Then, with three cheers for liberty, Mr Oliver was allowed to return home. He ranked as the third crown-officer in the colony. Where could you find "one of his Majesty's justices of the peace" to administer such an oath before such a "town-meeting"? A man was found to do that deed, and leave descendants to be proud of it; for, after three generations have passed by, the name of Richard Dana is still on the side of liberty.

No more of stamps in Boston at that time. In time of danger, it is thought "a good thing to have a man in the house." Boston had provided herself. There were a good many who did not disgrace the name. Amongst others, there was one of such "obstinacy and inflexible disposition," said Hutchinson, "that he could never be conciliated by any office or gift whatever." Yet Samuel Adams was "not rich, nor a bachelor." There was another, one John Adams, son of a shoemaker at Quincy, not a whit less obstinate or hard to conciliate with gifts. When he heard Otis in that great argument, he felt "ready to take up arms against the Writs of Assistance." One day, the twenty-second of December of that year, he writes in his journal:

"At home with my family, thinking." In due time, something came of his thinking. He wrote, "By inactivity we discover cowardice, and too much respect for the Act."

The Stamp Act was dead in New England and in all America. Very soon the Ministry were glad to bury their dead.

It was in such a spirit that Boston met the Writs of Assistance and the Stamp Act. What came of the resistance? When Parliament came together, the "great commoner" said,—every boy knew the passage by heart when I went to school,—"I rejoice that America has resisted. Three millions of people so dead to all the feelings of liberty as voluntarily to be slaves, would have been fit instruments to make slaves of all the rest." The Ministry still proposed to put down America by armies. Mr Pitt said: "America, if she fell, would fall like the strong man. She would embrace the pillars of the state, and pull down the Constitution along with her. But she would not fall." "I would advise," said he, "that the Stamp Act be repealed, absolutely, totally, and immediately;" "that the reason for the repeal be assigned; that it was founded on an erroneous principle." Repealed it was, "absolutely, totally, and immediately."

But the British Ministry still insisted on taxation without representation. Massachusetts continued her opposition. There was a merchants' meeting in Boston in favour of freedom. It assembled from time to time, and had a large influence. Men agreed not to import British goods: they would wear their old clothes till they could weave new ones in America, and kill no more lambs till they had abundance of wool. Boston made a non-importation agreement. Massachusetts wrote a "circular letter" to the other colonies, asking them to make common cause with her,—a circular which the king thought "of the most dangerous and factious character." On the seventeenth of June, 1768, the town of Boston instructed its four representatives, Otis, Cushing, Adams, and Hancock: "It is our unalterable resolution at all times to assert and vindicate our dear and invaluable rights, at the utmost hazard of our lives and fortunes."* This seemed to promise an-

* Town Records of that date.

other "seventeenth of June," if the Ministry persisted in their course.

On the fifteenth of May, 1770, she again issued similar instructions. "James I.," says the letter of instruction, "more than once laid down, that, as it was atheism and blasphemy in a creature to dispute what the Deity may do, so it is presumptuous and sedition in a subject to dispute what a king may do in the height of his powers." "Good Christians," said he, "will be content with God's will revealed in his word, and good subjects will rest in the king's will revealed in *his* law." That was the "No Higher Law Doctrine" of the time. See how it went down at Boston in 1770. "Surely," said the people of Boston, in town-meeting assembled, "nothing except the ineffable contempt of the reigning monarch diverted that indignant vengeance which would otherwise have made his illustrious throne to tremble, and hurled the royal diadem from his forfeit head."* Such was the feeling of Boston towards a government which flouted at the eternal law of God.

The people claimed that law was on their side; even Sir Henry Finch having said, in the time of Charles I., "The king's prerogative stretcheth not to the doing of any wrong." But, Boston said, "Had the express letter of the law been less favourable, and were it possible to ransack up any absurd, obsolete notions which might have seemed calculated to propagate slavish doctrines, we should by no means have been influenced to forego our birthright;" for "mankind will not be reasoned out of their feelings of humanity." "We remind you, that the further nations recede and give way to the gigantic strides of any powerful despot, the more rapidly will the fiend advance to spread wide desolation." "It is now no time to halt between two opinions." "We enjoin you at all hazards to deport... like the faithful representatives of a free-born, awakened, and determined people, who, being impregnated with the spirit of liberty in conception, and nurtured in the principles of freedom from their infancy, are resolved to breathe the same celestial ether, till summoned to resign the heavenly flame by that omnipotent God who gave it." That was the language of Boston in 1770.†

True there were men who took the other side; some of

* Town Records. † Ibid.

them from high and honourable convictions; others from sordid motives; some from native bigotry and meanness they could not help. But the mass of the people went for the rights of the people. It was not a mere matter of dollars and cents that stirred the men of Massachusetts then. True, the people had always been thrifty, and looked well to the "things of this world." But threepence duty on a pound of tea, six farthings on a gallon of molasses, was not very burdensome to a people that had a school before there was any four-footed beast above a swine in the colony —a people that once taxed themselves thirteen shillings and eight pence in a pound of income! It was the principle they looked at. They would not have paid three barley-corns on a hogshead of sugar, and admit the right of Parliament to levy the tax. This same spirit extended to the other colonies: Virginia and Massachusetts stood side by side; New York with Boston.

It was a dark day for New England when the Stamp Act became a law; but it was a much darker day when the Fugitive Slave Bill passed the Congress of the United States. The Acts of Trade and the Stamp Act were the work of foreign hands, of the ministers of England, not America. A traitor of New Hampshire was thought to have originated the Stamp Act; but even he did not make a speech in its favour. The author of the Act was never within three thousand miles of Boston. But the Fugitive Slave Bill was the work of Americans; it had its great support from another native of New Hampshire; it got the vote of the member for Boston, who faithfully represented the money which sent him there; though, God be thanked, not the men!

When the Stamp Act came to be executed in Boston, the ships hung their flags at half-mast; the shops were shut, the bells were tolled; ship, shop, and church all joining in a solidarity of affliction, in one unanimous lament. But, when the Fugitive Slave Bill came to Boston, the merchants and politicians of the city fired a hundred guns at noonday, in token of their joy! How times have changed! In 1765, when Huske of New Hampshire favoured the Stamp Act, and Oliver of Boston accepted the office of distributor of stamps, the people hung their busts in effigy on Liberty-tree; Oliver must ignominiously forswear his office. After

two of the Massachusetts delegation in Congress had voted for the Missouri Compromise in 1819, when they came back to Boston, they were hissed at on 'Change, and were both of them abhorred for the deed which spread slavery west of the great river. To this hour their names are hateful all the way from Boston to Lanesboro'. But their children are guiltless: let us not repeat the fathers' name. But what was the Stamp Act or the Missouri Compromise to the Fugitive Slave Bill! One was looking at a hedge, the other stealing the sheep behind it. Yet when the representative of the money of Boston, who voted for the bill, returned, he was flattered and thanked by two classes of men; by those whom money makes "respectable" and prominent; by those whom love of money makes servile and contemptible. When he resigned his place, Boston sent another, with the command, "Go thou and do likewise;" and he has just voted again for the Fugitive Slave Bill,—he alone of all the delegation of Massachusetts.

The Stamp Act levied a tax on us in money, and Boston would not pay a cent, hauled down the flags, shut up the shops, tolled the church-bells, hung its authors in effigy, made the third officer of the Crown take oath not to keep the law, cast his stamp-shop into the sea. The Slave Act levied a tax in men, and Boston fired a hundred guns, and said, "We are ready; we will catch fugitive slaves for the South. It is a dirty work, too dirty for any but Northern hands; but it will bring us clean money." Ship, shop, and church seemed to feel a solidarity of interest in the measure; the leading newspapers of the town were full of glee.

The Fugitive Slave Bill became a law on the eighteenth of September, 1850. Eighty-five years before that date there was a town-meeting in Boston, at which the people instructed their representatives in the General Assembly of Massachusetts. It was just after the passage of the Stamp Act. Boston told her servants "by no means to join in any measures for countenancing and assisting in the execution of the same [the Stamp Act]; but to use your best endeavours in the General Assembly to have the inherent and unalienable rights of the people of this province asserted, vindicated, and left upon the public record, that posterity may never have reason to charge the present times with the guilt of tamely giving them away."*

It was "voted unanimously that the same be accepted." This is the earliest use of the phrase "inherent and unalienable rights of the people" which I have yet found. It has the savour of James Otis, who had "a tongue of flame and the inspiration of a seer." It dates from Boston, and the eighteenth day of September, eighty-five years before the passage of the Fugitive Slave Bill. In 1850 where was the town-meeting of '65 ? James Otis died without a son; but a different man sought to "fence in" the Slave Act, and fence men from their rights.†

The passage of the Fugitive Slave Bill was a sad event to the coloured citizens of the State. At that time there were 8975 persons of colour in Massachusetts. In thirty-six hours after the passage of the bill was known here, five and thirty coloured persons applied to a well-known philanthropist in this city for counsel.‡ Before sixty hours passed by, more than forty had fled. The laws of Massachusetts could not be trusted to shelter her own children: they must flee to Canada. "This arm, hostile to tyrants," says the motto of the State, " seeks rest in the enjoyment of liberty." Then it ought to have been changed, and read, "This arm, once hostile to tyrants, confederate w.th them now, drives off her citizens to foreign climes of liberty."

The word "commissioner" has had a traditional hatred ever since our visitation by Sir Edmund Andros; it lost none of its odious character when it became again incarnate in a kidnapper. With Slave Act commissioners to execute the bill, with such "ruling" as we have known on the Slave Act bench, such swearing by "witnesses" on the slave stand, any man's freedom is at the mercy of the kidnapper and his "commissioned" attorney. The one can manufacture "evidence" or "enlarge" it, the other manufacture "law;" and, with such an administration and such creatures to serve its wish, what coloured man was safe? Men in peril have a keen instinct of their danger; the dark-browed mothers in Boston, they wept like Rachel for her first-born, refusing to be comforted. There was no

* Town Records. † Hon. Harrison Gray Otis. ‡ Mr Francis Jackson.

comfort for them save in flight: that must be not in the winter, but into the winter of Canada, which is to the African what our rude climate is to the goldfinch and the canary-bird.

Some of the coloured people had acquired a little property; they got an honest living; had wives and children, and looked back upon the horrors of slavery, which it takes a woman's affectionate genius to paint, as you read her book; looked on them as things for the memory, for the imagination, not as things to be suffered again. But the Fugitive Slave Bill said to every black mother, "This may be your fate; the fate of your sons and your daughters." It was possible to all; probable to many; certain to some, unless they should flee.

It was a dark bill for them; but the blackness of the darkness fell on the white men. The coloured men were only to bear the cross; the whites made it. I would take the black man's share in suffering the Slave Act, rather than the white man's sin in making it; ay, as I would rather take Hancock's than Huske's share of the history of the Stamp Act. This wicked law has developed in the Africans some of the most heroic virtues; in the Yankee it has brought out some of the most disgraceful examples of meanness that ever dishonoured mankind.

The Boston Massacre,—you know what that was, and how the people felt when a hireling soldiery, sent here to oppress, shot down the citizens of Boston on the fifth of March, 1770. Then the blood of America flowed for the first time at the touch of British steel. But that deed was done by foreigners; thank God, they were not Americans born; done by hirelings, impressed into the army against their will, and sent here without their consent. It was done in hot blood; done partly in self-defence, after much insult and wrong. The men who fired the shot were brought to trial. The great soul of John Adams stood up to defend them, Josiah Quincy aiding the unpopular work. A Massachusetts jury set the soldiers free,—they only obeyed orders, the soldier is a tool of his commander. Such was the Boston Massacre. Yet hear how John Hancock spoke on the fourth anniversary thereof, when passion had had time to pass away:—

"Tell me, ye bloody butchers! ye villains high and low!

ye wretches who contrived, as well as you who executed, the inhuman deed! do you not feel the goads and stings of conscious guilt pierce through your savage bosoms? Though some of you may think yourselves exalted to a height that bids defiance to the arms of human justice, and others shroud yourselves beneath the mask of hypocrisy, and build your hopes of safety on the low arts of cunning, chicanery, and falsehood; yet do you not sometimes feel the gnawings of that worm which never dies? Do not the injured shades of Maverick, Gray, Caldwell, Attucks, and Carr, attend you in your solitary walks, arrest you even in the midst of your debaucheries, and fill even your dreams with terror?

"Ye dark, designing knaves! ye murderers! parricides! how dare you tread upon the earth which has drank in the blood of slaughtered innocents, shed by your wicked hands? How dare you breathe that air which wafted to the ear of Heaven the groans of those who fell a sacrifice to your accursed ambition? But if the labouring earth doth not expand her jaws; if the air you breathe is not commissioned to be the minister of death; yet hear it, and tremble! the eye of Heaven penetrates the darkest chambers of the soul; traces the leading clue through all the labyrinths which your industrious folly has devised; and you, however you may have screened yourselves from human eyes, must be arraigned, must lift your hands, red with the blood of those whose deaths you have procured, at the tremendous bar of God."

But the Boston kidnapping was done by Boston men. The worst of the kidnappers were natives of the spot. It was done by volunteers, not impressed to the work, but choosing their profession,—loving the wages of sin,—and conscious of the loathing and the scorn they are all sure to get, and bequeath to their issue. They did it deliberat   it was a cold-blooded atrocity : they did it aggressively, not in self-defence, but in self-degradation. They did it for their pay : let them have it; verily, they shall have their reward.

When the Fugitive Slave Bill became a law, it seems to me the governor ought to have assembled the Legislature; that they should have taken adequate measures for protecting the eight thousand nine hundred and seventy-five persons thus left at the mercy of any kidnapper; that officers should have been appointed, at the public cost, to defend these helpless men, and a law passed, punishing any one who should attempt to kidnap a man in this commonwealth. Massachusetts should have done for justice what South Carolina has long ago done for injustice. But Massachusetts had often seen her citizens put into the jails of the North for no crime but their complexion, and looked on with a drowsy yawn. Once, indeed, she did send two persons, one to Charleston and the other to New Orleans, to attend to this matter; both of them were turned out of the South with insult and contempt. After that, Massachusetts did nothing; the commonwealth did nothing; the commonwealth did not even scold: she sat mute as the symbolic fish in the State-house. The Bay State turned non-resistant; "passive obedience" should have been the motto then. So, when a bill was passed, putting the liberty of her citizens at the mercy of a crew of legalized kidnappers, the governor of Massachusetts did nothing. Boston fired her hundred guns under the very eyes of John Hancock's house; her servile and her rich men complimented their representative for voting away the liberty of nine thousand of her fellow-citizens. Was Boston Massachusetts? It is still the governor.

As the government of Massachusetts did nothing, the next thing would have been for the people to come together in a great mass meeting, and decree, as their fathers had often done, that so unjust a law should not be kept in the old Bay State, and appoint a committee to see that no man was kidnapped and carried off; and, if the kidnappers still insisted on kidnapping our brothers here in Massachusetts, the people could have found a way to abate that nuisance as easily as to keep off the stamped paper in 1765. The commissioners of the Slave Act might as easily be dealt with as the commissioners of the Stamp Act.

I love law, and respect law, and should be slow to violate it. I would suffer much, sooner than violate a statute that was simply inexpedient. There is no natural reason, perhaps, for limiting the interest of money to six per cent., but as the law of Massachusetts forbids more, I would not take more. I should hate to interrupt the course of law, and put violence in its place.

"The way of ancient ordinance, though it winds,
Is yet no devious way. Straightforward goes
The lightning's path, and straight the fearful path
Of the cannon-ball. Direct it flies, and rapid;
Shattering that it may reach, and shattering what it reaches.
My son! the road the human being travels,—
That on which blessing comes and goes,—doth follow
The river's course, the valley's playful windings;
Curves round the corn-field and the hill of vines,
Honouring the h   .ounds of property!
And thus secure, though late, leads to its end."

But when the rulers have inverted their function, and enacted wickedness into a law which treads down the unalienable rights of man to such degree as this, then I know no ruler but God, no law but natural justice. I tear the hateful statute of kidnappers to shivers; I trample it underneath my feet. I do it in the name of all law; in the name of justice and of man; in the name of the dear God.

But of all this nothing was done. The governor did not assemble the Legislature, as he would if a part of the property in Massachusetts had thus been put at the mercy of legalized ruffians. There was no convention of the people of Massachusetts. True, there was a meeting at Faneuil Hall, a meeting chiefly of anti-slavery men; leading free-soilers were a little afraid of it, though some of them came honourably forward. A venerable man put his name at the head of the signers of the call, and wrote a noble-spirited letter to the meeting; Josiah Quincy was a Faneuil Hall name in 1859, as well as in 1765. It was found a little difficult to get what in Boston is called a "respectable man to preside. Yet one often true sat in the chair that night,—Charles F. Adams did not flinch, when you wanted a man to stand fire. A brave, good minister, whose large soul disdains to be confined to sect or party, came in from Cambridge, and lifted up his voice to the God who brought up Israel out of the iron house of bondage, and our fathers from thraldom in a strange land; thanking Him who created all men in His own image, and of one blood. Charles Lowell's prayer for all mankind will not soon be forgotten. The meeting was an honour to the men who composed it. The old spirit was there; philanthropy, which never fails; justice, that is not weary with continual defeat; and faith in God, which is sure to triumph at the last. But what a reproach was the meeting to Boston! "Respectability" was determined to kidnap.

At that meeting a Committee of Vigilance was appointed, and a very vigilant committee it has proved itself, having saved the liberty of three or four hundred citizens of Boston. Besides, it has done many things not to be spoken of now. I know one of its members who has helped ninety-five fugitives out of the United States. It would not be well to mention his name,—he has "levied war" too often,—the good God knows it.*

Other towns in the State did the same thing. Vigilance Committees got on foot in most of the great towns, in many of the small ones. In some places, all the people rose up against the Fugitive Slave Bill; the whole town a vigilance committee. The country was right; off the pavement, Liberty was the watchword; on the pavement, it was Money. But the government of Massachusetts did nothing. Could the eight thousand nine hundred and seventy-five coloured persons affect any election? Was their vote worth bidding for?

The controlling men of the Whig party and of the Democratic party, they either did nothing at all, or else went over in favour of kidnapping; some of them had a natural proclivity that way, and went over "with alacrity."

The leading newspapers in the great towns,—they, of course, went on the side of inhumanity, with few honourable exceptions. The political papers thought kidnapping would "save the Union;" the commercial papers thought it would "save trade," the great object for which the Union was established.

How differently had Massachusetts met the Acts of Trade and the Stamp Act! How are the mighty fallen! Yet, if you could have got their sacred ballot, I think fifteen out of every twenty voters, even in Boston, would have opposed the law. But the leading politicians and the leading merchants were in favour of the bill, and the execution of it.

There are two political parties in America: one of them is very large and well organized; that is the Slave-soil party. It has two great subdivisions; one is called Whig, the other Democratic: together they make up the

* It is not yet safe to mention his name. Feb. 22, 1855!

great national Slave-soil party. It was the desire of that party to extend slavery; making a national sin out of a sectional curse. They wished to "re-annex" Massachusetts to the department of the slave soil, and succeeded. We know the history of that party: who shall tell the future of its opponent? There will be a to-morrow after to-day.

The practical result was what the leading men of Boston desired: soon we had kidnappers in Boston. Some ruffians came here from Georgia, to kidnap William and Ellen Craft. Among them came a jailer from Macon, a man of infamous reputation, and character as bad as its repute; notoriously a cruel man, and hateful on that account even in Georgia. In the handbills, his face was described as "uncommon bad." It was worthy of the description. I saw the face; it looked like total depravity incarnate in a born kidnapper. He was not quite welcome in Boston; Massachusetts had not then learned to "conquer her prejudices," yet he found friends, got "a sort of a lawyer" to help him kidnap a man and his wife: a fee will hire such men any day. He was a welcome guest at the United States Hotel, which, however, got a little tired of his company, and warned him off. The commissioner first applied to for aid in this business seemed to exhibit some signs of a conscience, and appeared a little averse to stealing a man. The Vigilance Committee put their eye on the kidnapper: he was glad to escape out of Boston with a whole skin. He sneaked off in a private way; went back to Georgia; published his story, partly true, false in part; got into a quarrel in the street at Macon,—I traced out his wriggling trail for some distance back,—it was not the first brawl he had been in; was stabbed to what is commonly called "the heart," and fell unmistakably dead. Some worthy persons had told him, if he went to Boston, he would "rot in a Massachusetts jail;" others, that they "hoped it would turn out so, for such an errand deserved such an end." Poor men of Georgia! they knew the Boston of 1765, not of 1850;—the town of the Stamp Act, ruled by select men; not the city of the Slave Act, ruled by a "Mayor." Hughes came to save the "Union!"

That time the kidnappers went off without their prey. Somebody took care of Ellen Craft, and William took care of himself. They were parishioners of mine. Mr Craft was a tall, brave man; his countrymen, not nobler than he, were once bishops of Hippo and of Carthage. He armed himself, pretty well too. I inspected his weapons: it was rather new business for me; New England ministers have not done much in that line since the Revolution. His powder had a good kernel, and he kept it dry; his pistols were of excellent proof, the barrels true and clean; the trigger went easy; the caps would not hang fire at the snap. I tested his poniard; the blade had a good temper, stiff enough, yet springy withal; the point was sharp. There was no law for him but the law of nature; he was armed and equipped "as that law directs." He walked the streets boldly; but the kidnappers did not dare touch him. Some persons offered to help Mr Craft to purchase himself. He said, "I will not give the man two cents for his 'right' to me. I will buy myself, not with gold, but iron!" That looked like "levying war," not like conquering his prejudices for liberty! William Craft did not obey with "alacrity." He stood his ground till the kidnappers had fled; then he also must flee. Boston was no home for him. One of her most eminent ministers had said, if a fugitive came to him, "I would drive him away from my own door."

William and Ellen Craft were at the "World's Fair," specimens of American manufactures, the working-tools of the South; a proof of the democracy of the American State; part of the "outward evidences" of the Christianity of the American church. "It is a great country," whence a Boston clergyman would drive William Craft from his door! America did not compete very well with the European States in articles sent to the Fair. A "reaping machine" was the most quotable thing; then a "Greek slave" in marble; next an American slave in flesh and blood. America was the only contributor of slaves; she had the monopoly of the article; it is the great export of Virginia,—it was right to exhibit a specimen at the World's Fair. Visitors went to Westminster Abbey, and saw the monument of marble which Massachusetts erected to Lord George Howe, and thence to the Crystal Palace to see the man and woman whom Massachusetts would not keep from being kidnapped in her capital.

In due time came the "Union meeting," on the twenty-sixth day of November, 1850, in Faneuil Hall, in front of the pictures of Samuel Adams and John Hancock,—in the hall which once rocked to the patriotism of James Otis, thundering against Acts of Trade and Writs of Assistance, "more eloquent than Chatham or Burke." The Union meeting was held in the face and eyes of George Washington.

You remember the meeting. It was rather a remarkable platform; uniformly "Hunker," but decidedly heterogeneous. Yet sin abolishes all historical and personal distinctions. Kidnapping, like misery, "makes strange bed-fellows." Three things all the speakers on that occasion developed in common: A hearty abhorrence of the right; a uniform contempt for the eternal law of God; a common desire to kidnap a man. After all, the plat͏ͭ m did not exhibit so strange a medley as it seemed at ⊥st: the difference in the speakers was chiefly cutaneous, only skin-deep. The reading and the speaking, the whining and the thundering, were all to the same tune. Pirates, who have just quarrelled about dividing the spoil, are of one heart when it comes to plundering and killing a man.

That was a meeting for the encouragement of kidnapping; not from the love of kidnapping in itself, but for the recompense of reward. I will not insult the common sense of respectable men with supposing that the talk about the "dissolution of the Union," and the cry, "The Union is in peril this hour," was anything more than a stage-trick, which the managers doubtless thought was "well got up." So it was; but, I take it, the spectators who applauded, as well as the actors who grimaced, knew that the "lion" was no beast, but only "Simon Snug the joiner." Indeed, the lion himself often told us so. However, I did know two very "respectable" men of Boston, who actually believed the Union was in danger; only two, —but they are men of such incomprehensible exiguity of intellect, that their names would break to pieces if spoken loud.

Well, the meeting, in substance, told this truth: "Boston is willing; you may come here, and kidnap any black man you choose. We will lend you the marshal, the commissioner, the tools of perjury, supple courts of law, clergymen to bless the transaction, and editors to defend it!"

That was the plain English meaning of the meeting, of the resolutions and the speeches. It was so understood North and South.

At the meeting itself it was declared that the Union was at the last gasp; but the next morning the political doctors, the "medicine-men" of our mythology, declared the old lady out of danger. She sat up that day, and received her friends. The meeting was "great medicine;" the crisis was passed. The Fugitive Slave Bill could be "executed in Boston," where the Writs of Assistance and the Stamp Act had been a dead letter: a man might be kidnapped in Boston any day.

But the meeting was far from unanimous at the end. At the beginning a manly speech would have turned the majority in favour of the right. In November, 1850, half a dozen rich men might have turned Boston against the wicked law. But their interest lay the other side; and "where the treasure is, there will the heart be also." Boston is bad enough, but bad only in spots; at that time the spots showed, and some men thought all Boston was covered with the small-pox of the Union meeting: the scars will mark the faces of only a few. I wish I could heal those faces, which will have an ugly look in the eyes of posterity.

The practical result of the meeting was what it was designed to be: soon we had other kidnappers in Boston. This time they found better friends: like consorteth with like. A certain lawyer's office in Boston became a huckstery of kidnappers' warrants. Soon the kidnappers had Shadrach in their fiery furnace, heated seven times hotter than before for William and Ellen Craft. But the Lord delivered him out of their clutch; and he now sings "God save the Queen," in token of his delivery out of the hands of the kidnappers of "Republican" Babylon. Nobody knows how he was delivered; the rescue was officially declared "levying war," the rescuers guilty of "treason." But, wonderful to say, after all the violations of law by the court, and all the browbeating by the attorneys, and all the perjury and other "amendments and enlargement of testimony" by witnesses, not a man was found guilty of any crime. Spite of "Union meetings," there is some respect for Massachusetts law; spite of judicial attempts to pack a jury, it is still the great safeguard of the people; spite of preaching, there is some virtue left; and, though a minister would send back his mother into slavery, a Massachusetts jury will not a send a man to jail for such an act as that.

The case of Shadrach was not the last. Kidnappers came and kidnappers went: for a long time they got no spoil. I need not tell, must not tell, how they were evaded, or what help came, always in season. The Vigilance Committee did not sleep; it was in "permanent session" much of the whole winter; its eyes were in every place, beholding the evil and the good. The government at Washington did not like this state of things, and stimulated the proper persons, as the keeper of a menerie in private stirs up the hyenas and the cougars and the wolves, from a safe distance. There was a talk of "Sherman's flying-artillery" alighting at Boston; but it flew over and settled at Newport, I think. Next there was to be a "garrison of soldiers" to enforce the law; but the men in buckram did not appear. Then a "seventy-four gun ship was coming," to bombard Southack street, I suppose. Still it was determined that the "Union" was not quite safe; it was in danger of a "dissolution;" the "medicine-men" of politics and commerce looked grave. True, the Union had been "saved" again and again, till her "salvation" was a weariness; she "was nothing bettered, but rather grew worse." All winter long, the Union was reported as in a chronic spasm of "dissolution." So the "medicine-men" prescribed: A man kidnapped in Massachusetts, to be taken at the South; with one scruple of lawyer, and two scruples of clergyman. That would set the Union on her legs. Boston was to furnish all this medicine.

It was long before this city could furnish a kidnapped man. The Vigilance Committee parried the blow aimed at the neck of the fugitive. The country was on our side,— gave us money, help, men when needed. The guardians of Boston could not bear the taunt that she had not sent back a slave. New York had been before her; the "City of Brotherly Love," the home of Penn and Franklin, had assisted in kidnapping; it went on vigorously under the arm of a judge who appropriately bears the name of the great first murderer. No judge could be better entitled; Kane and kidnapping are names conjuring well. Should

Boston delay? What a reproach to the fair fame of her merchants! The history of Boston was against them; America has not yet forgotten the conduct of Boston in the matter of the Stamp Act and Acts of Trade. She was deeply guilty of the revolutionary war; she still kept its cradle of liberty, and the bones of Adams and Hancock,—dangerous relics in any soil; they ought to have been "sent back" at the passage of the Fugitive Slave Bill, and Faneuil Hall demolished. Bunker Hill Monument was within sight. Boston was suspected of not liking to kidnap a man. What a reproach it was to her!—8975 coloured persons in Massachusetts, and not a fugitive returned from Boston. September passed by, October, November, December, January, February, March; not a slave sent back in seven months! What a disgrace to the government of Boston, which longed to steal a man; to the representative of Boston, who had voted for the theft; to the Union meeting, which loved the Slave Act; to Mr Webster, who thought Massachusetts would obey "with alacrity,"—his presidential stock looked down; to his kidnappers, who had not yet fleshed their fangs on a fugitive. What a reproach to the churches of commerce, and their patron, Saint Hunker! One minister would drive a fugitive from his door; another send back his own mother: what was their divinity worth, if, in seven months, they could not convert a single parishoner, and celebrate the sacrament of kidnapping!

Yet, after all, not a slave went back from old Boston, though more than four hundred fled out of the city from the stripes of America, and got safe to the Cross of England; not a slave went back from Boston, spite of her representative, her government, her Union meeting, and her clerical advice. She would comfort herself against this sorrow, but her heart was faint in her. Well might she say, "The harvest is passed, the winter is ended, and we are not saved."

Yet the good men still left in Boston, their heart not wholly corrupt with politics and lust of gain, rejoiced that Boston was innocent of the great transgression of her sister-cities, and thought of the proud days of old. But wily men came here: it was alleged they came from the South. They went round to the shops of jobbers, to the mills of manufactures, and looked at large quantities of goods, pretending a desire to purchase to a great amount; now it was a "large amount of domestics," then "a hundred thousand dollars' worth of locomotives." "But then," said the wily men, "we do not like to purchase here; you are in favour of the dissolution of the Union." "Oh, no," says the Northerner; "not at all." "But you hate the South," rejoins the feigned customer. "By no means," retorts the dealer. "But you have not sent back a slave," concludes the customer, "and I cannot trade with you."

The trick was tried in several places, and succeeded. The story got abroad; it was reported that "large orders intended for Boston had been sent to New York, on account of the acquiescence of the latter city in the Fugitive Slave Bill." Trade is timid; gold is a cowardly metal; how the tinsel trembles when there is thunder in the sky! Employers threatened their workmen: "You must not attend anti-slavery meetings, nor speak against the Fugitive Slave Bill. The Union is in imminent danger."

The country was much more hostile to man-stealing than the city: it mocked at the kidnappers. "Let them try their game in Essex county," said some of the newspapers in that quarter. Thereupon commercial and political journals prepared to "cut off the supplies of the country," and "reduce the farmers and mechanics to submission." It was publicly advised that Boston should not trade with the obnoxious towns; nobody must buy shoes at Lynn. In 1774, the Boston Port Bill shut up our harbour: it was a punishment for making tea against the law. But "penurious old Salem," whose enterprise is equalled by nothing but her "severe economy," opened her safe and commodious harbour to the merchants of Boston, with no cost of wharfage! But the Boston of 1850 was not equal to the "penurious old Salem" of 1774!

It was now indispensable that a slave should be sent back. Trade was clamorous; the administration were urgent; the administration of Mr Fillmore was in peril; Mr Webster's reputation for slave-hunting was at stake; the Union was in danger; even the marshal's commission was on the point of "dissolution," it is said. A descent was planned upon New Bedford, where the followers of Fox and Penn had long hid the outcast. That attempt came to nothing. The Vigilance Committee made a long arm, and "tolled the bell" of Liberty Hall in New Bedford. You remember the ghastly efforts at mirth made by some newspapers on the occasion. "The Vigilance Committee knows everything," said one of the kidnappers.

It now became apparent that Boston must furnish the victim. But some of the magistrates of Boston thought the marshal was too clumsy to succeed, and offered him the aid of the city. So, on the night of the third of April, Thomas Sims was kidnapped by two police-officers of Boston, pretending to the by-standers that he was making a disturbance, and to him that he was arrested for theft. He was had into the "court" of the kidnappers the next morning, charged with being a slave and a fugitive.

You will ask, How did it happen that Sims did not resist the ruffians who seized him? He did resist; but he was a rash, heedless young fellow, and had a most unlucky knife, which knocked at a kidnapper's bosom, but could not open the door. He was very imperfectly armed. He underwent what was called a "trial," a trial without "due form of law;" without a jury, and without a judge; before a Slave Act Commissioner, who was to receive twice as much for sacrificing a victim as for acquitting a man! The Slave Commissioner decided that Mr Sims was a slave. I take it, nobody beforehand doubted that the decision would be against the man. The commissioner was to receive five dollars more for such a decision. The law was framed with exquisite subtlety. Five dollars is a small sum, very small; but things are great or little by comparison.

But, in doing justice to this remarkable provision of the bill, let me do no injustice to the commissioner, who decided that a man was not a man, but a thing. I am told that he would not kidnap a man for five dollars; I am told on good authority, that it would be "no temptation to him." I believe it; for he also is "a man and a brother." I have heard good deeds of his doing, and believe that he did them. Total depravity does not get incarnated in any man. It is said that he refused both of the fees in this case; the one for the "examination," and the other for the actual enslaving of Mr Sims. I believe this also: there is historical precedent on record for casting down a larger fee, not only ten, but thirty pieces of silver, likewise "the price of blood," money too base for a Jew to put in the public chest eighteen hundred years ago!

A noble defence was made for Mr Sims by three eminent lawyers, Messrs Charles G. Loring, Robert Rantoul, Jr., and Samuel E. Sewall, all honourable and able men. Their arguments were productions of no common merit. But of what use to plead law in such a "court" of the Fugitive Slave Bill; to appeal to the Constitution, when the statute is designed to thwart justice, and to destroy "the blessings of liberty?" Of what avail to appeal to the natural principles of right before the tool of an administration which denies that there is any law of God higher than the schemes of a politician? It all came to nothing. A reasonable man would think that the human body and soul were "free papers" from the Almighty, sealed with "the image and likeness of God;" but, of course, in a kidnapper's "court," such a certificate is of no value.

You all know the public account of the kidnapping and "trial" of Mr Sims. What is known to me in private, it is not time to tell: I will tell that to your children; no! perhaps your grandchildren.

You know that the arrest was illegal, the officers of Massachusetts being forbidden by statute to help arrest a fugitive slave. Besides, it appears that they had no legal warrant to make the arrest: they lied, and pretended to arrest him for another alleged offence. He was on "trial" nine days,—arraigned before a Slave Act Commissioner, —and never saw the face of a judge or any judicial officer but once. Before he could be removed to slavery, it was necessary that the spirit of the Constitution should be violated; that its letter should be broken; that the laws of Massachusetts should be cloven down; its officers, its courts, and its people, treated with contempt. The Fugitive Slave Bill could only be enforced by the bayonet.

You remember the aspect of Boston, from the fourth of April till the twelfth. You saw the chains about the Court-house; you saw the police of Boston, bludgeons in their hands, made journeymen kidnappers against their will. Poor fellows! I pitied them. I knew their hearts. Once on a terrible time,—it was just as they were taking Mr Sims from the Court-house, a year ago this day,—somebody reproached them, calling them names fitting their conduct, and I begged him to desist; a poor fellow clutched my arm, and said, "For God's sake don't scold us: we feel worse than you do!" But with the money of Boston against them, the leading clergy defending the crime against human nature, the city government using its brief authority, squandering the treasure of Boston and its intoxicating drink for the same purpose, what could a police officer or a watchman do but obey orders? They did it most unwillingly and against their conscience.

You remember the conduct of the courts of Massachusetts; the Supreme Court seemed to love the chains around the Court-house; for one by one the judges bowed and stooped and bent and cringed and curled and crouched down, and crawled under the chains. Who judges justly must himself be free. What could you expect of a court sitting behind chains; of judges crawling under them to go to their own place?—the same that you found. It was a very appropriate spectacle,—the Southern chain on the neck of the Massachusetts Court. If the Bay State were to send a man into bondage, it was proper that the Court-house should be in chains, and the judges should go under.

You remember the "soldiers" called out, the celebrated "Sims Brigade," liquored at Court Square and lodged at Faneuil Hall. Do you remember when soldiers were quartered in that place before? It was in 1768, when hireling "regulars" came, slaves themselves, and sent by the British Ministry to "make slaves of us all;" to sheathe their swords "in the bowels of their countrymen!" That was a sight for the eyes of John Hancock,—the "Sims Brigade," in Faneuil Hall, called out to aid a Slave Act Commissioner in his attempt to kidnap one of his fellow-citizens! A man by the name of Samuel Adams drilled the police in the street. Samuel Adams of the old time left no children. We have lost the true names of men; only Philadelphia keeps one.

You remember the looks of men in the streets, the crowds that filled up Court Square. Men came in from the country,—came a hundred miles to look on; some of them had fathers who fought at Lexington and Bunker Hill. They remembered the old times, when, the day after the battle of Lexington, a hundred and fifty volunteers, with the firelock at the shoulder, took the road from New Ipswich to Boston.

You have not forgotten the articles in the newspapers, Whig and Democratic both; the conduct of the "leading" churches you will never forget.

What an appropriate time that would have been for the Canadians to visit the "Athens of America," and see the conduct of the "freest and most enlightened people in the world!" If the great Hungarian could have come at that time, he would have understood the nature of "our peculiar institutions;" at least of our political men.

You remember the decision of the circuit judge,—himself soon to be summoned by death before the Judge who is no respecter of persons,—not allowing the destined victim his last hope, "the great writ of right." The decision left him entirely at the mercy of the other kidnappers. The Court-room was crowded with "respectable people," "gentlemen of property and standing;" they received the decision with "applause and the clapping of hands." Seize a lamb out of the flock, a wolf from a pack of wolves, the lambs bleat with sympathy, the wolves howl with fellowship and fear; but when a competitor for the Presidency sends back to eternal bondage a poor, friendless negro, asking only his limbs, wealthy gentlemen of Boston applaud the outrage.

"O judgment! thou art fled to brutish beasts,
And men have lost their reason!"

You remember still the last act in this sad tragedy,—the rendition of the victim. In the darkest hour of the night of the eleventh and twelfth of April, the kidnappers took him from his jail in Court Square, weeping as he left the door. Two kindly men went and procured the poor shivering boy a few warm garments for his voyage: I will not tell their names; perhaps their charity was "treason," and "levying war." Both of the men were ministers, and had not forgotten the great human word: "Inasmuch as ye have done it unto one of the least of these my brethren, ye have done it unto me." The chief kidnappers surrounded Mr Sims with a troop of policemen, armed with naked swords; that troop was attended by a larger crew of some two hundred policemen, armed with clubs. They conducted him, weeping as he went, towards the waterside; they passed under the eaves of the old State-house, which had rocked with the eloquence of James Otis, and shaken beneath the manly tread of both the Adamses, whom the cannon at the door could not terrify, and whose steps awakened the nation. They took him over the spot where, eighty-one years before, the ground had drunk in the African blood of Christopher Attucks, shed by white men on the fifth of March; brother's blood which did not cry in vain. They took him by the spot where the citizens of Massachusetts—some of their descendants were again at the place—scattered the taxed tea of Great Britain to the waters and the winds; they put him on board the "Acorn," owned by a merchant of Boston, who, once before, had kidnapped a man on his own account, and sent him off to the perdition of slavery, without even the help of a commissioner; a merchant to whom it is "immaterial what his children may say of him!"

"And this is Massachusetts liberty!" said the victim of the avarice of Boston. No, Thomas Sims, that was not "Massachusetts liberty;" it was all the liberty which the government of Massachusetts wished you to have; it was the liberty which the city government presented you; it was the liberty which Daniel Webster designed for you. The people of Massachusetts still believe that "all men are born free and equal," and "have natural, essential, and unalienable rights" "of enjoying and defending their lives and liberties," "of seeking and obtaining their safety and happiness." Even the people of Boston believe that; but certain politicians and merchants, to whom it is "immaterial what their children say" of them,—they wished you to be a slave, and it was they who kidnapped you.

Some of you remember the religious meeting held on the spot, as this new "missionary" went abroad to a heathen land; the prayer put up to Him who made of one blood all nations of the earth; the hymns sung. They sung then, who never sung before, their "Missionary Hymn:"

"From many a Southern river
And field of sugar-cane,
They call us to deliver
Their land from slavery's chain."

On the spot where the British soldiers slew Christopher

Attucks in 1770, other men of Boston resolved to hold a religious meeting that night. They were thrust out of the hall they had engaged. The next day was the Christian sabbath; and at night a meeting was held in a "large upper room," a meeting for mutual condolence and prayer. You will not soon forget the hymns, the Scriptures, the speeches, and the prayers of that night. This assembly is one of the results of that little gathering.

Well, all of that you knew before; this you do not know. Thomas Sims, at Savannah, had a fair and handsome woman, by the courtesy of the master called his "wife." Sims loved his wife; and, when he came to Boston, wrote, and told her of his hiding-place, the number in the street, and the name of the landlord. His wife had a paramour; that is a very common thing. The slave is "a chattel personal, to all intents, constructions, and purposes whatsoever." By the law of Georgia, no female slave owns her own virtue; single or married, it is all the same. This African Delilah told her paramour of her husband's hiding-place. Blame her not: perhaps she thought "the Union is in peril this hour," and wished to save it. Yet I doubt that she would send back her own mother; the African woman does not come to that; only a Doctor of Divinity and Chaplain of the Navy. I do not suppose she thought she was doing her husband any harm in telling of his escape; nay, it is likely that her joy was so full, she could not hold it in. The Philistine had ploughed with Sims's heifer, and found out his riddle: the paramour told the master Sims's secret: the master sent the paramour of Mr Sims's wife to Boston to bring back the husband! He was very welcome in this city, and got "the best of legal advice" at a celebrated office in Court-street.| Boston said, "God speed the paramour!" the government of Massachusetts, "God speed the crime!" Money came to the pockets of the kidnappers; the paramour went home, his object accomplished, and the master was doubtless grateful to the city of Boston, which honoured thus the piety of its founders!

He was taken back to Georgia in the "Acorn;" some of the better sort of kidnappers went with him to Savannah; there Sims was put in jail, and they received a public dinner. You know the reputation of the men: the workmen were worthy of their meat. In jail, Mr Sims was treated with great severity ; not allowed to see his relatives, not even his mother. It is said that he was tortured every day with a certain number of stripes on his naked back ; that his master once offered to remit part of the cruelty, if he would ask pardon for running away. The man refused, and took the added blows. One day, the jail-doctor told the master that Sims was too ill to bear more stripes. The master said, "Damn him! give him the lashes, if he dies;"—and the lashes fell. Be not troubled at that ; a slave is only a "chattel personal." Those blows were laid on by the speakers of the Union meeting; it was only "to save the Union." I have seen a clerical certificate, setting forth that the "owner" of Mr Sims was an "excellent Christian," and "uncommonly pious." When a clergyman would send back his own mother, such conduct is sacramental in a layman.

When Thomas Sims was unlawfully seized, and detained in custody against the law, the governor of Massachusetts was in Boston; the legislature was in session. It seems to me it was their duty to protect the man, and enforce the laws of the State; but they did no such thing.

As that failed, it seems to me that the next thing was for the public to come together in a vast multitude, and take their brother out of the hands of his kidnappers, and set him at liberty. On the morning of the sixth of March, 1770, the day after the Boston Massacre, Faneuil Hall could not hold the town-meeting. They adjourned to the Old South, and demanded "the immediate removal of the troops;" at sundown there was "not a red-coat in Boston." But the people in this case did no such thing.

The next thing was for the Vigilance Committee to deliver the man: the country has never forgiven the committee for not doing it. I am chairman of the executive committee of the Vigilance Committee; I cannot now relate all that was done, all that was attempted. I will tell that when the time comes. Yet I think you will believe me when I say the Vigilance Committee did all they could. But see some of the difficulties in their way.

There was in Boston a large number of crafty, rich, designing, and "respectable" men, who wanted a man kidnapped in Boston, and sent into slavery; they wanted that for the basest of purposes,—for the sake of money; they wanted the name of it, the reputation of kidnapping a man. They protected the kidnappers,—foreign and domestic; egged them on, feasted them. It has been said that fifteen hundred men volunteered to escort their victim out of the State; that some of them are rich men. I think the majority of the middle class of men were in favour of freedom; but, in Boston, what is a man without money? and, if he has money, who cares how base his character may be? You demand moral character only of a clergyman. Some of the richest men were strongly in favour of freedom; but, alas! not many, and for the most part they were silent.

The city government of that period I do not like to speak of. It offers to a man, as cool as I am, a temptation to use language which a gentleman does not wish to apply to any descendant of the human race. But that government, encouraging its thousand and five hundred illegal groggeries, and pretending a zeal for law, was for kidnapping a man; so the police-force of the city was unlawfully put to that work; soldiers were called out; the money of the city flowed freely, and its rum. I do not suppose that the kidnapping was at all disagreeable to the "conscience" of the city government; they seemed to like it, and the consequences thereof.

The prominent clergy of Boston were on the same side. The dollar demanded that; and whither it went, thither went they. "Like people, like priest," was a proverb two thousand five hundred years ago, and is likely to hold its edge for a long time to come. Still there were some very noble men among the ministers of Boston: we found them in all denominations.

Then the courts of Massachusetts refused to issue the writ of *Habeas Corpus*. They did not afford the smallest protection to the poor victim of Southern tyranny.

Not a sheriff could be got to serve a writ; the high sheriff refused, all his deputies held back. Who could expect them to do their duty when all else failed?

The Legislature was then in session. They sat from January till May. They knew that eight thousand nine hundred and seventy-five citizens of Massachusetts had no protection but public opinion, and in Boston that opinion was against them. They saw four hundred citizens of Boston flee off for safety; they saw Shadrach captured in Boston; they saw him kidnapped, and put in jail against their own law; they saw the streets filled with soldiers to break the laws of Massachusetts, the police of Boston employed in the same cause; they saw the sheriffs refuse to serve a writ; they saw Thomas Sims kidnapped and carried from Boston; and, in all the five months of the session, they did not pass a law to protect their fellow-citizens; they did not even pass a "resolution" against the extension of slavery! The Senate had a committee to investigate the affair in Boston. They sat in the Senate-hall, and were continually insulted by the vulgarest of men; insulted not only with impudence, but impunity, by men who confessed that they were violating the laws of Massachusetts.

Massachusetts had then a governor who said he "would not harbour a fugitive slave." What did he do? He sat as idle as a feather in the chair of state; he left the sheriffs as idle as he. While the laws of Massachusetts were broken nine days running, the successor of John Hancock sat as idle as a feather in the chair of state, and let kidnapping go on! I hate to say these things. The governor is a young man, not without virtues; but think of such things in Massachusetts!

This is my public defence of the Vigilance Committee. The private defence shall come, if I live long enough.

It was on the nineteenth day of April that Thomas Sims was landed at Savannah, and put in the public jail of the city. Do you know what that day stands for in your calendar? Some of your fathers knew very well. Ten miles from here is a little monument at Lexington, "sacred to liberty and the rights of mankind," telling that on the 19th of April, 1775, some noble men stood up against the army of England, "fired the shot heard round the world," and laid down their lives " in the sacred cause of God and their country." Six miles further off is another little monument at Concord; two miles further back, a third, all dating from the same day. The war of revolution began at Lexington, to end at Yorktown. Its first battle was on the nineteenth of April. Hancock and Adams lodged at Lexington with the minister. One raw morning, a little after daybreak, a tall man, with a large forehead under a three-cornered hat, drew up his company of seventy men on the green, farmers and mechanics like himself; only one is left now, the boy who "played" the men to the spot. They wheeled into line to wait for the regulars. The captain ordered every man to load "his piece with powder and ball." "Don't fire," were his words, "unless fired upon; but, if they want a war, let it begin here."

The regulars came on. Some Americans offered to run away from their post. The captain said, "I will order the first man shot dead that leaves his place." The English commander cried out, "Disperse, you rebels; lay down your arms and disperse." Not a man stirred. "Disperse, you damned rebels!" shouted he again. Not a man stirred. He ordered the vanguard to fire; they did so, but over the heads of our fathers. Then the whole main body levelled their pieces, and there was need of ten new graves in Lexington. A few Americans returned the shot. British blood stained the earl grass, which "waved with the wind." "Disperse and take care of yourselves," was the captain's last command! And, after the British fired their third round, there lay the dead, and there stood the soldiers; there was a battle-field between England and America, never to be forgot, never to be covered over. The "mother-country" of the morning was the "enemy" at sunrise. "Oh, what a glorious morning is this!" said Samuel Adams.

The nineteenth of April was a good day for Boston* to land a fugitive slave at Savannah, and put him in jail, because he claimed his liberty. Some of you had fathers in the battle of Lexington, many of you relations; some of you, I think, keep trophies from that day, won at Concord or at Lexington. I have seen such things,—powder-horns, shoe-buckles, a firelock, and other things, from the nineteenth of April, 1775. Here is a Boston trophy from April nineteenth, 1851. This is the coat of Thomas Sims.* He wore it on the third of April last. Look at it. You see he did not give up with alacrity, nor easily " conquer" his "prejudices" for liberty. See how they rent the sleeve away! His coat was torn to tatters. "And this is Massachusetts liberty!"

* Here the coat was exhibited.

Let the kidnappers come up and say, "Massachusetts! knowest thou whether this be thy son's coat or not?"

Let Massachusetts answer: "It is my son's coat! An evil beast hath devoured him. Thomas is without doubt rent in pieces!"

Yes, Massachusetts! that is right. It was an evil beast that devoured him, worse than the lion which comes up from the swelling of Jordan: it was a kidnapper. Thomas was rent with whips! Go, Massachusetts! keep thy trophies from Lexington. I will keep this to remind me of Boston, and her dark places, which are full of cruelty.

After the formation of the Union, a monument was erected at Beacon Hill, to commemorate the chief events which led to the American Revolution, and helped secure liberty and independence. Some of you remember the inscriptions thereon. If a monument were built to commemorate the events which are connected with the recent "Salvation of the Union," the inscriptions might be:—

Union saved by Daniel Webster's Speech at Washington, March 7, 1850.
Union saved by Daniel Webster's Speech at Boston, April 30, 1850.
Union saved by the Passage of the Fugitive Slave Bill, Sept. 18, 1850.
Union saved by the arrival of Kidnapper Hughes at Boston, Oct. 19, 1850.
Union saved by the "Union Meeting" at Faneuil Hall, Nov. 26, 1850.
Union saved by kidnapping Thomas Sims at Boston, April 3, 1851.
Union saved by the Rendition of Thomas Sims at Savannah, April 19, 1851.—
"*Oh, what a glorious morning is this!*"

SICUT PATRIBUS SIT DEUS NOBIS.*

The great deeds of the American Revolution were also commemorated by medals. The Boston kidnapping is worthy of such commemoration, and would be an appropriate subject for a medal, which might bear on one side a bas-relief of the last scene of that act: the Court-house in chains; the victim in the hollow square of Boston police, their swords and bludgeons in their hands. The motto might be—THE GREAT OBJECT OF GOVERNMENT IS THE PROTECTION OF PROPERTY AT HOME.† The other side might bear a Boston church, surrounded by shops and taverns taller than itself, with the twofold inscription: NO HIGHER LAW; and, I WOULD SEND BACK MY OWN MOTHER.

What a change from the Boston of John Hancock to the

* The Latin words are the motto on the Seal of Boston.
† Remark of Mr Webster.

Boston of the Fugitive Slave Bill; from the town which hung Grenville and Huske in effigy, to the city which approved Mr Webster's speech in defence of slave-catching! Boston tolled her bells for the Stamp Act, and fired a hundred holiday cannons for the Slave Act! Massachusetts, all New England, has been deeply guilty of slavery and the slave-trade. An exile from Germany finds the chief street of Newport paved by a tax of ten dollars a head on all the slaves landed there; the little town sent out Christian New England rum, and brought home heathen men—for sale. Slavery came to Boston with the first settlers. In 1639, Josselyn found here a negro woman in bondage refusing to become the mother of slaves. There was much to palliate the offence: all northern Europe was stained with the crime. It did not end in Westphalia till 1739. But the consciences of New England never slept easy under that sin. Before 1641, Massachusetts ordered that a slave should be set free after seven years' service, reviving a merciful ordinance of the half-barbarous Hebrews a thousand years before Christ. In 1645, the General Court of Massachusetts sent back to Guinea two black men illegally enslaved, and made a law forbidding the sale of slaves, except captives in war, or men sentenced to sale for crime. Even they were set free after seven years' service. Still slavery always existed here, spite of the law; the newspapers once contained advertisements of "negro-babies to be given away" in Boston! Yet New England never loved slavery: hard and cruel as the Puritans were, they had some respect for the letter of the New Testament. In 1700, Samuel Sewall protested against "the selling of Joseph;" as another Sewall, in 1851, protested against the selling of Thomas. There was a great controversy about slavery in Massachusetts in 1766; even Harvard College took an interest in freedom, setting its young men to look at the rights of man! In 1767, a bill was introduced to the General Assembly to prevent "t' ᚋ unnatural and unwarrantable custom of enslaving mankind." It was killed by the Hunkers of that time. In 1774, a bill of a similar character passed the Assembly, but was crushed by the veto of Governor Hutchinson.

In 1788, three men were illegally kidnapped at Boston by "one Avery, a native of Connecticut," and carried off to Martinico. Then we had John Hancock for governor, and he wrote to all the governors of the West India Islands in favour of the poor creatures. The Boston Association of Congregational Ministers petitioned the Legislature to prohibit Massachusetts ships from engaging in the foreign or domestic slave-trade. Dr Belknap was a member of the Association,—a man worthy to have Channing for a successor to his humanity. The legislature passed a bill for the purpose. In July the three men were brought back from the West Indies: Dr Belknap says, "It was a day of jubilee for all the friends of justice and humanity."

What a change from the legislature, clergy, and gover or of 1788 to that of 1851! Alas! men do not gather figs of thistles. The imitators of this Avery save the Union now: he saved it before it was formed. How is the faithful city become a harlot! It was full of judgment: righteousness lodged in it, but now murderers.

What is the cause of this disastrous change! It is the excessive love of money which has taken possession of the leading men. In 1776, General Washington said of Massachusetts: "Notwithstanding all the public spirit that is ascribed to this people, there is no nation under the sun that I ever came across, which pays greater adoration to money than they do." What would he say now? Selfishness and covetousness have flowed into the commercial capital of New England, seeking their fortune. Boston is now a shop, with the aim of a shop, and the morals of a shop, and the politics of a shop.

Thomas Jefferson said: Governments are instituted amongst men to secure the natural and unalienable right to life, liberty, and the pursuit of happiness. All America said so on the fourth of July, 1776. But we have changed all that. Daniel Webster said, at New York, 1850: "The great object of government is the protection of property at home, and respect and renown abroad." John Hancock had some property to protect; but he said the design of government is "security to the persons and the properties of the governed." He put the persons first, and the property afterwards; the substance of man before his accidents. Hancock said again: "It is the indispensable duty of every member of society to promote, as far as in him lies, the prosperity of every individual." The governor of

Massachusetts says, "I would not harbour a fugitive." A clergyman says, I would send back my own mother! If the great object of government is the protection of property, why should a governor personally harbour a fugitive, or officially protect nine thousand coloured men? Why should not a clergyman send to slavery his mother, to save the Union, or to save a bank, or to gain a chaplaincy in the navy? But, if this be so, then what a mistake it was in Jesus of Nazareth to say, "A man's life consisteth not in the abundance of things that he possesseth!" Verily the meat is more than the life; the body less than raiment! Christ was mistaken in his "beware of covetousness:" he should have said, "Beware of philanthropy; drive off a fugitive; send back your mother to bondage. Blessed are the kidnappers, for they shall be called the children of God."

Even Thomas Paine had a Christianity which would choke at the infidelity and practical atheism taught in the blessed name of Jesus in the Boston churches of commerce to-day. The gospel relates that Jesus laid his hands on men to bless them—on the deaf, and they heard; on the dumb, and they spoke; on the blind, and they saw; on the lame, and they walked; on the maimed and the sick, and they were whole. But Christian Boston lays its hand on a whole and free man, and straightway he owns no eyes, no ears, no tongue, no hands, no foot: he is a slave!

In 1761, the Massachusetts of John Hancock would not pay three pence duty on a pound of tea, to have all the protection of the British Crown: ninety years later, the Boston of Daniel Webster, to secure the trade of the South, and a dim, delusive hope of a protective tariff, will pay any tax in men. It is no new thing for her citizens to be imprisoned at Charleston and New Orleans, because they are black. What merchant cares? It does not interrupt trade. Five citizens of Massachusetts have just been sent into bondage by a Southern State. Of what consequence is that to the politicians of the commonwealth? Our property is worth six hundred million dollars. But how much is a man worth less than a dollar! The penny wisdom of "Poor Richard" is the great gospel to the city which cradled the benevolence of Franklin.

Boston capitalists do not hesitate to own Southern plantations, and buy and sell men; Boston merchants do not scruple to let their ships for the domestic slave-trade, and carry the child from his mother in Baltimore, to sell him to a planter in Louisiana or Alabama; some of them glory in kidnapping their fellow-citizens in Boston. Most of the slave-ships in the Atlantic are commanded by New England men. A few years ago, one was seized by the British government at Africa, "full of slaves;" it was owned in Boston, had a "clearance" from our harbour, and left its name on the books of the insurance offices here. The controlling men of Boston have done much to promote, to extend, and to perpetuate slavery. Why not, if the protection of property be the great object of government? why not, if interest is before justice? why not, if the higher law of God is to be sneered at in state and church?

When the Fugitive Slave Bill passed, the six New England States lay fast asleep: Massachusetts slept soundly, her head pillowed on her unsold bales of cotton and of woollen goods, dreaming of "orders from the South." Justice came to waken her, and whisper of the peril of nine thousand citizens; and she started in her sleep, and, being frighted, swore a prayer or two, then slept again. But Boston woke,—sleeping, in her shop, with ears open, and her eye on the market, her hand on her purse, dreaming of goods for sale,—Boston woke broadly up, and fired a hundred guns for joy. O Boston, Boston! if thou couldst have known, in that thine hour, the things which belong unto thy peace! But no: they were hidden from her eyes. She had prayed to her god, to money; he granted her the request, but sent leanness into her soul.

Yet at first I did not believe that the Fugitive Slave Bill could be executed in Boston; even the firing of the cannons did not convince me; I did not think men bad enough for that. I knew something of wickedness; I knew what love of money could do; I had seen it blind most venerable eyes. I knew Boston was a Tory town; the character of upstart Tories—I thought I knew that: the man just risen from the gutter knocks down him that is rising. But I knew also the ancient history of Boston. I remembered the first commissioner we ever had in New England,—Sir Edmund Andros, sent here by the worst of the Stuarts "to rob us of our charters in North America."

He was a terrible tyrant. The liberty of Connecticut fled into the "Great oak at Hartford:"—

"The Charter Oak it was the tree
That saved our blessèd liberty."

"All Connecticut was in the oak." But Massachusetts laid her hands on the commissioner,—he was her governor also,—put him in jail, and sent him home for trial in 1689. William of Orange thought we "served him right." The name of "commissioner" has always had an odious meaning to my mind. I did not think a commissioner at kidnapping men would fare better than Sir Edmund kidnapping charters. I remembered the Writs of Assistance, and thought of James Otis; the Stamp Act, "Adams and Liberty" came to my mind. I did not forget the way our fathers made tea with salt water. I looked up at that tall obelisk; I took courage, and have since reverenced that "monument of piled stones." I could not think Mr Webster wanted the law enforced, spite of his speeches and letters. It was too bad to be true of him. I knew he was a bankrupt politician, in desperate political circumstances, gaming for the Presidency, with the probability of getting the vote of the county of Suffolk, and no more. I knew he was not rich: his past history showed that he would do almost anything for money, which he seems as covetous to get as prodigal to spend. I knew that "a man in falling will catch at a red-hot iron hook." I saw why Mr Webster caught at the Fugitive Slave Bill: it was a great fall from the coveted and imaginary Presidency down to actual private life at Marshfield. It was a great fall. The Slave Act was the red-hot iron hook to a man "falling like Lucifer, never to hope again." The temptation was immense. I could not think he meant to hold on there; he did often relax his grasp, yet only to clutch it the tighter. I did not like to think he had a bad heart. I hoped he would shrink from blasting the head of a single fugitive from that dreadful "thunder" of his speech; that he would not like to execute his own law. Men in Boston said it could not be executed. Even cruel men that I knew shuddered at the thought of kidnapping a man who fills their glasses with wine. The law was not fit to be executed: that was the general opinion in Boston at first. So, when kidnapper Hughes came here for William Craft, even the commissioner applied to was a little shy of the business. Yet that commissioner is not a very scrupulous man. I mean in the various parties he has wriggled through, he has not left the reputation of any excessive and maidenly coyness in moral matters, and a genius for excessive scrupulousness as to means or ends. Even a hunker minister informed me that he "would certainly aid a fugitive." But, after the Union Meeting, the clouds of darkness gathered together, and it set in for a storm; the kidnappers went and rough-ground their sword on the grindstone of the church, a navy chaplain turning the crank; and all our hopes fell to the ground.

> "Vice is a monster of such frightful mien,
> As, to be hated, needs but to be seen;
> But seen too oft, familiar with her face,
> We first endure, then pity, then embrace.".

The relentless administration of Mr Fillmore has been as cruel as the law they framed. Mr Webster has thrust the red-hot iron hook into the flesh of thousands of his fellow-citizens. He and his kidnappers came to a nation scattered and peeled, meted out and trodden down; they have ground the poor creatures to powder under their hoof. I wish I could find an honourable motive for such deeds, but hitherto no analysis can detect it, no solar microscope of charity can bring such a motive to light. The end is base, the means base, the motive base.

Yet one charge has been made against the Government, which seems to me a little harsh and unjust. It has been said the administration preferred low and contemptible men as their tools; judges who blink at law, advocates of infamy, and men cast off from society for perjury, for nameless crimes, and sins not mentionable in English speech; creatures "not so good as the dogs that licked Lazarus's sores; but, like flies, still buzzing upon anything that is raw." There is a semblance of justice in the charge: witness Philadelphia, Buffalo, Boston; witness New York. It is true for kidnappers the Government did take men that looked "like a bull-dog just come to man's estate;" men whose face declared them, "if not the devil, at least his twin-brother." There are kennels of the courts wherein there settles down all that the law breeds most foul, loathsome, and hideous and abhorrent to the eye of day; there this contaminating puddle gathers its noisome ooze, slowly, stealthily, continually, agglomerating its fetid mass by spontaneous cohesion, and sinking by the irresistible gravity of rottenness into that abhorred deep, the lowest, ghastliest pit in all the subterranean vaults of human sin. It is true the Government has skimmed the top and dredged the bottom of these kennels of the courts, taking for its purpose the scum and sediment thereof, the Squeers, the Fagins, and the Quilps of the law, the monsters of the court. Blame not the Government; it took the best it could get. It was necessity, not will, which made the selection. Such is the stuff that kidnappers must be made of. If you wish to kill a man, it is not bread you buy: it is poison. Some of the instruments of Government were such as one does not often look upon. But, of old time, an inquisitor was always "a horrid-looking fellow, as beseemed his trade." It is only justice that a kidnapper should bear "his great commission in his look."

In a town full of British soldiers in 1774, on the anniversary of the Boston Massacre, John Hancock said:—

"Surely you never will tamely suffer this country to be a den of thieves. Remember, my friends, from whom you sprang. Let not a meanness of spirit, unknown to those whom you boast of as your fathers, excite a thought to the dishonour of your mothers. I conjure you by all that is dear, by all that is honourable, by all that is sacred, not only that ye pray, but that you act; that, if necessary, ye fight, and even die, for the prosperity of our Jerusalem. Break in sunder, with noble disdain, the bonds with which the Philistines have bound you. Suffer not yourselves to be betrayed by the soft arts of luxury and effeminacy into the pit digged for your destruction. Despise the glare of wealth. That people who pay greater respect to a wealthy villain than to an honest, upright man in poverty, almost deserve to be enslaved: they plainly show that wealth, however it may be acquired, is, in their esteem, to be preferred to virtue.

"But I thank God that America abounds in men who are superior to all temptation, whom nothing can divert from a steady pursuit of the interest of their country, who are at once its ornament and safeguard. And sure I am I should not incur your displeasure, if I paid a respect so justly due to their much-honoured characters, in this place; but, when I name an Adams, such a numerous host of fellow-patriots rush upon my mind, that I fear it would take up too much of your time, should I attempt to call over the illustrious roll: but your grateful hearts will point you to the men; and their revered names, in all succeeding times, shall grace the annals of America. From them let us, my friends, take example; from them let us catch the divine enthusiasm; and feel, each for himself, the godlike pleasure of diffusing happiness on all around us; of delivering the oppressed from the iron grasp of tyranny; of changing the hoarse complaint and bitter moans of wretched slaves into those cheerful songs which freedom and contentment must inspire. There is a heartfelt satisfaction in reflecting on our exertions for the public weal, which all the sufferings an enraged tyrant can inflict will never take away, which the ingratitude and reproaches of those whom we have saved from ruin cannot rob us of. The virtuous assertor of the rights of mankind merits a reward, which even a want of success in his endeavours to save his country, the heaviest misfortune which can befall a genuine patriot, cannot entirely prevent him from receiving."

But, in 1850, Mr. Webster bade Massachusetts "conquer her prejudices." He meant the "prejudices" in favour of justice, in favour of the unalienable rights of man, in favour of Christianity. Did Massachusetts obey? The answer was given a year ago. "Despise the glare of wealth," said the richest man in New England in 1774: the "great object of government is the protection of property," said "the great intellect" of America in 1850! John Hancock, seventy-eight years ago, said, "We dread nothing but slavery:" Daniel Webster, two years ago, said Massachusetts will obey the Fugitive Slave Bill "with alacrity." Boston has forgotten John Hancock.

In 1775, Joseph Warren said, "Scourges and death with tortures are far less terrible than slavery." Now it is "a great blessing to the African." Said the same Warren, "The man who meanly submits to wear a shackle contemns the noblest gift of Heaven, and impiously affronts the God that made him free." Now clergymen tell us that kidnappers are ordained of God, and passive obedience is every man's duty! The town of Boston in 1770 declared,

"Mankind will not be reasoned out of the feelings of humanity." In 1850 the pulpit of Boston says, Send back your brother.

The talk of dissolution is no new trick. Hear General Warren, in the spirit of 1775: "Even anarchy itself, that bugbear held up by the tools of power, is infinitely less dangerous to mankind than arbitrary government. Anarchy can be but of short duration; for, when men are at liberty to pursue that course which is most conducive to their own happiness, they will soon come into it, and from the rudest state of nature order and good government must soon arise. But tyranny, when once established, entails its curses on a nation to the latest period of time, unless some daring genius, inspired by Heaven, shall, unappalled by danger, bravely form and execute the design of restoring liberty and life to his enslaved and murdered country." Now a man would send his mother into slavery to save the Union!

Will Boston be called on again to return a fugitive? Not long since, some noble ladies in a neighbouring town, whose religious hand often reaches through the darkness to save men ready to perish, related to me a fresh tale of woe. Here is their letter of the first of March:—

"Only ten days ago, we assisted a poor, deluded sufferer in effecting his escape to Canada, after having been cheated into the belief by the profligate captain who brought him from the South, that he would be in safety as soon as he reached Boston. . . . He had accumulated two hundred dollars, which he put into the captain's hands, upon his agreeing to secrete him, and bring him to Boston. The moment the vessel touched the wharf, the scoundrel bade the poor fellow be off in a moment; and he then discovered his liability to be pursued and taken. It was then midnight and the cold was intense. He wandered about the streets, and in the morning strolled into the ———— Depot, and came out to ———— in the earliest cars. On reaching this town, he had the sense to find out the only man of colour who lives here, ————, a very respectable barber. Mr ———— sheltered him that day and the following night; and early the next morning a sufficient sum had been collected for him to pay his passage to Canada, and supply his first wants after arriving there; but, in the mean while, the villainous captain bears off his hard earnings in triumph."

I must not give the names of the ladies: they are liable to a fine of a thousand dollars each, and imprisonment for six months.* It was atrocious in the captain to steal the two hundred dollars from the poor captive; but the Government of the United States would gladly steal his body, his limbs, his life, his children, to the end of time. The captain was honourable in comparison with the kidnappers. Perhaps he also wished to "Save the Union."—Sicut Patribus sit Deus Nobis!

What a change from the Boston of our fathers! Where are the children of the patriots of old? Tories spawned their brood in the streets: Adams and Hancock died without a child. Has nature grown sterile of men? is there no male and manly virtue left? are we content to be kidnappers of men? No. Here still are noble men, men of the good old stock; men of the same brave, holy soul. No time of trial ever brought out nobler heroism than last year. Did we want money, little Methodist churches in the country, the humanest churches in New England, dropped their widow's mite into the chest. From ministers of all modes of faith but the popular one in money, from all churches but that of commerce, there came gifts, offers of welcome, and words of lofty cheer. Here in Boston, there were men thoroughly devoted to the defence of their poor, afflicted brethren; even some clergymen faithful among the faithless. But they were few. It was only a handful who ventured to be faithful to the true and right. The great tide of humanity, which once filled up this place, had ebbed off: only a few perennial springs poured out their sweet and unfailing wealth to these weary wanderers.

Yet Boston is rich in generous men, in deeds of charity, in far-famed institutions for the good of man. In this she is still the noblest of the great cities of the land. I honour the self-sacrificing, noble men; the women whose loving-kindness never failed before. Why did it fail at this time? Men fancied that their trade was in peril. It was an idle fear; even the dollar obeys the "Higher Law," which its worshippers deny. Had it been true, Boston had better lose every farthing of her gold, and start anew with nothing but the

* It is still unsafe to mention their names! January, 1855.

wilderness, than let her riches stand between us and our
fellow-man. Thy money perish, if it brutalize thy heart!
I wish I could believe the motives of men were good
in this; that they really thought the nation was in peril.
But no; it cannot be. It was not the love of country
which kept the "compromises of the Constitution" and
made the Fugitive Slave Bill. I pity the politicians who
made this wicked law, made it in the madness of their
pride. I pity that son of New England, who, against his
nature, against his early history, drew his sword to sheathe
it in the bowels of his brother-man.* The melancholiest
spectacle in all this land, self-despoiled of the lustre which
would have cast a glory on his tomb, and sent his name a
watchword to many an age,—now he is the companion of
kidnappers, and a proverb amongst honourable men, with a
certainty of leaving a name to be hissed at by mankind.
 I pity the kidnappers, the poor tools of men almost as
base. I would not hurt a hair of their heads; but I would
take the thunder of the moral world, and dash its bolted
lighting on this crime of stealing men, till the name of kidnapping should be like Sodom and Gomorrah. It is piracy
to steal a man in Guinea; what is it to do this in Boston?
 I pity the merchants who, for their trade, were glad to
steal their countrymen; I wish them only good. Debate
in yonder hall has shown how little of humanity there is in
the trade of Boston. She looks on all the horrors which
intemperance has wrought, and daily deals in every street;
she scrutinizes the jails,—they are filled by rum; she looks
into the alms-houses, crowded full by rum; she walks her
streets, and sees the perishing classes fall, mowed down by
rum; she enters the parlours of wealthy men, looks into the
bridal chamber, and meets death: the ghosts of the slain
are there,—men slain by rum. She knows it all, yet says,
"There is an interest at stake!"—the interest of rum;
let man give way! Boston does this to-day. Last year
she stole a man; her merchants stole a man! The sacrifice of man to money, when shall it have an end? I pity
those merchants who honour money more than man. Their
gold is cankered, and their soul is brass,—is rusted brass.
They must come up before the posterity which they affect
to scorn. What voice can plead for them before their own

* Mr Webster.

children? The eye that mocketh at the justice of its son, and scorneth to obey the mercy of its daughter, the ravens of posterity shall pick it out, and the young eagles eat it up!

But there is yet another tribunal: "After the death the judgment!" When he maketh inquisition for the blood of the innocent, what shall the stealers of men reply? Boston merchants, where is your brother, Thomas Sims? Let Cain reply to Christ.

Come. Massachusetts! take thy historic mantle, wrought all over with storied memories of two hundred years, adorned with deeds in liberty's defence, and rough with broidered radiance from the hands of sainted men; walk backwards, and cover up and hide the naked public shame of Boston, drunk with gain, and lewdly lying in the street. It will not hide the shame. Who can annul a fact? Boston has chronicled her infamy, and on the iron leaf of time, —ages shall read it there!

Then let us swear by the glory of our fathers and the infamy of this deed, that we will hate slavery, hate its cause, hate its continuance, and will exterminate it from the land; come up hither as the years go by, and here renew the annual oath, till not a kidnapper is left lurking in the land; yes, till from the Joseph that is sold into Egypt, there comes forth a man to guide his people to the promised land. Out of this "Acorn" a tall oak may grow.

Old mythologies relate, that, when a deed of sin is done, the souls of men who bore a kindred to the deed come forth and aid the work. What a company must have assisted at this sacrament a year ago! What a crowd of ruffians, from the first New England commissioner to the latest dead of Boston murders! Robert Kidd might have come back from his felon-grave at "Execution Dock," to resume his appropriate place, and take command of the "Acorn," and guide her on her pirate-course. Arnold might sing again his glad Te Deum, as on that fatal day in March. What an assembly there would be,—"shapes hot from Tartarus."

But the same mythologies go fabling on, and say that at such a time, the blameless, holy souls who made the virtues blossom while they lived, and are themselves the starriest flowers of heaven now, that they return to bless the old familiar spot, and witness every modern deed; and, most of all, that godly ministers, who lived and laboured for their flocks, return to see the deed they cannot help, and aid the good they bless. What a gathering might there have been of the just men made perfect! The patriots who loved this land, mothers whose holy hearts had blessed the babes they bore; pure men of lofty soul who laboured for mankind,—what a fair company this State could gather of the immortal dead! Of those great ministers of every faith, who dearly loved the Lord, what venerable heads I see: John Cotton and the other "famous Johns;" Eliot, bearing his Indian Bible, which there is not an Indian left to read; Edwards, a mighty name in East and West, even yet more marvellous for piety than depth of thought; the Mathers, venerable men; Chauncy and Mayhew, both noble men of wealthy soul; Belknap, who saw a brother in an African; Buckminster, the fairest, sweetest bud brought from another field, too early nipped in this; Channing and Ware, both ministers of Christ, who, loving God, loved too their fellow-men! How must those souls look down upon the scene! Boston delivering up—for lust of gold delivering up—a poor, forsaken boy to slavery; Belknap and Channing mourning for the church!

I turn me off from the living men, the living courts, the living churches,—no, the churches dead; from the swarm of men all bustling in the streets; turn to the sainted dead. Dear fathers of the State; ye blessed mothers of New England's sons;—O holy saints who laid with prayer the deep foundations of New England's church, is then the seed of heroes gone? New England's bosom, is it sterile, cold, and dead? "No!" say the fathers, mothers, all,— "New England only sleeps; even Boston is not dead! Appeal from Boston drunk with gold, and briefly mad with hate, to sober Boston in her hour to come. Wait but a little time; have patience with her waywardness; she yet shall weep with penitence that bitter day, and rise with ancient energy to do just deeds of lasting fame. Even yet there's justice in her heart, and Boston mothers shall give birth to men!"

Tell me, ye blessed, holy souls, angels of New England's church! shall man succeed, and gain his freedom at the last? Answer, ye holy men; speak by the last great angel of the church who went to heaven. Repeat some noble word you spoke on earth!

Hear their reply:—

> "Oppression shall not always reign:
>   There comes a brighter day,
> When Freedom, burst from every chain,
>   Shall have triumphant way.
> Then Right shall over Might prevail,
>   And Truth, like hero armed in mail,
> The hosts of tyrant Wrong assail,
>   And hold eternal sway.
>
> What voice shall bid the progress stay
>   Of Truth's victorious car?—
> What arm arrest the growing day,
>   Or quench the solar star?
> What reckless soul, though stout and strong,
> Shall dare bring back the ancient wrong,—
> Oppression's guilty night prolong,
>   And Freedom's morning bar?
>
> The hour of triumph comes apace,—
>   The fated, promised hour,
> When earth upon a ransomed race
>   Her bounteous gifts shall shower.
> Ring, Liberty, thy glorious bell!
> Bid high thy sacred banners swell!
> Let trump on trump the triumph tell
>   Of Heaven's redeeming power!" *

---

* These are the words of Henry Ware, jun., the last minister, eminent for religion, who had died in Boston.

THE LAW OF GOD AND THE STATUTES OF MEN.

A SERMON

PREACHED AT

THE MUSIC HALL, IN BOSTON,

ON SUNDAY, JUNE 18, 1854.

Thou shalt worship the Lord thy God, and him only shalt thou serve.
MATT. iv. 10.

LAST Sunday I spoke of trust in God, endeavouring to show that it involved an absolute confidence in the purposes of God, and an absolute confidence in the means thereunto, and consequently the practical use thereof.

There is a matter of very great consequence connected herewith, namely, this—the relation between a man's religion and his allegiance to the Church and the State. So this morning I ask your attention to a sermon of our Duty to the Laws of God, and our Obligation to the Statutes of Men. It is a theme I have often spoken of; and what I shall say this morning may be regarded as occasional, and supplementary to the much I have said, and printed, likewise, before.

In its primitive form, religion is a mere emotion; it is nothing but a sentiment, an instinctive feeling; at first vague, shadowy, dim. In its secondary stage it is also a thought; the emotion has travelled from the heart upwards to the head: it is an idea, an abstract idea, the object whereof transcends both time and space, and is not cognizable by any sense. But finally, in its ultimate form, it becomes likewise an act. Thus it spreads over all a man's life, inward and outward too; it goes up to the tallest heights of the philosopher's speculation, down to the lowest deeps of human consciousness; it reaches to the minute details of our daily practice. Religion wraps all our life in its own wide mantle; takes note of the private conduct of the individual man, and the vast public concerns of the greatest nation and the whole race of mankind. So the sun, ninety-six million miles away, comes every morning and folds in its warm embrace each great and every little thing on the round world.

Religion is eminently connected with the creeds and the statutes of the people, wherein the nation comes to the consciousness of itself and of its duty. To comprehend the relation which it bears to these creeds and statutes, let us look at the matter a little more narrowly, going somewhat into detail; and to understand it the more completely, let us go back to the first principles of things.

There is a God of infinite perfection, who acts as perfect cause and perfect providence of all things,—making the universe from a perfect motive, of perfect material, for a perfect purpose, and as a perfect means thereunto. Of course, if the universe be thus made, there must be power and force enough of the right kind in it to accomplish the purposes of God; and this must be true of both parts of the universe,—the world of matter, and the world of man. Else, God is not a perfect cause and providence, and has not made the universe from a perfect motive, of perfect material, for a perfect purpose, and as a perfect means thereto.

Now, there are certain natural modes of operation of these forces and powers which God has put in the universe; the natural powers of matter and of man are meant to act in a certain way, and not otherwise. These modes of operation I will call laws, natural laws; they exist in the material world and in the human world. They are a part of the universe. These laws must be observed and kept as means to the end that is proposed.

In the world of matter these laws are always kept, for the actual of nature and the ideal of nature are identical; they are just the same. When this leaf which I drop falls from my hand, it moves by the law which the Infinite God meant it should fall by, and keeps that exactly. In nature —the world of matter—this always takes place, and the actual of to-day is the ideal of eternity,—for there everything is accomplished with no finite, private, individual will; all is mechanism, the brute, involuntary, unconscious action of matter passively obedient to the mind and will of God. There God is the only actor; all else is tool: He is the only workman; nature is all engine and God the engineer. Accordingly, in the world of matter there is a harmony of forces; but not a harmony of purpose, of will, of thought, of feeling,—because there is only one purpose, will, thought, feeling. God alone is the consciousness of the material world; matter obeys His laws, but wills not, knows not. The ideal of nature resides in God's consciousness; only its actual in itself. The two are one; but the material things do not know of that oneness; only God knows thereof. Nature knows nothing of God, nothing of His laws, nothing of itself;—because therein God is the only cause, the only providence, the only consciousness.

On the other hand, in the human world, man is an actor as well as a tool; he is in part engine, in part also engineer. The ideal of man's conduct, character, and destination, resides in God; but thence it is transferred to the mind of man by man's own instinct and reflection; and it is to become actual by man's thought, man's will, man's work. The human race comes to consciousness in itself, and not merely to consciousness in God. So in virtue of the superior nature and destination of man, between him and God there is to be not merely a harmony of forces, but a harmony of feeling, thought, will, purpose, and thence of act. Man is to obey the natural laws as completely as that leaf obeyed them, falling from my hand. But, unlike the leaf, man is to know that he obeys; he must will to obey. So he is to form in his own mind an ideal of the character which he should observe, and then by his own will he is to make that ideal his actual. This is the dignity of man,— he is partial cause and providence of his own affairs.

In general, man has powers sufficient to find out the natural mode of operation of all his human forces, all the natural laws of his conduct, his natural ideal. Narrow this down to a small compass, and take one portion of these powers,—the moral part of man, and thereof this only, —that portion which relates to his dealing with his fellow-men.

There is a moral faculty called conscience. Its function

is to inform us of the moral ideal; to transfer it from God's mind to our mind; to inform us what are the natural modes of operation, the rules of conduct in our relation with other men. Conscience does this in two ways.

First, by instinctive moral action. Here conscience acts spontaneously and anticipates experience, acts in advance of history, and spontaneously projects an ideal which is derived from the moral instinct of our nature. This is the transcendent way of learning the moral law. And let me add, it is the favourite way of young and enthusiastic persons; the favourite way, likewise, of meditative and contemplative men, who dwell apart from mankind, and look at principles, which are the norm of action, more than at the immediate or ultimate effect of special measures.

The other way is by reflective moral action. Here we learn the moral laws by experiment; by observation, trial, experience, we find out what suits the conscience of the individual and the conscience of mankind. This is the inductive way, and it is the favourite mode of the great mass of men, practical men who live in the midst of affairs.

Each of these methods has its advantage, both their special limitations and defects. We require both of these, —the process of moral instinct which shoots forward and forecasts the ideal, and the process of moral induction which comes carefully afterwards and studies the facts, and sees what conduct squares with conscience, and how it looks after the act has been done as well as before.

In these two ways we learn the natural mode of operation and the natural rules of conduct which suit our moral nature; that is, we discover the moral laws which are writ in the nature and constitution of man, and are thence historically made known in the consciousness of man.

When they are understood, we see that they are the laws of God, a part of the universe, a part of the purpose of God, a part of the means which He has provided for accomplishing His purpose.

These laws are not of man's making, but of his finding made. He no more makes them than the blacksmith makes the heaviness of his iron, or the astronomer makes the moon eclipse the sun. A man may heed these laws, or heed them not; make them, or unmake them,—that is beyond his power.

Neither the individual nor the race acquires a consciousness of these moral laws all at once. It is done progressively by you and me; progressively by the human race, learning here a little, and there a little. The natural moral ideal is not all at once transferred from God's mind to man's. We learn the laws of our moral nature like the laws of matter, slowly,—little by little. A good man is constantly making progress in the knowledge of God's natural moral laws; mankind does the same. The race to-day knows more of the natural moral laws of our constitution than the human race ever knew before. A thousand years hence, no doubt, mankind will know a great deal more of this natural moral ideal than we know to-day. Accordingly, speaking after the events of history, the moral ideal of mankind is continually rising. It may not be always rising in the same man, who goes on for a while, then becomes idle, or old, or wicked, and goes down: nor always be rising in the same nation; that also advances for a while, then sins against God sometimes, and goes down to ruin. But, take the human race as a whole, the moral ideal of mankind is constantly rising higher and higher.

The next thing is to obey these laws, consciously, knowing we obey them; voluntarily, willing to obey, and make the moral ideal the actual of life for the individual and the race. This also is done progressively; not all at once, but by slow degrees. The moral actual of the human race is constantly rising higher and higher. Just in proportion as the ideal shoots up the actual follows after it, though on slow and laborious wings. If you look microscopically at the condition of mankind at intervals of only a hundred years, you will see that there is a moral progress from century to century; but separate your points of observation by a thousand years instead of a century, the moral progress of the race is so obvious that no unprejudiced man can fail to see it when he opens his natural eyes and looks. I will not say it is so with every special nation, for a nation may go back as well as forward; but it is so with the human race as a whole. so with mankind.

Religion,—which begins in feeling, proceeds to thought, and thence to action,—in its highest form is the keeping of all the laws which God writ in the constitution of man: in other words, it is the service of God by the normal use, discipline, development, enjoyment, and delight of every limb of the body, every faculty of the spirit, every power which we possess over matter or over mankind,—each in its due proportion, all in their complete harmony. That is the whole and complete religion.

Now leaving out of sight for a moment the matter of mere sentiment, in religion reducing itself to practice there are two things,—to wit, first, intellectual ideas, doctrines of the mind, things to be believed ; secondly, moral duties, doctrines of the conscience, things to be done. Each man in his private individual capacity, as Edwin or Richard, has his own intellectual ideas, things to be believed ; his own moral duties, things to be done. To be faithful to himself he must believe the one and must do the other. It is a part of his personal religion to believe the truths which he knows, to do the duties that he acknowledges.

But man is social as well as solitary. So men, in their collective capacity as churches, towns, nations, come to the conclusion that they have certain intellectual ideas which ought to be believed, certain moral duties which ought to be done. As an expression of this fact, men assembling in bodies for purposes called religious, as churches, make up a collection of ideas connected with religion which are deemed true. They call this a creed. It is a collection of things to be believed, and so it is also a rule of intellectual conduct in matters pertaining to religion.

They likewise assemble in bodies for a purpose more directly practical, as towns, as nations, and make a collection of duties which are deemed obligatory. They call this collection of duties a constitution or a code of statutes.

I will use the word statute to mean what is commonly called a law, made by men : that is to say, a rule of practical conduct devised by men in authority. I keep the word law to describe the natural mode of operation which God wrote in the constitution of material or human nature, and the word statute for that rule of conduct which man makes and adds thereunto.

This is a legitimate aim in making the creed,—to preserve all known religious truth, and diffuse it amongst men. But it is not legitimate to aim at hindering the attainment of new religious truth, or to hinder efforts for the attainment of new religious truth.

This is a legitimate aim in making the statutes, to preserve all known moral duty, and diffuse it amongst men; and thereby secure to each man the enjoyment of all his natural rights, so that he may act according to the natural mode of operation of his powers. But it is not legitimate to hinder the attainment of new moral duty, or efforts after that. The creed should aim at truth, all truth, and should be a step towards it. The statutes should aim at justice, all justice, to insure all the rights of each, and should be a step in that direction, not away from it.

Both the creeds and statutes may be made as follows:—

First, they may be made by men who are far before the people, men who get sight of truths and duties in advance of mankind. Then these men set to mankind a hard lesson, but one which is profitable for instruction, for doctrine, for reproof, that the man of God may be thoroughly furnished to every good work. In such cases the creed or statute is educational; it is prepared for the pupil, set by a master.

Or, secondly, these creeds and statutes may be made by men who are just on a level with the average of the people. Then they are simply expressional of the moral character and attainments of the average men. They are educational to the hindmost, expressional to the middlemost, and merely protectional to the foremost,—of no service as helping them forward, only as protecting them from being disturbed, interrupted, and so drawn backwards by those who are behind.

Or, thirdly, these creeds and statutes may be made by crafty men who are below the moral average of the people; made not as steps towards truth and justice, but as means for the private personal ambition of such as make the statutes or the creeds; by men who are endowed with force of body, and rule over our flesh by violence, or with force of cunning, and rule over our minds by sophistry and fraud. In this case the creed or statute is a step backwards, aims not at truth and justice, but at falsehood and wrong, and is simply debasing,—debasing to the mind and conscience. Here it is not a teacher giving lessons to the pupil; it is not a pupil undertaking to set a lesson to another who knows as much as he does; it is a scoundrel setting a lesson of wickedness to the saint and the sinner.

Laws may be made in any one of these three ways, and no more; the categories are exhaustive.

Now see the relation of each individual man to the creed of his nation or church. By his moral nature man is bound to believe what to him appears true. His mind demands it as intellectual duty, his conscience demands it as moral duty; it is a part of his religion; faithfulness to himself requires this.

But he is likewise morally bound to reject everything that to him seems false. He can close his mind and not think about the matter at all, and so he may seem to believe when he does not; or he can actually think the other way, and lie about it and pretend to believe. But if he is faithful, he must believe what to him seems true, and must reject what to him seems untrue.

If a man does this, the public creed of the people or church may be a help to him, because while it embodies both the truths that men know and the errors which they likewise suppose to be true, he accepts from the creed what he deems true, and rejects what he deems false. The false that he rejects, harms him not; the true which he accepts is a blessing. But there is this trouble,—the priest, who has made, invented, or imported the creed, claims jurisdiction over the minds of men and bids the philosopher "Accept our creed." "No!" answers the philosopher, "I cannot! my reason forbids." "Then, down with your reason!" thunders the priest, "there is no truth above our creed! The priest and creed are not amenable to reason; reason is amenable to them!" What shall be done? Shall the philosopher submit, and seem to believe? Shall he think the other way, and yet pretend to believe, and lie? or shall he openly and unhesitatingly reject what seems false? Ask these prophets of the Old Testament what we shall do! ask Socrates, Anaxagoras, Paul, Luther, Jesus! ask the Puritans of England, the Huguenots of France, the Covenanters of Scotland, which we shall do! whether we shall count human reason amenable to the priest, or the priest amenable to human reason. Sometimes a whole nation violates its mind, and submits to the priest's creed. The many mainly give up thinking altogether,—they can do it and have done it; the few think, but lie outwardly, pretending belief. Then there comes the intellectual death of the nation; the people are cut off from new accessions of truth, and intellectually they die out. "Where there is no vision the people perish," says the Old Testament; and there is not a word in the Bible more true. Tear a rose-bush from the ground and suspend it in the air, will it thrive? Just as much will man's mind thrive when plucked away from contact with truth. Do you want historic examples? Look at Mahometan countries compared with Christian. Whilst the Koran was in advance of the Mahometans there was a progress in the nations which accepted it. There arose great men. But now when men have lived up to the Koran, and are forbidden to think further, science dies out, all original literature disappears, there is no great spiritual growth. In the whole Mahometan world this day there is not a single man eminent for science or literature; not a great Mahometan orator, poet, or statesman, amongst all the many millions of Mahometans on the round world. Look at a Catholic in comparison with a Protestant country. Compare Catholic Spain, Portugal, Italy, with England, Scotland, Germany, noble Protestant countries, and see the odds. In the Catholic countries the priest has laid himself down at the foot of the tree, and says, "Root into me, and you shall have life." Compare Catholic Brazil with Protestant New England. Nay, in New England, go into the families of private men, families where bigotry of the various denominations, Nothingarian, Unitarian, as well as Trinitarian—for there is also a "Nothingarian" bigotry—has put its cold, hard hand, and forbidden freedom of thought; —compare the children born and bred there with such as are born and bred in families where freedom of thought is not only tolerated but encouraged, and see the difference. The foremost men of this country in science, literature, statesmanship, are men who have spurned that Pharisaic meanness, which chains a man's mind and fetters his conscience.

It is as important to accumulate the thoughts of many men, as to consolidate their property for building a railroad, a factory, or a town. No single man is so rich as the whole people of Massachusetts; and though before all others in some speciality, no one man is so rich in thought as mankind. To aggregate the knowledge of a hundred men, each mastering some special subject, is of great value; it embodies the result of very much thinking, which may thus be hoarded up for future use. That is a good thing; and as each truth is a means of power, it quickens other men and helps them to think. Such is the effect of the scientific associations of Christendom, from the Boston Society of Natural History to the French Academy,—perhaps the most learned and accomplished body of men on earth. That is a legitimate function of bodies of men coming together, each dropping his special wisdom into the human treasury, for the advantage of the whole.

But, on the other hand, the consolidation of the opinions of men who are not seeking for truth to liberate mankind, but for means to enthral us withal, will embody falsehood and also retard the progress of mankind by hindering free thought. This will be the result wherever the actual creed is taken for total,—embracing all truth now known; as final,—embracing all truth that is to be known; and as unquestionable, the ultimate standard of truth.

I just said there was not a single eminent man of science or letters in any Mahometan country; not a great scholar, philosopher, or historian. Yet there is talent enough born into Mahometan countries,—as much as in Christian nations of the same race; but it has not opportunity for development; the young Hercules is choked in his cradle. Look at the Catholics of the United States in comparison with the Protestants. In the whole of America there is not a single man born and bred a Catholic distinguished for anything but his devotion to the Catholic Church: I mean to say there is not a man in America born and bred a Catholic, who has any distinction in science, literature, politics, benevolence, or philanthropy. I do not know one; I never heard of a great philosopher, naturalist, historian, orator, or poet amongst them. The Jesuits have been in existence three hundred years; they have had their pick of the choicest intellect of all Europe,—they never take a common man when they know it,—they subject every pupil to a severe ordeal, physical and intellectual, as well as moral, in order to ascertain whether he has the requisite stuff in him to make a strong Jesuit out of. They have a scheme of education masterly in its way. But there has not been a single great original man produced in the company of Jesuits from 1545 to 1854. They absorb talent enough, but they strangle it. Clipped oaks never grow large. Prune the roots of a tree with a spade, trim the branches close to the bole, what becomes of the tree? The bole itself remains thin and scant and slender. Can a man be a conventional dwarf and a natural giant at the same time? Case your little boy's limbs in metal, would they grow? Plant a chestnut in a tea-cup, do you get a tree? Not a shrub even. Put a priest, or a priest's creed, as the only soil for a man to grow in; he grows not. The great God provided the natural mode of operation:—do you suppose He will turn aside and mend or mar the universe at your or my request? I think God will do no such thing.

Now see the relation of the individual to the statutes of men. There is a natural duty to obey every statute which is just. It is so before the thing becomes a statute. The legislator makes a decree; it is a declaration that certain things must be done, or certain other things not done. If the things commanded are just, the statute does not make them just; does not make them any more morally obligatory than they were before. The legislator may make it very uncomfortable for me to disobey his command when that is wicked; he cannot make it right for me to keep it when wicked. All the moral obligation depends on the justice of the statute, not on its legality; not on its constitutionality; but on the fact that it is a part of the natural law of God, the natural mode of operation of man. The statute no more makes it a moral duty to love men and not hate them, than the multiplication table makes twice two four: the multiplication table declares this; it does not make it. If a statute announces, "Thou shalt hate thy neighbour, not love him," it does not change the natural moral duty, more than the multiplication table would alter the fact if it should declare that twice two is three. Geometry proves that the three angles of a triangle are equal to two right angles: it does not make the equality between the two.

Now, then, as it is a moral duty to obey a just statute because it is just, so it is a moral duty to disobey any statute which is unjust. If the statute squares with the law of God, if the constitution of Morocco corresponds with the constitution of the universe, which God writ in my heart,—then I am to keep the constitution of Morocco; if not, disobey it, as a matter of conscience.

Here, in disobedience, there are two degrees. First, there is passive disobedience, non-obedience, the doing nothing for the statute; and second, there is active disobedience, which is resistance, the doing something, not for the statute, but something against it. Sometimes the moral duty is accomplished by the passive disobedience, doing nothing; sometimes, to accomplish the moral duty, it is requisite to resist, to do something against the statute. However, we are to resist wrong by right, not wrong by wrong.

There are many statutes which relate mainly to matters of convenience. They are rules of public conduct indeed, but only rules of prudence, not of morals. Such are the statutes declaring that a man shall not vote till twenty-one; that he shall drive his team on the right-hand side of the street; that he may take six per cent. per annum as interest, and not sixty; that he may catch alewives in Taunton River on Fridays, and not on Thursdays or Saturdays. It is necessary that there should be such rules of prudence as these; and while they do not offend the conscience every good man will respect them; it is not immoral to keep them.

The intellectual value of a creed is, that while it embodies truth it also represents the free thought of the believer who has come to that conclusion, either by himself alone, or as he has been voluntarily helped thitherward by some person who knows better than he. In that case his creed is the monument of the man's progress, and is the basis for future progress. It is to him, in that stage of his growth, the right rule of intellectual conduct. But when the creed is forced on the man, and he pretends to believe and believes not, or only tacitly assents, not having thought enough to deny it,—then it debases and enslaves the man.

So the moral value of a statute is, that while it embodies justice it also represents the free conscience of the nation. Then also it is a monument of the nation's moral progress, showing how far it has got on. It is likewise a basis for future progress, being a right rule for moral conduct. But when the statute only embodies injustice, and so violates the conscience, and is forced on men by bayonets, then its moral value is all one; it is against the conscience. If the people consent to suffer it, it is because they are weak; and if they consent to obey it, it is because they are also wicked.

When the foremost moral men make a statute in advance of the people, and then attempt to enforce that law against the consent of the majority of the people, it is an effort in the right direction and is educational; then I suppose the best men will try to execute the law, and will appeal to the best motives in the rest of men. But even in such a case, if ever this is attempted, it should always be done with the greatest caution, lest the leader go too fast for his followers, undertaking to drag the nation instead of leading them. You may drag dead oxen, drive living oxen; but a nation is not to be dragged, not to be driven, even in the right direction; it is to be led. A grown father, six feet high, does not walk five miles the hour with his child two years old; if he does, he must drag his boy; if he wants to lead him he must go by slow and careful steps, now and then taking him over the rough places in his arms. That must be done when the lawmaker is very far in advance of the people; he must lead them gently to the right end.

But when a wicked statute is made by the hindmost men in morals, men far in the rear of the average of the people, and urging them in the wrong direction; when the statute offends the conscience of the people, and the rulers undertake by violence to enforce the statute, then it can be only mean men who will desire its execution, and they must appeal to the lowest motives which animate mean men, and will thus debase the people further and further.

The priest makes a creed against the mind of the people, and says, "There is no truth above my creed! Down with your reason! it asks terrible questions." So the Catholic is always taught by authority. The priest does not aim to convince the reason; not at all! He says to the philosophers, "This is the doctrine of the Church. It is a true doctrine, and you must believe it, not because it is true,—you have no right to ask questions,—but because the Church says so." The tyrant makes a statute, and says, "There is no law above this." The subject is not to ask, "Is the statute right? does it conform to the constitution of the universe, to God's will reflected in my conscience?" He is only to inquire, "Is it a statute-law? what does the judge say? There is no higher law."

That is the doctrine which is taught to-day in almost every political newspaper in this country, Whig and Democratic; and in many of the theological newspapers. But the theological newspapers do not teach it as a principle and all at once; they teach it in detail, as a measure, telling us that this or that particular statute is to be observed, say conscience what it may. It is assumed that the legislator is not amenable to the rules of natural justice. He is only to be checked by the constitution of the land, not the constitution of the universe.

See how the principle once worked. Pharaoh made a statute that all the new-born boys of Hebrew parentage should be killed as soon as they were born. That was the statute; and instructions were given to the nurses, "If it be a son, then ye shall kill him." Did it become the moral duty of nurse Shiprah and nurse Puah to drown every new-born Hebrew baby in the river Nile? Was it the moral duty of Amram and Jochebed to allow Moses to be killed? It is only a legitimate application of the principle laid down by "the highest authorities" in America,— what are called the highest, though I reckon them among the lowest.

King Darius forbade prayer to any God or man except himself. Should the worshippers of Jehovah hold back their prayer to their Creator? Daniel was of rather a different opinion. A few years ago a minister of a "prominent church" in this city was told of another minister who had exhorted persons to disobey the Fugitive Slave Bill, because it was contrary to the law of God and the principles of right. "What do you think of it?" said the questioner, who was a woman, to the Doctor of Divinity. "Very bad!" replied he, "this minister ought to keep the statute, and he should not advise men to disobey it." "But," said the good woman, "Daniel, we are told, when the law was otherwise, prayed to the Lord! prayed right out loud three times a day, with his window wide open! Did he do right or wrong? Would not you have done the same?" The minister said, "If I had lived in those times,—I think—I should—have shut my window." There was no higher law!

King Herod ordered all the young children in Bethlehem to be slain. Was it right for the magistrates to execute the order? for the justices of the peace to kill the babies? for the fathers and mothers to do nothing against the massacre of those innocents? The person who wrote the account of it seems to have been of rather a different opinion.

King Henry the Eighth of England ordered that no man should read the English Bible. Reading the Bible in the kingdom was made a felony,—punishable with death, without benefit of clergy. Was it the duty of Dr Franklin's humble fathers to refuse to read their Bibles? They did read them, and your fathers and mine also, I trust. King Pharaoh, Darius, Herod, Henry the Eighth, could not make a wrong thing right. If a mechanic puts his wheel on the upper side of the dam, do you suppose the Merrimack is going to run up into New Hampshire to turn his mill? Just as soon as the great God will undo his own moral work to accommodate a foolish and wicked legislator.

Suppose it was not the king, a one-headed legislator, but the majority of the nation, a legislator with many heads, who made the statutes, would that alter the case? Once, when France was democratic, the democracy ordered the butchery of thousands of men and women. Was it a moral duty to massacre the people?

I know very well it is commonly taught that it is the moral duty of the officers of government to execute every statute, and of the people to submit thereto, no matter how wicked the statute may be. This is the doctrine of the Supreme Court of the United States of America, of the executive of the United States; I know very well it is the doctrine of the majority of the legislature in both houses of Congress; it is the doctrine of the churches of commerce; —God be praised, it is not the doctrine of the churches of Christianity, and there are such in every denomination, in many a town; even in the great centres of commerce there are ministers of many denominations, earnest, faithful men, who declare openly that they will keep God's law, come what will of man's statute. This is practical piety; the opposite is practical atheism. I have known some speculative atheists. I abhor their doctrines; but the speculative atheists that I have known all recognize a law higher than men's passions and calculations; the law of some power which makes the Universe and sways it for noble purposes and to a blessed end.

Then comes the doctrine:—While the statute is on the books it must be enforced: it is not only the right of the legislator to make any constitutional statute he pleases, but it is the moral and religious duty of the magistrate to enforce the statute; it is the duty of the people to obey. So in Pharaoh's time it was a moral duty to drown the babies in the Nile; in Darius' time to pray to King Darius, and him only; in Herod's time to massacre the children of Bethlehem; in Henry the Eighth's time to cast your Bible to the flames. Iscariot only did a disagreeable duty.

It is a most dreadful doctrine; utterly false! Has a legislator, Pharaoh, Darius, Herod, Henry the Eighth, a single tyrant, any moral right to repudiate God, and declare himself not amenable to the moral law of the universe? You all answer, No! Have ten millions of men out of nineteen millions in America a right to do this? Has any man a moral right to repudiate justice and declare himself not amenable to conscience and to God? Where did he get the right to invade the conscience of mankind? Is it because he is legislator, magistrate, governor, president, king? a right to do wrong!

Suppose all the voluptuaries of America held a congress of lewdness at New Orleans, and said, "There is no law higher than the brute instinctive passion of lust in men," —then would the pimps, and bawds, and lechers have the moral right to repudiate conscience and crush purity out of the nation?

Imagine that all the misers, and sharpers, and cheats held a convention of avarice at New York or Boston, and made statutes accordingly, declaring, "There is no law higher than covetousness,"—would they have the moral right to lie, and steal, and cheat, and "crush out" all the honest men?

Fancy all the ruffians and man-killers assembled in San Francisco,—it would be a fit place, for there were twelve hundred murders committed there in less than four years, —held a convention of violence, and sought to organize murder, and declared, "There is no law higher than the might of the lifted arm,"—would they have the moral right to kill, stab, butcher whomsoever they pleased?

But that is supposing all this wickedness done without the form of an elected legislature. Then suppose the actual legislatures of the nation should revise the Constitution and delegate the power to those persons to do that work and make statutes for the protection of lewdness, fraud, and butchery,—would it then be the moral duty of the rulers to enforce those statutes; and of the people to submit? Just as much as it is the moral duty of men to enforce any wicked statute made under the present Constitution of the United States and by the present legislators. The principle is false. It is only justified on the idea that there is no God, and this world is a chaos. But yet it is taught; and only last Sunday the minister of a "prominent church" taught that every law must be executed, right or wrong, and thanked the soldiers who, with their bayonets, forced an innocent man to slavery. No matter how unjust a statute is, it must be enforced and obeyed so long as it is on the law book!

Human law in general is a useful and indispensable instrument; but because a special statute has been made for injustice, is it to be used for injustice? Massachusetts has some thousands of muskets in the arsenal at Cambridge; but because they were made to shoot with, shall I take them to kill my neighbours; shall the governor order the soldiers to shoot down the citizens? It is no worse to do injustice with a gun than to do injustice with a statute. It is not merely the means by which the wicked end is reached that is wicked, it is the end itself; and if the means is a thing otherwise good, the wicked end makes its use atrocious. What is the statute in the one case but a tool, and the gun a tool in the other case? The instrument is not to be blamed, and the statute is no more to be used for a wicked purpose than the gun; a State statute no more than a State gun. Medicine is a very useful thing. But will you, therefore, go into an apothecary's shop and take his drugs at random? If you are killed by a poison it is no better because called "medicine."

But the notion that every statute must be enforced is historically false. Who enforces the Sunday law in Massachusetts? Every daily newspaper you will read tomorrow morning violates the statutes of Massachusetts to-day. It would not be possible to enforce them. Of all the sixty millions of bank capital in Massachusetts, within twelve months, every dollar has violated the statute against usury. Nobody enforces these acts. Half the statutes of New England are but sleeping lions to wait for the call of the people: nobody wakes them up every day. Some have been so long fast asleep that they are dead.

When the nation will accept every creed which the priest makes, because it is made for them, then they are tools for the priest, intellectually dead; and they are fit to have Catholic tyrants rule over them in the church. When the nation is willing to accept a statute which violates the nation's conscience, the nation is rotten. If a statute is right, I will ask how I can best obey it. When it is wrong, I will ask how I can best disobey it,—most safely, most effectually, with the least violence. When we make the priest the keeper of our creed, the State the master of our conscience, then it is all over with us.

Sometimes a great deal of sophistry is used to deceive the consciences of men and make them think a wicked law is just and right. There are two modes of procedure for reaching this end.

One is to weaken the man's confidence in his own moral perceptions by debasing human nature, declaring "that conscience is a most uncertain guide for the individual," and showing that all manner of follies and even wickedness have been perpetrated in its name. So all manner of follies have been taught in the name of reason, and foolish undertakings have been set a going by prudent and practical men. But is that sufficient argument for refusing to trust the science of the philosopher and the common sense of practical men?

The other way is to pretend that the obnoxious statute is "consistent with morality and religion." Thus the most wicked acts have been announced in the name of God. The Catholics claimed divine authority for the Inquisition; the Carthaginians alleged the command of God as authority for sacrificing children to Melkarte. In the Law Library at Cambridge, a copy of the English Bible in folio was once the first book in the collection: a Professor then used often to point to the Bible and say, "That is the foundation of the law. It all rests on the word of God!" So every wicked statute, each "ungodly custom become a law," had a divine authority! The same experiment is often tried with the Fugitive Slave Bill—it is declared "divine," having "the sanction of the Law, and the Prophets, and the Gospel."

With these two poisons do men corrupt the public fountains of morality!

Religion is the only basis for everything. It must go everywhere, into the man's shop, into the seamstress' workroom, must steer the sailor's ship. Reverence for the Infinite Mind, and Conscience, and Heart, and Soul, who is Cause and Providence of this world,—that must go up to the highest heights of our speculation, down to the lowest deeps of our practice. Take that away, and there is nothing on which you can depend, even for your money; or for your liberty and life. Without a reverence for the higher law of God everything will be ruled by interest or violence. The Church will collapse into nothing, the State will go down to ruin!

All around us are monuments of men who, in the name of truth broke the priest's creed, defied the king's statute in the spirit of justice. Look at them! There is a little one at Acton where two men gave their lives for their country; another at Concord; one at Lexington,—a little pile of dear old mossy stone, "Sacred to Liberty and the Rights of Mankind;" another at West Cambridge; another at Danvers,—all commemorative of the same deed; and on yonder hill there is a great stone finger pointing to God's higher law, and casting its shadow on the shame of the two sister cities. All New England is a monument to the memory of those men who trusted God's higher law, and for its sake put an ocean three thousand miles wide between them and their mothers' bones. It is this which makes Plymouth Rock so dear. Our calendar is dotted all over with days sacred to the memory of such men. What are the First of August, the Twenty-second of December, the Nineteenth of April, the Seventeenth of June, the Fourth of July, but bright red-letter days in our calendar, marked by the memory of men who were faithful to God, say the statutes of tyrants what they may say?

Nay, what else are these venerable days, called Christmas, Easter, Pentecost, and the Catholic saints' days throughout the Christian year?

There is one thing which this Bible teaches in almost every page, and that is reverence for the higher law of God. The greatest men who wrote here were only men; to err is human, we all learn by experiment, and they were mistaken in many things; but all teach this, from the littlest to the greatest, from Genesis to Revelation,—RELIGION BEFORE ALL OTHER THINGS, REVERENCE FOR GOD ABOVE ALL! It was that for which Jesus bowed his head on the cross, and "sat down at the right hand of God."

There is an Infinite God! You and I owe allegiance to Him, and our service of Him is the keeping of every law which he made;—keeping it faithfully, earnestly, honestly. That is Religion, and to those who do it, on every thundering cloud which passes over their heads, He will cast his rainbow, girdling it with sevenfold magnificence and beauty, and on that cloud take them to His own kingdom of heaven, to be with Him for ever and for ever.

THE NEBRASKA QUESTION.

SOME THOUGHTS

ON THE

NEW ASSAULT UPON FREEDOM IN AMERICA, AND THE GENERAL STATE OF THE COUNTRY IN RELATION THEREUNTO,

SET FORTH IN A DISCOURSE PREACHED AT THE MUSIC HALL, IN BOSTON, ON SUNDAY, FEBRUARY 12, 1854.

The dark places of the earth are full of the habitations of cruelty.—PSALM lxxiv. 20.

BEFORE next Sunday it will be nine years since I first spoke to you in this city, coming at your request. In the first discourse I spoke of the Necessity of Religion for the Conduct of the Individual and the State. Since that time several crises have occurred in our national affairs which have led me to endeavour to apply the great principles of Religion to the political measures of this nation. It is something more than a year since any such event has called forth such treatment in this place. But now another assault has been made upon the liberty of man, in America, and so to-day I ask your attention to some thoughts on the new assault upon freedom in America, and the general state of the country in relation thereunto.

To comprehend the matter clearly, and the cause and the consequences of this special iniquity now contemplated, we must begin far off and study the general course of human conduct in America,—the last new continent left as a stage for the development of mankind.

The transfer of the Anglo-Saxon tribe to this Western

continent is one of the most important events which has taken place in the last thousand years. Since the Protestant Reformation, which helped forward the ideas that were the banner of the march, nothing has proved so significant as the westward movement of this swarm of men, not so much coming as driven out from the old close-pent European hive, and then settling down on the new continent.

A few Romano-Celtic Frenchmen had already moored their venturous shallops in the American water, and pitched their military tents in what was else only the great wilderness of North America, roamed over by wild beasts and wild men, also the children of the woods.

The Spanish tribe had come before either, and with military greediness were eating up the wealthy South. But Spain could set only a poor and perishing scion in the new world. That was always an evil tree to graft from, not producing good fruit. Besides, an old nation, in a state of decay, founds no healthy colonies. The children of a decomposing State, time-worn and debauched, though with a whole continent before them—what could they accomplish for mankind? They inherited the idleness, the ferocity, the military avarice, the superstition and heinous cruelty, of a people never remarkable for any high traits of character. Two thousand years ago, the Celto-Iberic tribe mingled with the Roman; then with the Visi-Goth, the Moor, the Jew—war proclaiming the savage nuptials,—and modern Spain is the issue of this six-fold juncture. This composite tribe of men had once some martial vigour; nay, some commercial enterprise, but it has done little to advance mankind by the invention of new ideas, the organization thereof, or the administration of what others devised and organized; the meanest and most cruel of the Christian nations, to-day she seems made but of the leavings of the world. To Columbus, adventurous Italy's most venturous son, she gave, grudgingly, three miserable ships, wherewith that daring genius sailed through the classic and mediæval darkness which covered the great Atlantic deep, opening to mankind a new world, and new destination therein. No Queen wore ever a diadem so precious as those pearls which Isabella dropped into the Western sea, a bridal gift whereby the Old World, well endowed with Art and Science, and the hoarded wealth of experience, wed America, rich only in her gifts from nature and her hopes in time. The three most valuable contributions Spain has made to mankind are the *Consolato del mare*, the Barcelonian bud whence modern mercantile law has slowly blossomed forth; the three scant ships a wealthy nation furnished to the Genoese navigator whom the world's instinct pushed Westward in quest of continents; and *Don Quixote*, a masterly satire on a form of folly then old-fashioned and fast getting extinct. These are the chief contributions Spain has dropped into the almsbox of the world. Coarse olives, huge onions, strong red wine—these are the offerings of the Spanish mind in the world's fair of modern times. Since the days of Seneca and Lucan, perhaps Servetus is her foremost man, fantastic-minded yet rich in germs of fertile thought. Moorish and Hebrew greatness has indeed been cradled on her soil, but thereof Spain was not the mother.

Long before the Anglo-Saxons, the Spaniard came to America; greedy of money, hungering for reputation—the glory of the Gascon stock. He brought the proud but thin and sickly blood of a decaying tribe; the traditionary institutions of the past—Theocracy, Monarchy, Aristocracy, Despotocracy, the dominion of the master over the exploitered slave. He brought the mass-book and legends of unnatural saints,—the symbols of superstition and ecclesiastic tyranny; the sword,—the last argument of Spanish kings, the symbol of military depotism; fetters and the bloodhound. He brought no great ideas, new trees started in the old nursery of the past; no noble sentiments, the seed-corn of ideal harvests yet to be. He shared only the material momentum of the human race which dashed his Eastern body on the Western world. He butchered the Indians who disbelieved "the immaculate conception of our blessed Lady" as taught by men of most Titanic, all-devouring lust. He set up the Inquisition, and soon had monks and nuns believing what heathen Guatemozin would have found bitterer than fire. The Spaniard attempted to found no institution which was an improvement on what he left behind—he reproduced only the Church, the State, the

‎mmunity, and Family, of the middle ages. He hated arts, letters, liberty; even the mass of the people seemed t care nothing for freedom of body or of mind.

The Spaniard settled in the fairest parts of the new-found land, amongst tribes already far advanced toward civilization—the world's foremost barbarians. He slew them with merciless rapacity; took their stone-built cities; occupied their land better tilled than the gardens of Castile; he seized their abundant gold; stole their wives and their maidens. At home the people were wonted to bull-fights, wherein the valiant *Matador* risks his own worthless body, and to *Autos da Fe*, where the cowardly priests burn their freethinking sister without hazarding their own nuisance of a life; in America the Spaniard rioted in the murder of men. The pictured horrors of De Bry report only a drop of the blood so torturously shed; yet two hundred and fifty years ago they terrified all Europe—Latin, German, French, English, Dutch.

To America, Spain transferred the superstition and tyranny of mediæval Europe, its four-fold despotism,— ecclesiastical, political, social, domestic. She reinvented negro slavery. Six thousand years ago, before the "flood," yea, before mythological Cain had been conceived by a Hebrew head, Egypt, it seems, was guilty of this crime. In the middle ages negro slavery was an art well nigh lost. Spain, first, of the Christian nations, enforced religion with the knife, and beheaded men for heresy; she rolled the Inquisition as a sweet morsel under her tongue; her sovereigns, who extinguished the brand which smoked on the national hearth yet warm with Gothic liberty, who butchered the Moors and banished the plundered Jews, were for such services styled "the Catholic!" Spain re-annexed negro slavery to herself, and therewith stained the soil of America. Therein she broke not the continuity of her history, the succession of rapine, piracy, cruel outpouring of blood. Not Italian Columbus, but Iberian Cortes and Pizarro, were the types of Spain; not Las Casas, but Torquemada.

Behold now the condition of Spanish America. Its most flourishing part is an empire, with the house of Braganza at its head—an imitation of the old world, a despotism throned on bayonets. There are two empires in Tropic

America—Hayti and Brazil; the foremost tradition of Africa, the hindmost of Europe set down on American soil. The negro empire appears the most successful, the most promising. There alone is no hereditary slavery. Over Cuba, France and England still hold up the feeble hands of Spain—whence at last freedom seems dropping into the slave's expectant lap. The rest of Spanish America has the form of a republic—a republic whose only permanent constitution is a cartridge-box, which blows up once a year. Look at Mexico—I am glad she is going swiftly back to the form of despotism; she is capable of no other reality. How the Western vultures fly thitherward! Where the carcase of a nation rots there will the fillibusters be gathered together. Every raven in the hungry flock of American politicians looks that way, wipes his greedy beak, prunes his wings, and screams "Manifest Destiny!"

In South America there are ten "Republics." They cover three and a half millions of square miles, and contain twelve million men. But they do less for mankind than Holland; nay, Basil and Zurich do more for the human race than these "Republics," which only blot the continent. No idea is cradled in Spanish America; no books are written there; none read but books of "Devotion," which ignorance long since wrote. Old Spain imports from France the filthiest novels of the age; new Spain only the yet more deadly books of Catholic "Devotion." The "laws" of the Chilian "Republic" are printed in Spain, where no Chilian ship ever sailed. The Amazon has eighty thousand miles of navigable water,—near a hundred thousand, say some, the survey is conjectural,—and drains into the lap of America, a tropic basin, the largest, the richest on the globe, with more good land than all Europe owns; therein streams larger than the Danube discharge their freight. But only a single steamer disturbs the alligator on its mighty breast—that steamer built and owned at New York. Pará at its mouth is more than three hundred years old, yet has not twenty thousand souls. If the South American "Republics" were to perish this day, the world would hardly lose a valuable experiment in Spanish political or social life, hardly a visible promise of future prosperity; so badly flourish the Spanish scions set in the green soil of America, and surrounded by the old institutions of the middle ages. Slavery is the one idea of the Spanish tribes—here African, there Indian or Caucasian.

One hundred and thirty years after Genoese Columbus had planted the Spanish Cross in the new world—" sword in hand and splendidly arrayed,"—from a little vessel, leaky, and with a "wrack in the main beam amidships," the Anglo-Saxons dropped their anchor in Massachusetts bay, circled then with savage woods; they drew up a "compact," chose their "Governor" for one year; rested and worshipped on Sunday; the next day landed at "New Plymouth," thanking God. They came, a slip from a young tree full of hardy life. Four stout roots—Angle, Saxon, Danish, Norman—united their old fantastic twists and joined in this one tough and rugged stem, then quadruply buttressed below, now how widely branched abroad in every climate of the world! Fresh blood was in those Anglo-Saxon veins; strong, red, heathen blood, not long before inoculated with Christianity which yet took most kindly in all Teutonic veins.

These pilgrims had in them the ethnologic idiosyncrasy of the Anglo-Saxon—his restless disposition to invade and conquer other lands; his haughty contempt of humbler tribes, which leads him to subvert, enslave, kill, and exterminate; his fondness for material things, preferring use to beauty; his love of personal liberty, yet coupled with most profound respect for peaceful and established law; his inborn skill to organize things to a mill, men to a company, a community, tribes to a federated State; and his slow, solemn, inflexible, industrious, and unconquerable will.

They brought with them much of the tradition of the human race, the guidings and warnings of experience; a great deal of superstition, of tyranny not a little,—ecclesiastical, political, social, domestic. They brought the sword,—that symbol of military despotism must yet fight on freedom's side; but they loved better the axe, the wooden shovel—the best they had,—the plough, the swine, the ox, tools of productive industrial civilization, types of toil and co-operative freedom. For the Mass-book they had the Bible: it was a free Bible; let him read that listeth.

No doubt the Bible contained the imperfection of the men and ages concerned in writing it. The hay tastes of the meadow where it grew, of the weather when it was made, and smells of the barn wherein it has been kept; nay, the breath of the oxen housed underneath comes down to market in every load. But in its many-coloured leaves, the Bible likewise holds the words of great men, free and making free; it was full of the old blossoms of piety, and rich in buds for new and glorious life, ay, and beauty too. The cup of prophets mainly, not of priests, it ran over with water of life from the mythologic well in the wilderness and Bethesda's pool which angels stirred to healing power;— it gave men vigorous strength and hardy life. Instead of the bloodhound, the pilgrims sent the schoolmaster to his work;—they put their fetters on the little streams that run among the hills, and those river-gods must saw, and grind, and spin for mortal men; not the Inquisition, but the printing press, was the type and symbol of this Northern work.

They had the traditions of the human race, but also its momentum acquired in the movement of many a thousand years. They brought the best political institutions the world had then known. They had the English common law,—which had slowly got erected in the practice of this liberty-loving people, its Cyclopean walls built up by the Lesbian rule,—with its forms and precedents, its methodical schemes of procedure, itself a popular *judicium rusticum;* they had the habit of local self-government; the right— though then not well understood—of popular legislation, also founded in immemorial usage; dim notions and the certain practice of representative government—the democracy of law-making; the trial by jury—the democracy of law-administration. They brought Congregational Protestantism—the democracy of Christianity, involving, what they neither granted nor knew, the universal right of search for truth and justice, the natural right to take or reject, as a man's own spirit should require.

Besides the organized institutions—visible as tools of industry or politics, or invisible in literature, science, settled and admitted principles of private morality or of public law,—which represent the history and achievements of mankind, they brought also ideas not organized in either form of institution, and sentiments not then translated into conscious thought. These represented man's natural instinct of progress and the momentum he had gained in history; they were to become institutions and facts in future time.

When the Puritan founded his colonies in New England, there were other Anglo-Saxon settlements on the Atlantic coast. Jamestown was founded in 1607. Other settlements followed. The same Anglo-Saxon blood flowed South as well as North; the same traditions and institutions were with both. But the Anglo-Saxons North brought institutions, ideas, and feelings quite unlike those of their Southern fellows. The motive for immigrating was altogether unlike. New England was a religious colony,—mainly composed of persecuted men who fled Westward because they had ideas which could not be set up in the Eastern world. Thrice the May-flower crossed the sea, coming to Plymouth, to Salem, to Boston; each time bringing veritable pilgrims who came from a religious motive, and sought religious ends. This was likewise the case with the primitive settlers of Pennsylvania. The South was not settled by religious colonies. The primitive difference in the seed has continually appeared in the growth thence accruing; in the policy and the character of the South and North. The same year which brought the Puritan Pilgrims to New England bore a quite different freight to Virginia. In 1620, a Dutch captain carried thither some twenty Africans who were sold as slaves into perpetual bondage—themselves and their children. Thus the old sin of Egypt, half omitted and half forgotten in classic and mediæval times, rediscovered by the Spaniards, and fixed by despots—a loathly plague-spot—on the tropic regions of America, was brought North, adopted by the Anglo-Saxons of the South, and set a going at Jamestown. It excited no astonishment. All the "Christian" world then sold prisoners of war for slaves. Thus early did Negro Slavery become an "institution" of the South.

But all things are double: in the Anglo-Saxon North there were two contending elements. One represented old institutions, and wished to stop therewith. It loved despotocracy in the family, aristocracy in the community, monarchy in the State, and theocracy in the Church: it opposed the natural human rights of the servant in the family, of the labourer in the community, of the people in the State, of the layman in the Church; it favoured the rule of the master, the lord, the king, the priest. This element was old, ancestral, stationary, if not retrogressive; it was also powerful. In this the Anglo-Saxon and the Spaniard were alike.

The other element was the instinct for progressive development; the sentiments not idealized into conscious thoughts; the ideas not organized into institutions. There was a feeling of the equality of all men in the substance of their human nature, and consequently in all natural rights, howsoever diverse in natural powers, in transmitted distinction and riches, or in acquired culture, money, and station. Now and then this feeling had broken out in a "Jack Cade's insurrection," or a "Peasants' war." But in the seventeenth century it found no distinct expression as a thought. Perhaps it was not an idea with any man a hundred and fifty years ago; it was the stuff ideas are made of. What other feelings are there, one day to become ideas, then acts, the world's victorious life! Lay down your ear to the great ocean of humanity, and as the Spirit of God moves on the face of this deep, listen to the low tone of the great ground swell, and interpret the ripple at the bottom of the sea, while, all above, the surface is calm as a maiden's dreamless sleep. In these days, what is it that we hear at the bottom of the world as the eternal tide of human history meets with the sand bars cast down in many an ancient storm! Thereof will I speak not now.

This feeling came slowly to an idea. With many stumblings and wanderings it went forth, blindfold as are all the instinctive feelings—whereunto only God not man is eye,—not knowing whither it went or intended to go. See what has been done, or at least commenced.

I. They protested against Theocracy in the church. "Let us have a church without an altar or a bishop; a service with no mass-book, no organ, no surplice, each congregation subject only to the Lord, not to man," said the Puritan—and he had it: "Yea," answered the Quaker, "and with no hireling minister, no outward sacrament, no formal prayer of words; the church is they that love the Lord; it takes all the church to preach all the gospel, and without that cannot all mankind be saved!" "No vicarious sprinkling of babies, but the voluntary plunging of men," cried the Anabaptist. Thereat the theocratic Puritan lifted his hands and scourged the Baptist and smote the Quaker stone dead. But the palm-tree of toleration sprang out of Mary Dyer's grave. The theocracy got routed in many a well-contested fight; in this city of the Puritans, the Catholic, the Quaker, the Anabaptist, the Jew, and the Unitarian may worship or worship not, just as they will. But this fight is not over; yet it is plain how the battle is going. The theocracy is doomed to the cave of Pope and Pagan. Let us give it our blessing—as it goes. The Puritan fled from episcopal England to tolerant Holland, to the wilderness of America. But he brought more than Puritanism along with him,—humanity came in the same ship. The great warfare for the right of man's nature to transcend all the accidents of his history, began in the name of religion—the instinct whereunto is the deepest in us, the innermost kernel and germinal dot in the human spirit; Luther's hammer shook the world. During midwinter, in Switzerland, when the snow overhangs heavily from every cliff, if the traveller but clap his hands and shout aloud, the mountains answer with an avalanche. When Martin lifted up his voice amid the mediæval snows of Europe, half Christendom came down in that great landslip of churches. Other snows have since fallen; other voices will be lifted up; other church-slides will follow—for every mountain shall be levelled, and the valleys filled. The Bible took the place of the Mass-book, the minister of the priest, the independent society of the Papal church. The glorious liberty of the children of God is to be the final result of all.

II. Next came the protest against Monarchy. The Anglo-Saxons never loved single-headed, absolute despotism. How the barons fought against it! But it was left for "His Majesty's faithful Commons" to do the work. The dreadful axe of Puritanic Oliver Cromwell shore off the divine right of kings, making a clean cut between the vicarious government of the middle ages, and the personal self-rule of modern times. On the 30th of January, 1648, the executioner held up the head of Charles I. with a "Behold the head of a traitor," and "Royalty disappeared in front of Whitehall :" a ghastly, dreadful sight. Peasant Luther pushed the Latin Mass-book aside with his German Bible, saying, "Thus I break the succession of the priests." With his sword Cromwell, the brewer, pushed aside the Crown of England, "Thus I break the succession of Kings." New England loved Cromwell; and while dwelling in the wilderness exercised the rights of sovereignty many times before it was known what she did, both destroying and building,—as likewise do all of us,—greater and wiser than she knew. Luther's hammer broke also the neck of kings, who disappear, and in their place came up governors and presidents not born to adverse rule, but voted in for official service.

III. Then came the protest against 'Aristocracy. God made men not in classes but as individuals—each man a person with all the substantive rights of humanity : the same law must serve for all; all must be equal before it and the social institutions of the community. That was the dim utterance of many a man who grumbled in his beard :—

"When Adam delved and Eve span
Where was then the gentleman?"

How idly they dreamed—looking back for the Paradise that lay before them! But between it and them Pison, Gihon, Hiddekel, and a fourth stream, nameless as yet, rolled torrents of blood; and a fiery sword of selfishness turned every way to keep men from the tree of life, whose very leaves are for the healing of the nations—could they but get to it. Could they—ay! Can they not?

Little by little, man's nature prevailed over Aristocracy, one accident of his development. The Anglo-Saxon Briton had restricted the nobility he brought with him from the continent ;—only the eldest son inherits his father's land, title, and rank, the later-born all commoners. The Anglo-Saxon American broke up primogeniture : the children are equal in blood and rank; the first son has no more of his father in him than the last; all must share equally in his goods. Rank is not heritable. If a coward, the captain's son is no captain; by human substance, eminent manhood, bravery, skill, is the new man made captain; not by the historic accident of legitimate descent from an old captain. To be born well is to be well born; tall men are of a high family. The corporal's child, yea, the sons of rank and file, are also men. In the woods of nature, new humanity takes precedence of all the artificial distinctions of old time. The crime of the father must work no attainder in the baby's blood; by the sour grapes of his own eating only shall a man's teeth be set on edge. Estates must not be entailed in perpetuity. Land must be held in fee-simple, with no quit-rents, or other servitudes of vassalage; on terms which all can understand. The vicarious land-tenures of the middle ages are for ever broken. All men may hold land; and cheaply convey it to whom they will. For the first time the majority have a stake in the public hedge; the mediæval "noble," the conventional "gentleman," gradually withdraws and moves out from New England. "It is not a good place for gentlemen," so a governor wrote two hundred years ago. Everybody is "Mr;" then "Esquire." The born magistrate vanishes, the "select men" are annually voted in. Still the social aristocracy, bottomed on accident, is far from being ended. But it rests no longer on the immovable accident of birth, but on the changeable block of money, and like that can be struggled for and acquired by all. It rests on golden sands or fickle votes.

IV. There yet remains the protest against Despotocracy —the adverse rule of the master over the servant, the hostile subordination of the weak to the strong in the family. In a military despotism, war confers dignity: "it is the part of a man to fight," says Homer, "of a slave to work;" and they "who exercise lordship are called benefactors." In a Theocracy, the priest is a sacred person: his work is "divine service," he enters the temple; but the people are profane, and must stand without; their work is menial! In a Theocracy, Monarchy, Aristocracy—founded and maintained by violence or cunning—labour is thought degrading; the labourer is for the State, not it also for him. This exploitering of the weak by the strong belongs to the essence of those three institutions. Domestic slavery coheres therewith, and in dark ages this adverse rule of the strong over the weak appears in all the collective action of men—ecclesiastical, political, social, domestic; the god, the king, the noble, the master, the husband, the father, —all are tyrants; all rule is despotism—the strong for his interest coercing the weak against theirs. In such a soil, slavery is at home, and grows rank and strong.

But in an industrial community, with a printed Bible bought by the parish and belonging thereunto; with a minister chosen by the laymen's votes, ordained by their hands, paid by their free-will offerings, nay, educated, perhaps, by their charity, criticized by their judgment, removable at their will; with a creed voted in by the congregation—and voted out when they change their mind; with no monarch ruling by divine right, but only a governor chosen by the people at their annual meeting; with no "nobles," no "gentlemen," but an elected assembly, a general court,—sworn on a constitution made by the people,—democratically making laws; with magistrates chosen by the people, or responsible thereto; with democratic trial by jury for all men; with the idea that a man's nature is before all the accidents of his ancestry or estate—the old domestic Despotocracy must gradually become impossible. Labour will be thought honourable—idleness a disgrace. Productive activity will be deemed a glory, and riches its result, the greatest of all mere outside and personal distinctions. The tools must be for whoso can handle them. So the threefold movement, destroying the triple tyranny already mentioned, must presently achieve the emancipation of man from all personal servitude and domestic subordination: the substance of man must be inaugurated above the accidents of his history. This must be done not only in the Church, the State, the community, but also in the family. It must set the bondman free. If the Church, State, and community rest on natural law, so likewise must the family as well.

To accomplish this, two things were needful. This was the first.

1. To affirm as a principle and establish in measures the idea that all men, rich and poor, strong and weak, are equal in all their natural rights; that as the accident of birth makes no man priest, king, or noble, with a right, thence derived, to rule over men against their will in the

Church, State, or community; so the accident of superior power gives no man a right in the family to hold others in bondage and subordination, for his advantage and against theirs. It is only to admit that all are MEN, for manhood carries all human rights with it, as land the crops, and the substance its primary qualities. It seems a small thing to do;—especially for men able to dispense and make way with the other mediæval forms of vicarious rule—theocracy, monarchy, and aristocracy. How easy it seemed to inaugurate personality and individualism in the family! But as matters were, this was the most difficult thing of all. For the priests, the kings, the nobles did not come over— only the tradition thereof, and the habit of subordination thereto, with a few feeble scions of the sacerdotal, royal, and noble stocks—and preaching against these always was popular,—while the masters came over in large numbers, bringing their slaves. They brought the substance of Despotocracy along with them, not merely its tradition. To preach against that was always a "sin" to the American Church. But man wants unity of consciousness. Accordingly, in New England good men began early to feel that absolute and perpetual slavery was a wicked thing. Had not the letter of the Old Testament and of certain passages in the New blinded their eyes, I think the Puritan would have seen more clearly than he did see. Still, with so much of the spirit of the Old Testament in him, he could not but see it was wrong to steal men for the purpose of making them slaves and their children after them. So slavery was always a contradiction in the consciousness of New England. The white slaves became free on expiration of their term of service, or were set free before. There were many such. The red men would not work—and were let alone, or quietly shot down. The Indians killed the white man and scalped him; the Puritan omitted the scalping—it was not worth his while; the scalp was of no use.

The slavery of the blacks never prevailed extensively in New England. It was not found very profitable. True it prevailed: it had the laws and the tradition of the elders on its side. But it was yet felt, known, and confessed to be at variance with the ecclesiastical, political, and social ideas of the people. There was always a good deal of conscience in New England. The religious origin of the first colonies is not yet a forgotten fact. The Puritan still looked up to a higher law. Did he keep his powder dry? He also trusted in God. Coveting the end, he looked for the means thereto. The gain from the compulsory labour of the African slave was not motive enough to keep up the contradiction in the New England consciousness. So before the Revolution this institution was much weakened, and with that disappeared from New England; and soon after vanished out of all the States which she bore or taught.

2. ...e other thing was to affirm as a principle and establish as a measure the natural equality of men and women in all that pertained to human rights. It was only to affirm that woman is human, and has the same quality of human substance with man. If difference in condition, as rich and poor, or ability, as strong or weak, does not affect the substance of manhood, and the rights thence accruing, no more does difference of sex, masculine or feminine, make one master and the other slave. Not only the proletary, the servant, the slave, but exploitered woman also must rise as Despotocracy goes down.

In the Southern part of the North American continent other Anglo-Saxon colonies got planted and grew up. None of them was a religious settlement; the immigrants came not for the sake of an idea too new or too great for toleration at home. They came as adventurers, seeking their fortune; not as pilgrims, to found the " Kingdom of Heaven on earth." The Southern settlers had not the New England hostility to mediæval institutions. Theocracy, monarchy, aristocracy, were not so unwelcome further South. In 1671, the Governor of Virginia said that she " had no free schools nor printing-press. Learning has brought disobedience, and heresy, and sects into the world, and printing has divulged them, and libels against the best governments. God keep us from both!" Despot.cracy had its home in the Southern States. African slavery came to Virginia in the same year which brought the pilgrims to Plymouth. It suited the idleness of the self-indulgent master, and became an institution fixed and beloved in the Southern colonies, so diverse in their ideas from the stern but bigoted North. Still the ideas of the age found their way to these colonies—and led to acts. There also was a protest against Theocracy, Monarchy, Aristocracy, and even against Despotocracy. Mutuality of origin, community of position—that is all the Northern and Southern colonies at first had in common. Sentiments, ideas, institutions, were quite diverse. By and by a little trade helped unite the two. The South wanted slaves. The North—especially Rhode Island—overcame its scruples, and, spite of the Old Testament, stole men in Africa to sell them at enormous profit in the colonies of the South.

This great human protest againt that four-fold despotism continually went on—no man understanding the great battle between the substance of man's progressive nature and the stationary institutions which were the accidents of his history. At length, things came to such a pass that connection between New America and Old England could not be borne. Between the old and new there had ceased to be that mutuality of sentiment and idea which makes unity of institutions and unity of action possible. The daughter was too strong to bear patiently the dictation and the yoke of her parent; the mother was too distant and two feeble to enforce her selfish commands.

America published to the world a part of the new ideas which lay in her mind. The Declaration of Independence contained the American programme of political principles. The motive thereto is to be found in the general human instinct for progress, but more especially in the old Teutonic spirit, the love of individual liberty, which has marked the ancient Germans, and still more eminently their Anglo-Saxon descendants, as well in Christian as in heathen times. The form of speech—self-evident maxims, universal truths resting on the consciousness of mankind—seems derived from European writers on natural law; the influence of continental free-thinkers is obvious therein. But the first express declaration, that there are natural, unalienable rights in man, seems to have been made a few years before, in New England, in Boston. Is it here thought an honour to the town?—Nay, perhaps a disgrace!

Here is the American programme of political principles: All men are endowed by their Creator with certain natural rights; these rights can be alienated only by the possessor thereof; in respect thereto all men are equal; amongst them are the right to life, liberty, and the pursuit of happiness; it is the function of government to preserve all these natural, unalienable, and equal rights for each man; government is amenable to the people, deriving its sanction from the consent of the governed.

In time of peace the thirteen distinct colonies could not have united in that Declaration of principles. The political ideal was a severe criticism on the actual legislation of the Americans. Talk of natural law and equal rights when every colony held slaves in perpetual bondage! when the North stole men in Africa to sell them in Carolina! But America was then in her agony and bloody sweat. European despotism was the angel which strengthened her. External violence pressed the colonies together into a confederation of States; that alone gave unity of action when there was no unity of humane sentiment or political idea. The union was only military—for defence.

The New conquered; but the Old did not die. Not every Tory went over to the British side. After the war was over, the nation must organize itself on that new platform of principles. But, alas, much of the old selfishness remained—theocratic, monarchic, aristocratic, and still more despotocratic; it would appear in the new government. There was no real unity of idea between the extreme South and the North, between Carolina and Connecticut. Nothing is done by leaps. In organizing the independence won in battle, the people proclaimed their programme of political purpose. It is the preamble to the Constitution: "To form a more perfect union, establish justice, insure domestic tranquillity, provide for the common defence, promote the general welfare, and secure the blessings of liberty." The purpose was as noble as the principles. But the means to that end, the Constitution itself, is by no means unitary; it is a provisional compromise between the ideal political principles of the Declaration, and the actual selfishness of the people North and South; it is a measure which did not so much suit the ideal right, as it favoured one great actual tyranny. National theocracy was given up. How could the Americans allow a "national religion"? Monarchy went also to the ground; the Puritan bosom that bore Cromwell—

"Would have brooked
Th' eternal devil to keep his state....
As easily as king."

Aristocracy found more favour, but likewise perished; "no title of nobility shall be granted;" honours are not devisable. Despotocracy, the worst institution of the middle ages—the leprosy of society—came over the water : the slave survived the priest, the noble, the king. Must the axe of a more terrible Cromwell shear that also away? Shall it be a black Cromwell? History points to St Domingo. The future also has much to teach us. The declaration of principles and of purposes would annihilate slavery; the Constitution nowhere forbids it, but broods over that egg which savage selfishness once laid. How could the liberty-loving North join with Carolina, which rejoiced to fetter men? The unity of action was no longer military—it was commercial, union for trade. Thus the idea of America became an act!

The truths of the Declaration went abroad to do their work. The French Revolution followed with its wide-reaching consequences, so beneficial to mankind; it still goes on. The ground-swell has come near the surface, and all the European sea now foams with tumult. Foreign opposition withdrew; America was left to herself, the sole republic of the world, with the wilderness for her stage and scene, and her great ideas for plot. The two antagonistic elements, the old selfishness which loves those four traditions of the past, the new benevolent instinct of progress which seeks the development of all man's nobler powers, were to fight their battle, while with hope and fear the world looks on. The New World has now broken with the Old—once and for ever.

The peculiar characteristics of the Anglo-Saxon appear now more prominent in the American than in the Britons; yet he is not altered, only developed. The love of individual liberty triumphs continually; the white man becomes more democratic—in Church, State, community, and family. The invasive character appears in the individual and national thirst for land and our rapid geographic spread. Materialism shows itself in the swift growth of covetousness, in the concentration of the talent and genius of the nation upon the acquisition of riches. The power to organize things and men comes out in the machines, ships, and mills, in little and great confederations, from a lyceum to the Federal Union of thirty-one States. The natural exclusiveness appears in the extermination of the red man, in the enslavement of the black man, in the contempt with which he is treated—turned out of the tavern, the church, and the grave-yard. The lack of high qualities of mind is shown in the poverty of American literature, the meanness of American religion, in the neglect and continual violation of the idea set forth in our national programme of principles and purpose. Since the Revolution, the immediate aim of America appears to have changed.

At first, during the period of America's colonization and her controversy with England, and her affirmation and establishment of her programme of political principles,— the great national work of the disunited provinces was a struggle for local self-government against despotic centralization beyond the sea. It was an effort against the vicarious rule of the middle ages, which allowed the people no power in the State, the laity none in the Church, the servant none in the family. It was a great effort—mainly unconscious—in favour of the direct government of each State by itself, of the whole people by the whole people; a national protest against Theocracy, the subordination of man in religious affairs to the accident of his history; Monarchy, the subordination of the mass of men to a single man; Aristocracy, the subordination of the many to the few, of the weak to the strong; yes, in part also against Despotocracy, the subordination of the slave who toils to the master that enjoys,—in their rights they were equal. This forced men to look inward at the natural rights of man; outward at the general development thereof in history. It led to the attempt to establish a Democracy, which, so far as measures are concerned, is the government of all, for all, by all; so far as moral principle is concerned, it is the enactment of God's justice into human laws. There was a struggle of the many against the few; of man's nature, with its instinct of progressive and perpetual development, against the accidents of man's history. It was an effort to establish the eternal law of God against the provisional caprice of tyrants. I do not mean to say that these great purposes and ideas existed consciously in the minds of men. They were in men's character, not in their convictions; they came out in their life more than in their speech. They were in men as botany is in this plant, as chemistry in this drop of water, as gravitation which rounds it to a globe and brings it to the ground. But the camelia knows not the botany it lives; the drop of water knows nothing of the chemistry which has formed it, arranging its particles "by number and measure and weight;" it knows not the gravitation which brings it to the ground. So it was the great soul of humanity that stirred in our fathers' heart; it was the providence of God working by the men who formed the State.

From 1620 to 1788 there was a rapid development of ideas. But since that time the outward pressure has been withdrawn. The nation is no longer called to protest against a foreign foe; no despot forces us to fall back on the great principles of human nature, and declare great universal truths. Even the Anglo-Saxon people are always metaphysical in revolution. We have ceased to be such, and have become material. We have let the programme of political principles and purposes slip out of the nation's consciousness, and have betaken ourselves, body and soul, to the creation of riches. Wealth is the great object of American desire. Covetousness is the American passion. This is so—nationally in the political affairs of the country; ecclesiastically, socially, domestically, individually. Our national character, political institutions, geographic situation,—all favour the accumulation of riches. I thank God that we are thus rich!

No country was ever so rich before, nor got rich so fast; in none had wealth ever such power, or was so esteemed. It is counted as the end of life, not as the material basis to higher forms thereof. It has no conventional check in the institutions of the land, and only two natural checks in the heart of the people. One is the talent and genius—intellectual, moral, affectional, and religious—that is born in rare men; and the other is the desire, the caprice, the opinion, of the great majority of men, who oppose their collective human will against the material glitter of mere accumulated money. But money can buy intellectual talent and intellectual genius; at least it can buy American talent and American genius. Money, and the men of cultivated minds whom it buys, can deceive the people, so that the majority shall follow the dollar wherever it rolls. The clink of the dollar,—that is the *reveille*, the morning drum-beat, for the American people. In America money is inaugurated as a power to control all other powers. It has itself become an "Institution"—master of all the rest.

Three of those bad institutions that I named, whereof our fathers brought the traditions from the old world, have mainly perished. The mediæval Theocracy has gone out from the Protestant Church; Monarchy has wholly faded from the consciousness of the people; Aristocracy, sitting unmovable on her cradle, has had her heart pierced through and through by the gigantic spear of American industry horsed on a steam-engine. Money has taken the place of all three. It has got inaugurated into the Church,—it is a Church of commerce; in the State—it is a State of commerce; in the Community not less,—it is a society of commerce; and money wields the triple power of those three old masters, Theocracy, Monarchy, Aristocracy. It is the almighty dollar.

In the American Church, money is God. The peculiar sins of money, and of the rich, they are never preached against; it is a Church of commerce, wealth its heaven and the millionaire its saint; its ministers should be ordained, not "by the imposition of hands," but of bank-bills—of small denomination. In the American State, money is the Constitution : officers ought to be sworn on the federal currency; they should make the sign of the dollar ($) as their official symbolic cross; it is a State of commerce. In the community, money is nobility; it is transmissible social power; it is Aristocracy, it makes a man who has got it a vulgar "gentleman;" it is a society of commerce. Nay, in the family, money is thought better than love, and the daughter who fascinates and coaxes and courts and weds a bag of gold, gets the approbation of her mother and her father's benediction, "Many daughters have done virtuously, but thou excellest them all."

"None but the *rich* deserve the fair."

The fourth bad institution whose tradition our fathers brought, Despotocracy, the rule of the master over the slave whom he exploiters,—that has no, yet shared the fate of Theocracy, Monarchy, and Aristocracy. It is still preserved; it leagues itself with money, and builds up anew in America the old corrupt family of the middle ages. In New York, it clothes the white flunkeys of the Hon. Dives Gotrich with an imitated livery; in New Orleans, and in more than half the land, it takes those whom nature has clothed in a sable livery, and makes them its slaves. Despotocracy alone could not accomplish this. The wickedness is foreign to the American idea of a State, a community, or a Church. But leaguing with money, which has taken the place of all those old institutions, it is this day the strongest power in the nation.

Money having taken the place of these three institutions, it must be politically represented in the nation by a party; for a party is the provisional organization of a tendency. So there is a pa by organized about the dollar as its central nucleus and idea. The dollar is the germinal dot of the Whig party; its motive is pecuniary; its motto should be, to state it in Latin, *pecunia pecuniata*, money moneyed, money made. It sneers at the poor; at the many; has a contempt for the people. It legislates against the poor, and for the rich; that is, for men pecuniarily strong; the few who are born with the desire, the talent, and the conventional position to become rich. "Take care of the rich, and they will take care of the poor," is its secret maxim. Everything must yield to money; that is to have universal right of way. Down with mankind! the dollar is coming! The great domestic object of government, said the greatest expounder of this party, "is the protection of property;"—that is to say, the protection of money moneyed, money got. With this party there is no absolute right, no absolute wrong. Instead thereof, there is expediency and inexpediency. There is no law higher than the power to wield money just as you will. Accordingly a millionaire is reckoned by this party as the highest production of society. He is the Whig ideal; he alone has att ned "the measure of the stature of a perfect man."

Singular to say, most of the great public charities of America have been founded by men of this party; most of the institutions of learning, the hospitals and asylums of all kinds. Drive out Nature with a dollar, still she comes back.

But man is man, can a dollar stop him? For ever? The instinct of development is as inextinguishable in man as the instinct of perpetuation in blackbirds and thrushes, who build their procreant nests under all administrations, theocratic or democratic. So there is another party which represents the majority of the people; that majority who have not money which is coveted, only the covetous desire thereof. This represents the acquisitive instinct of the people; not acquired wealth; not money moneyed, but money moneying,—*pecunia pecunians*, to state it Latin-wise. This is the Democratic party. It loves money as well as the Whig party, but has got less of it. However, with all its love of money, it has something of the momentum of the nation, something also of the instinct of mankind.

To the Whig party belong the rich, the educated, the decorous; the established,—those who look back, and count the money got. To the other party belong the young, the poor, the bold, the adventurous, everybody that is in want, everybody that is in debt, everybody who complains. The audacious are its rulers; often men destitute of lofty character, of great ideas, of justice, of love, of religion—bold, smart, saucy men. This party sneers at the rich, and hates them; of course it envies them, and lusts for their gold. It talks loudly against oppression in all corners of the world, except our own. The other party talks favourably of oppression, and shows its good side.

The Democratic party appeals to the brute will of the majority, right or wrong; it knows no higher law. Its statesmanship is the power to enact into permanent institutions the transient will of the majority: that is the ultimate standard. Popular and unpopular, take the place of right and wrong—*vox populi, vox Dei*; the vote settles what is true, what right. It regards money made and hoarded as the foe of human progress, and so is hostile to the millionaire. The Whig calls on his lord, "Money, help us!" To get money, the Democrat can do all things through the majority strengthening him.

The Catholic does homage to the wafer which a baker made, and a celibate priest addressed in Latin; it is to him the body of the Catholic God. The Protestant worships the Bible, a book written with ink, in Hebrew and Greek, "translated out of the original tongues, appointed to be read in churches." To him it is the word of God, the Protestant God. In the same way the Whig party worships money: it is the body of the Whig god; there is no higher law. T' ɔ Democratic party worships the opinion of the majority: it is the voice of the Democrat's god; there is no higher law. To the Whig party,—no matter how the money is got, by smuggling opium or selling slaves,—it is *pecunia pecuniata*,—money moneyed. To the Democratic party it is of no consequence what the majority wishes, or whom it chooses: Polk is as strong as Jackson— when voted in; and Pierce as great as Jefferson,—for office makes all men equally tall. Once the Democracy manfully protested against England's impressing American sailors —but refused to protect a coloured seaman;—and now it basely protests against America making any black man free. Once it went to war—righteously, perhaps, for aught I know—in order to take a marblehead fisherman out of a British ship, where he had been wickedly imprest ɔd. Now the same Democracy covets Cuba and Mexico, and seeks to make slaves out of millions of men, and spread slavery everywhere. If the majority wan : to violate the Constitution of America and the Declaration of Independence, or the constitution of the universe and the declaration of God, why! the cry is—"there is no high ɜr law!" "the greatest good of the greatest number!"—What shall become of the greatest good of the smaller number?

There is, therefore, no vital difference between the Whig party and the Democratic party; no difference in moral principle. The Whig inaugurates the money got; the Democrat inaugurates the desire to get the money. That is all the odds. So in the times that try the passions, which are the souls of these parties, the Democrat and the Whig meet on the same Baltimore platform. One is not higher and the other lower; they are just alike. There is only a hand rail between the two, which breaks down if you lean on it, and the parties mix. In common times, it becomes plain that a Democrat is but a Whig on time; a Whig is a Democrat arrived at maturity; his time has come. A Democrat is a young Whig who will legislate for money as soon as he has got it; the Whig is an old Democrat who once hurrahed for the majority—"Down with money! that is a despot! and up with the desire for it! Down with the rich, and up with the poor!" The young man, poor, obscure, and covetous, in 1812 was a Democrat, went a-privateering against England; rich, and accordingly ' one of our eminent citizens," in 1851 he was a Whig, and went a-kidnapping against Ellen Craft and Thomas Sims.

Bedini's hand is "thicker than itself with brother's blood." Young Democrats very properly burnt him in effigy. Old Democrats, wanting to be president, took him to their hearts. The young ones will also grow up in time to honour such future Nuncios of the Pope. I once new a crafty family which had two sons; both men of ability, and of remarkable unity of "principle." The family invested one in each party, and as it had a *head* on either side of the political penny thrown into the air, the family was sure to win. A New England family, wise in its generation.

Now, I do not mean to say that all Democrats or all Whigs are of this way of thinking. Quite the contrary. There is not a Whig or a Democrat who would confess it. The majority, so far as they have convictions, are very different from! this; but the Whig would say in his convention, that I told the truth of the Democratic party; the Democrat, in his convention, would say, I told the truth of the Whigs. These ideas,—they reside in the two parties, as botany in this camelia, as chemistry in the water, as in the drop the gravitation which brings it to the ground: not a conviction, but a fact. Each of these parties has great good to accomplish. Both seem indispensable. Money must be looked after. It is a valuable thing; the human race could not do without property. It is the ladder whereby we scale the heavens of manhood. But property alone is good for nothing. The will of the majority must be respected. I honour the ideas of the Democratic party, and of the Whig party, so far as they are just. But man is not made merely for money; the majority are the standard of power, not of right. There is a law of God which directs the chink of every dollar; it cannot roll except by the laws of the

Eternal Father of earth and heaven. What if the majority enact iniquity into a statute! Can millions make wrong right? Justice is the greatest good of all.

With little geographical check or interference from other nations, we are going on solving our problem of "manifest destiny." Since the establishment of Independence, America has made a rapid development. Her population has increased with unexampled rapidity; her territory has enlarged to receive her ever greatening family; riches have been multiplied faster even than their possessors. But some of the least lovely qualities of the Anglo-Saxon tribe have become dreadfully apparent. We have exterminated the Indians; we keep no treaties made with the red men; they keep all. The national materialism and indifference to great universal principles of right shows itself clearer and clearer. Submission to money or the majority is the one idea that pervades the nation. There are few great voices in the American churches which dare utter the Eternal Justice of the Infinite God and rebuke the wickedness of the nation, or talk as with a trumpet, COME UP HIGHER. We have taken a feeble tribe of men and made them slaves; we kidnap the baby newly born; tear him from his mother's arms, to sell him like swine in the market; the children of Jefferson and Madison are slaves in the Christian republic. The American treats his African victims with the intensest scorn. Even in Boston, spite of Constitution and Statute law, they are ignominiously thrust out of the common school. The clergy are the anointed defenders of slavery. The Whig party loves slavery as a tool for making money; the Democratic party, however, has the strongest antipathy to the African, and uses him for the same purpose. How many great American politicians care for him?

To obtain any considerable office in America, a man must conciliate one of these two—the money power or the majority power. But the particular body which sways the destinies of the nation, or its politics, is an army of slaveholders, some three hundred thousand strong. They direct the money; they sway the majority; and are the controlling force in America. They have been so for more than sixty years. I cannot now stop and weary you with showing how they acquired the power, and how they administer it.

In the history of mankind, this is the first attempt to found a State on the natural rights of man. It is not to be supposed that there should be national unity of action on so high a platform as that which the genius of Adams and Jefferson presented for the people then militant against oppression. There is a contradiction in the consciousness of the nation. In our industrial civilization, under the stimulus of love of wealth, and its consequent social and political power, we have made such a rapid advance in population and riches as no nation ever made. The lower powers of the understanding have also had a great development. We can plan, organize, and administer material means for material ends, as no nation has ever done. But it is not to be supposed that any people could pass all at once from the military civilization, with its fourfold despotism, to an industrial civilization with Democracy in its Church, State, community, and family. How slowly we learn; with what mistakes do we come to the true idea, and how painfully enact it into a deed! But see what results have come to pass.

In 1776, there were about 784,093 miles of territory; now there are 3,347,451. Then there were about two and a half millions of people; now there are four and twenty. In 1790, the annual revenue of America was less than four millions of dollars. Last year it was more than sixty-one. Then we had less than 698,000 slaves; now we have more than 3,204,000. In 1776, slavery was exceptional; the nation was ashamed of it. In 1774, Mr Jefferson had more democratic and Christian ideas than all Virginia has now. He said, "The abolition of domestic slavery is the greatest desire of the American people." In the first draft of the Declaration of Independence, he condemned England for fastening slavery upon us, forbidding us to abolish the slave-trade. He trembled when he remembered that "God is just." The leading men of the nation disliked slavery on principle. Some excused themselves for it,— "England forced it on us;" some thought it "expedient as a measure;" all thought it wrong as a principle.

During the Revolution, the white slaves who had been

soldiers, became free; there has not been any white slavery—of the old kind—since '76. I know some families in this city whose parents came to America as slaves—white slaves, I mean. They were bought in England; they were sold in America—sold under cruel laws. I should not like to mention their names; but in 1850, they were the most desperate Hunkers that could be found. Born of slaves, the iron had entered their contaminated souls, and they sought to enslave your brethren and my parishioners. These were the children of white slaves. The Indians were set free by laws. In most of the States, attempts were made to free the blacks. All the New England States set them free;—partly by the programme of principles in their Constitutions; partly by the decisions of courts; partly by statute law, enacted by the legislature. New York, New Jersey, Pennsylvania, soon followed. In twelve years after the Declaration of Independence, seven of the thirteen States had begun efforts to abolish slavery for ever. The truths of the Declaration carried forward New England and other Northern States; nay, the momentum of the Revolution carried the whole of Congress forward, and ere long, America performed two great acts, restricting Despotocracy—establishing freedom and not bondage. Here they are.

I. In 1787, the general government had jurisdiction over the North-Western territory, and decreed that therein slavery should never exist, to all time, save as a punishment for crime "duly convicted." On that spot, there have since grown up five great States; Ohio, Indiana, Illinois, Michigan, and Wisconsin. Five great States, with four and a half millions of men, and not a slave. Near a million children went to the schools of those States last year, and there is not a slave. Out of 239,345 square miles, there is not an inch of slave soil, except what stands in the shoes of Senator Douglas and his coadjutors. That is the first thing.

II. In 1808, America abolished the slave-trade. Before that it was carried on from the harbours of New England; Boston, Bristol, Newport, New York, added to their wealth by enslaving men. These were the great ports whence men cleared for Africa, to take in a cargo of slaves. It is still carried on from New York and Boston—but secretly; then it was openly done. Some of you, whose hoary heads dignify and give a benediction to this audience, may perhaps remember the great Rhode Island slave-trader, who occasionally visited this city, and if your eyes ever saw him, I know that your hearts—then hot with youth—recoiled with indignation at such a sight—a stealer of men! He seemed to be born for a slave-trader; he had a kidnapper's name on him at his birth. He was called *Wolf!*

These are the two acts of the Federal government against slavery since the Declaration of Independence. That is all that America has done against slavery, in eight and seventy years. She has multiplied her population tenfold, her revenue fifteenfold, and has abolished the slave-trade, and prohibited slavery in the North-Western territory. Now see what has been done in favour of slavery.

I. This is the first step: in 1787, America inaugurated slavery into the Constitution.

1. She left it in the slave States, as part of the "Republican" Institutions.

2. Next, she provided that the owners of slaves should have their property represented in Congress, five slaves counting the same as three freemen; and, at this day, in consequence of this iniquitous Act, for the 3,204,000 slaves which she has stolen and unjustly holds, the South has delegates in Congress equal to the representation of almost two millions of freemen in New England.

3. It was agreed, also, that slaves escaping from the service of their masters into a free State, should not thereby recover their freedom, but should be "delivered up."

Here were three concessions made to slavery at first. They were at variance with the programme of principles in the Declaration; the programme of purpose in the Constitution's preamble. They were known to be at variance with the religion of Jesus in the New Testament; at variance with the laws of Nature and of God. The Convention was ashamed of the whole thing, and added hypocrisy to its crime: it did not dare mention the word slave. That was the first great step against freedom. It has cost us millions of people. We should have had a population counting millions more. It has cost us hundreds of millions of money. The Whig is poorer, the Democrat has a smaller majority. Ay, it has cost us what is worth more than both money and human life—it has cost manhood; it has caused us crime, falseness to our nature and our God. Just now the "Christian Republic" commits a greater offence against the fundamental principles of all morality, all religion, than the Russian or the Turk, or any Pagan despotism in the wide world!

How came it? The North wanted a special privilege of navigation; and it let slavery into the Constitution for that pitiful price. Mr Gorham, a representative from Massachusetts, a Boston man, in the Convention, declared that Massachusetts wanted Union, not to defend herself, she could do so, and had done so, and had defended others along with her; but she wanted a special privilege to trade. I am ashamed to confess it,—that was the Massachusetts which had just come out of the Revolutionary war. Here was a "compromise" between the covetousness of the North, wanting a special privilege of navigation, and the idleness of the South, wishing to eat but not to earn. Between these two mill-stones the African man was crushed into a slave—a mere chattel "to all intents, constructions, and purposes whatsoever." That was the first step.

II. In 1792, America admitted Kentucky as a new State, made out of old soil, and established slavery therein. That was the first act of Congress establishing new slavery so far as she had power. Since then America has thrice repeated the experiment;—in 1796, establishing slavery in Tennessee; in 1817, in Mississippi; and in 1819, in Alabama—three new States made afresh out of old slave soil. That was the second step.

III. In 1793, America adopted slavery as a Federal institution; undertook herself, the Federal government, to seize and deliver up the fugitive slave. She took no such charge of other fugitive "property." She was not field-driver for horses and mules, only the hog-reeve for fugitive men, "endowed by their Creator with certain unalienable rights," "to life, liberty, and the pursuit of happiness." That was the third step; and the great "Expounder of the Constitution" declared it was "wholly unconstitutional;" every freeman, who thinks with a free mind, I am confident will say the same.

IV. In 1803, Louisiana was purchased from France and organized into a territory, with slavery in it. This was the first attempt of America to carry the hateful institution upon new soil, acquired since the Declaration of Independence. In 1812, Louisiana was admitted as a State with slavery in it; the first slave State made out of new soil, acquired after the Declaration. Hitherto slavery had been confined to the Atlantic slope of the continent; in 1792, the Federal government established it in the valley of the Mississippi; in 1803, for the first time, she carried it west of the great river. That was the fourth step.

V. In 1819-20, Missouri was organized as a State; in 1821, admitted with slavery in it. Before this time, slavery had receded from the North. On the Atlantic, it did not reach up to the fortieth parallel of latitude; on the Mississippi, it sunk below the thirty-seventh. But by admitting Missouri, it all at once rose to the fortieth parallel of latitude. Here, however, there was a great battle. The South wanted slavery to extend all the way from the Gulf of Mexico to the British line. The North wanted to restrict slavery by the Mississippi river, and not carry it west. A few Northern men were brought up; nothing is more marketable than Northern politicians, Whig or Democrat, it makes no odds, both are lieges of the almighty dollar. Wickedness prevailed; Missouri came in with her slaves. However, there was a "Compromise;" the celebrated Missouri Compromise, by which slavery was restricted in the Louisiana territory north of 36° 30'. Then, all the territory South thereof was made over to that institution. In 1836, Arkansas was organized as a territory, and came in as a State with slavery. In the territory of Louisiana, bought in 1803, there are now 423,172 slaves. That was the fifth step.

VI. In 1845, Florida was admitted as a slave State, with a constitution providing that the "general assembly shall have no power to pass laws emancipating slaves," or to forbid emigrants to bring their slaves with them. Here, slavery was extended over territory acquired for that purpose from Spain in 1819-21; made perpetual therein. It went down to the Gulf of Mexico, reaching far in. That was the sixth step.

VII. In 1845, Texas was "reannexed" and admitted as a State. This was territory whence the Mexicans had banished slavery. Slavery was in the Constitution of Texas; was carried west of the territory purchased of France, and spread over 325,520 square miles. It was established in a territory forty-three times greater than Massachusetts, by and by to be carved into more slave States. This was the first time that America had ever established slavery in any land whence any government had positively driven it out. That was the seventh step.

VIII. In 1848, at the conclusion of the war for plundering Mexico, by conquest and treaty we acquired California, Utah, and New Mexico—a territory of more than 596,000 square miles. This was coveted as new ground for the extension of slavery. The Mexican war was begun and continued for slavery; the land was to be slave soil. This was the first time we had conquered new land in battle for the sake of putting slavery on it. That was the eighth step.

IX. In 1850, you remember the cry, "The Union is in danger!"—How lustily men roared, "The Union is in danger!"—How the politicians talked, and the ministers! The "pedlars of oratory" took the stump. You remember the "Boston eloquence" that screamed, and tottered and stood a tiptoe, and spread its fingers, and tore its hair, and invaded the very heavens with its scary speech;— "The Union is in danger—this hour!" The celebrated Compromise measures were passed. So far as it concerns this question, they consisted of the Fugitive Slave Bill— of which I do not think you wish *me*, at least, to speak again; of the establishment of a territorial government in

New Mexico and Utah, extending slavery over 407,667 square miles,—a territory larger than fifty-three States of the size of Massachusetts; it paid Texas ten millions of money as a gift to slavery.

That was the greatest step of all since slavery was inaugurated in the Constitution. It was the most insulting to the North; it was most revolting to our political ideas and the principles of our professed religion. You remember the stir, and tumult, and storm. You have not forgotten the promise that "agitation was to cease." In 1852, the Whigs decided to "discountenance" agitation; and the Democrats, being stronger and more audacious, declared that they would resist all attempts to renew the agitation on the question of slavery, in Congress or out, in whatsoever shape. That was the ninth great step.

In 1776, African slavery existed in all the thirteen States. In a few years it shrunk southward. In 1790, the end of Delaware in 40° was its northern Atlantic limit; on the Mississippi, it fell away to less than 37°. Below the snaky line which separates Delaware, Maryland, Virginia, and Kentucky on the south, from New York, Pennsylvania, and Ohio, on the north, east of the "Father of Waters," on the Atlantic slopes of the continent—the monster had scope and verge enough. North and west of these limits he dared not show his head. But in that year, America bought of Maryland and Virginia a field "ten miles square," as capital of the United States; in 1800, the seat of government was transferred from Philadelphia to the district of Columbia; in 1802, Congress re-enacted the slave codes of Virginia and Maryland, extending them over the capital of the nation. Behold, the Federal government of the sole Christian Republic of the world has its head-quarters on slave soil! Congress had gone South—ominous change! Since that day, no State has abolished slavery. It still exists in the six old States, Delaware, Maryland, Virginia, North Carolina, South Carolina, and Georgia. It has spread into Kentucky, Tennessee, Alabama, Mississippi, four new States in twenty years made out of the territory of the old States. It has been put anew into Louisiana, Missouri, Arkansas, Florida, Texas,—five new States made out of territory acquired for extending the area of slavery. It has been carried to Utah and New Mexico,—land plundered from Mexico for this purpose. The white polygamy of Joe Smith, and the black polygamy of men yet more shameless, there flourish side by side. It has spread over 1,051,528 square miles, where there was no legal slavery at all in 1788. It has blotted the Mississippi Valley with more than 1,580,000 slaves. It has put slavery in a population of 8,250,808 white persons, which else would never have had an entailment of this curse upon their property, their education, and their morality, and their religion!

Why was all this? Has the South the most money, and so can buy up the North? the most votes, and so can scare us by overwhelming numbers? Not at all; the South is poor in money; in numbers she is weak. The North is strong in both. The South wanted slavery, the North did not want freedom for the African. Before 1808, Northern clergymen occasionally ventured their little savings in the slave-trade: since 1808, they obey with alacrity all attempts of the slave power to blaspheme the higher law of God! At each step, the South becomes more imperious, more insulting. She has served us right! Nine times she has demanded a sacrifice—nine times the North has granted the demand. In some twenty-four millions of men, every seventh man is a slave; the children of Jefferson and Madison are sold at public vendue. Senator Foote roared in the Capitol; his father's sons were slaves in the same street! It is "a great country;" a "Union" worth saving!

But who is to blame for all this? The North has had the majority in the Federal councils from the beginning. It is the North who is to blame for these nine steps—for establishing, spreading, fostering, and perpetuating the worst institution wherewith the Spaniard has dared to blot the Western continent. Who put slavery in the Constitution, made it Federal? who put it in the new States? who got new soil to plant it in? who carried it across the Mississippi—into Louisiana, Florida, Texas, Utah, New Mexico? who established it in the capital of the United States? who adopted slavery and volunteered to catch a runaway, in 1798, and repeated the act in 1850,—in defiance of all law, all precedent, all right? Why, it was the North. "Spain armed herself with bloodhounds," said Mr Pitt, "to extirpate the wretched natives of America."

In 1850, the Christian Democracy set worse bloodhounds afoot to pursue Ellen Craft; offered them five dollars for the run, if they did not take her; ten if they did! The price of blood was Northern money; the bloodhounds—they were kidnappers born at the North, bred there, kennelled in her church, fed on her sacraments, blessed by her priests! In 1778, Mr Pitt had a yet harsher name for the beasts wherewith despotic Spain hunted the red man in the woods—he called them *"Hell Hounds."* But they only hunted "savages, heathens, men born in barbarous lands." What would he say of the pack which in 1851 hunted American Christians, in the "Athens of America," and stole a man on the grave of Hancock and Adams—all Boston looking on, and its priests blessing the deed!

The slave power is now ready to take the tenth step. It wants these things; the acquisition of Cuba, the Mesilla Valley, the enslavement of Nebraska. Of the first and second I shall not now say anything. The third is a most important matter. It is an attempt to establish slavery in a new country. First, in a country where it never existed to any extent. There is only one American in the territory known to have ever held a slave. That is a missionary who went thither from Boston, and, for a thousand dollars, bought a man in Missouri, to serve as help for his sick wife,—the only slave ever held by an American in Nebraska, so far as Senator Douglas is informed; and of all men the most, he ought to know.

Next, it is an attempt by the Federal government to establish it in a territory where it has been prohibited by the Federal government itself, by the solemn enactment of Congress, made thirty-three years ago, at a time when all the North swore solemnly that it would not suffer slavery to come north another inch.

Do you know what is the population of Nebraska? There are not one thousand Americans in it. There is a delegate from Nebraska at Washington. He had *seventy votes, out of this vast territory!* There were two competitors, and I suppose there could not have been more than two hundred votes cast; I doubt if there were one hundred.

It is an immense territory, 95,000 square miles; larger than sixty-two States of the size of Massachusetts. It contains as much land as all the thirteen States that fought the Revolution, and more than 121,000 square miles besides. Draw a line from Trieste to Amsterdam,—Nebraska is larger than the part of Western Europe thus cut off. It contains more than all the fourteen Free States east of the Mississippi,—Maine, New Hampshire, Vermont, Massachusetts, Rhode Island, Connecticut, New York, New Jersey, Pennsylvania, Ohio, Michigan, Indiana, Illinois, and Wisconsin—and 83,393 square miles over and above. It reaches from the western boundary of Missouri to the Rocky Mountains. It extends from 37° north latitude to 49°—twelve degrees of latitude; and from 94° longitude to 114°—twenty degrees of longitude. Its waters run to the Gulf of Mexico, to the Pacific Ocean, and to Hudson's Bay. The blood of the slave will reach "Greenland's icy mountains," and stain the waters at the mouth of Baffin's Bay; the Saskatchawan, its great northern river, will drain the slave soil into Lake Winnepeg, and the keel of Captain Kane's ship, returning from his adventurous quest in the Arctic sea, will pass through waters that are darkened by the last great crime of America!

The slave power has long been seeking to extend its jurisdiction. It has eminently succeeded. It fills all the chief offices of the nation; the presidents are slave presidents; the supreme court is of slave judges, every one; the district judges,—you all know Judge Sprague, Judge Grier, Judge Kane. In all that depends on the political action of America, the slave power carries the day. In what depends on industry, population, education, it is the North. The slave power seeks to extend its institutions at the expense of humanity. The North works with it. In this century, the South has been foiled in only two efforts,—to extend slavery to California and Oregon: nine times it has succeeded.

Now see why the South wishes to establish slavery in Nebraska.

1. She wishes to gain a direct power in Congress. So she wants new slave States, that she may have new slave Senators to give her the uttermost power in the Senate of the United States.

2. Next, she wishes indirectly to gain power by directly checking the rapid growth of the free States of the North.

If Nebraska is free, the tide of immigration will set thither, as once to Ohio, Michigan, Illinois; as now to Wisconsin, Iowa, Minesota. There will be a rapid increase of freemen, with their consequent wealth, education, ideas, democratic institutions, free States, with consequent political power.

All this the South wishes to avoid; for the South—I must say it—is the enemy of the North. She is the foe to Northern industry—to our mines, our manufactures, and our commerce. Thrice, in my day, has she sought to ruin all three. She is the foe to our institutions—to our democratic politics in the State, our democratic culture in the school, our democratic work in the community, our democratic equality in the family, and our democratic religion in the Church. Hear what a great slave organ says of religion :—"The Bible has been vouchsafed to mankind for the purpose of keeping us out of hell-fire and getting us into heaven by the mysteries of faith and the inner life— not to teach us ethnology, government," &c. It is the Editor of the Richmond Examiner who says that, the American Chargé at Turin.

I say the South is the enemy of the North. England is the *rival* of the North, a powerful rival, often dangerous; sometimes a mean and dishonourable rival. But the South is our *foe*,—far more dangerous, meaner, and more dishonourable. England keeps treaties; the South breaks faith. She broke faith individually, and Webster lies there a wreck on the shore of his own estate; breaks it nationally, "and renews the agitation!" I always knew she would; I never trusted her lying breath; I warned my brothers and sisters against it: now she fulfils the expectation. She is the enemy of our material welfare and our spiritual development. Her success is our ruin. Our welfare shames her institutions, her ideas, and is the destruction to her "peculiar institution." She has been beaten in her effort to blot the territory of Oregon with slavery; but she never surrenders. This I honour in the South,—she is always true to her own institution, and her own idea. I honour the man who, on Plymouth Rock, when the sons of the Puritans crouched and shrunk down, and scarce one brave word could get spoken for humanity and the great rights of man which our fathers brought across the sea,—I honour the Southern man who stood up and claimed that slavery should be protected, on Plymouth Rock, and told one Northern candidate for the Presidency that he also had once offered and volunteered to shoulder his musket, "the old Middlesex musket," and march South to put down an insurrection of slaves. I say, I honour a man's fidelity to his own principle, even if it is a base one.

Such are the two general reasons why the South wishes slavery in this new territory. But here is a third reason, quite special.

3. There must be communication with the West. Three railroads are possible; one lies through Mexican territcry, but we have not got it, for the Gadsden treaty is not yet a fact accomplished:—two others lie through Nebraska territory. One or the other of them must be built. If Nebraska is free soil, the slave master cannot take his slave across, for the law of the free soil makes the black man free. But if Nebraska is a slave State, then the master can go there and carry his "chattels personal,"—coffles of men, droves of women, herds of children, attended by the "missionary from Boston," and the bloodhounds of the kidnapper. She wants right of way for her institution; a slave railroad from the Mississippi to the Pacific. Such are the reasons why she wants to establish slavery there.

See what encourages the South to make new encroachments. She has been eminently successful in her former demands, especially with the last. The authors of the Fugitive Slave Bill did not think that enormity could be got through Congress: it was too atrocious in itself, too insulting to the North. But Northern men sprang forward to defend it—powerful politicians supported it to the fullest extent. The worse it was, the better they liked it. Northern merchants were in favour of it—it "would conciliate the South." Northern ministers in all the churches of commerce baptized it, defended it out of the Old Testament, or the New Testament. The Senator of Boston gave it his mighty aid,—he went through the land a huckster of slavery, peddling Atheism: the Representative of Boston gave it his vote. Their constituents sustained both! All the great cities of the North executed the bill. The leading journals of Boston advised the merchants to withhold all commercial intercourse from towns which opposed kidnapping. There was a "Union Meeting" at Faneuil Hall. You remember the men on the platform: the speeches are not forgotten. The doctrine that there is a law of God above the passions of the multitude and the ambition of their leaders, was treated with scorn and hooting: a loud guffaw of vulgar ribaldry went up against the justice of the Infinite God ! All the great cities did the same. Atheism was inaugurated as the first principle of Republican government; in politics, religion makes men mad ! Mr Clay declared that "no Northern gentlemen will ever help return a fugitive slave!" What took place at Philadelphia? New York? Cincinnati?—nay, at Boston ? The Northern churches of commerce thought slavery was a blessing, kidnapping a "grace." The Democrats and Whigs vie with each other in devotion to the Fugitive Slave Bill. The "Compromises" are the golden rule. The North conquered her prejudices. The South sees this, and makes another demand. Why not? I am glad of it. She serves us right.

There is one thing more which helps her. The South, weak in numbers, weak in money, has yet a certain unity of idea,—that of slavery. She has the political skill to control the money and the numbers of the North. She always makes the Presidents. As the Catholic priest takes a bit of baker's bread, and says, "Bread thou art, become a God!" and the dough is God,—so the South takes any man and transubstantiates him,—"Thou art a man! become a President!" And by political transubstantiation Polk and Pierce are Presidents, to be "lifted up," to be exhibited," set on high, and worshipped accordingly. Now the Northern lump covets exceedingly this Presidential transubstantiation; but to attain thereunto, it must be of the right leaven for the South. A new President is presently to be kneaded together, to be baked to the requisite hardness, transubstantiated, and then set up in 1856. Several old *Ephraims*, alas ! cakes "not turned," begin to swell, and bubble, and crack, and break, hoping presently to be in condition to be transubstantiated. Some Northern dough is leavening itself to suit the Southern taste. Alas! "It is not in man that walketh to direct his steps." Many are leavened, but few rise. A Northern man, a bold adventurer, a bar-room politician of Illinois, born in Vermont, they say, has long coveted presidential transubtantiation. He has tempered his measures of meal with Southern leaven: he is a slave-holder—not born so; he courted slavery and "married on;" he has stirred into his character a great amount of appropriate leaven,—the "emptyings" of Southern firkins, the leavings of Southern feasts, the yeasty scum and froth of the Southern consciousness where slavery heats and swelters and keeps up a perpetual fermentation. In 1852, all his leaven was of no avail; even the heat of the Baltimore Convention could not make him rise to the requisite degree. Now he adds more potent leaven, and drugs his Northern dough, hoping the lump will rise a presidential loaf!

Mr. Douglas has made his bid for the Presidency. He claims that the Missouri Compromise was abolished in 1850. Nobody knew it then; not he himself: it is his last discovery.' Then he claims that Congress has no right to say that slavery shall not be in the territory.

So the question is, shall we let slavery into the two great territories of Kanzas and Nebraska? That is a question of political economy. Here it is. Shall men work with poor industrial tools, or with good ones? Shall they have the varied industry of New England and the North, or the slave labour of Virginia and Carolina? Shall their land be worth five dollars and eight cents an acre as in South Carolina, or thirty dollars and a half as in Connecticut? Shall the people all be comfortable, engaged in honest work, which enriches while it elevates; or shall a part be the poorest of the world that a few may be idle and rich?

It is a question of political morality. Shall the government be a commonwealth where all are citizens, or an aristocracy where man owns his brother man? Shall there be the schools of Ohio, or the ignorance of Tennessee? Shall it be a virtue and a dignity to teach, as it is in the public schools of Boston; a great charity, as some of you are administering in private schools for the ignorant and poor; or shall it be a crime, as in Virginia, where Mrs Douglas, by sentence of court, is now serving out her time in the House of Correction, for teaching a black child its letters? Shall there be the public libraries, newspapers, lectures, lyceums, of Massachusetts; or the ignorance, the ignoble sloth, of Mississippi and Alabama? Ay! it is a question of domestic morality. Shall a man have a right to his own limbs, his liberty, his life? Shall the mother own the babe that is born from her bosom? Shall she be a maid, and keep her innocence and her honour? Shall she be a wife, faithful to him that she loves, or shall she be the instrument of a master's lust, who has the law to enforce rape and violence? That is the question.

It is a great religious question. Shall the passions and ambition of base men have rule in Nebraska, or the natural law of the most high God? The Unitarian Autumnal Convention at Worcester debated the great question, whether men should have a Litany in the churches. The American Tract Society, the American Missionary Society, have questions of similar magnitude, which come before them. *This* is not thought a religious question. It is only one which concerns the welfare of millions of men, in hundreds of years yet to come; ay, thousands! The prayer of the Puritan, his self-denial, his trust in God, and love of the right,—they are the best inheritance New England ever got—shall we extend the best institutions of New England to Nebraska; or shall we send there the slave-driver with his whip, with his bloodhound, with his politician and his ——! shall I say the next word? I pass it by. That question must be answered in a month; in one short month; ay! perhaps, in a week.

In sixty years, Virginia has not doubled her population, while New York has ten times the population of 1790. The most valuable export of Virginia, is her slaves, enriched by the "best blood of the old dominion;" the "Mother of Presidents" is also the great slave-breeder of America. Since she ceased to import bondmen from Africa, her slaves become continually paler in the face; it is the "effect of the climate"—and Democratic institutions. One quarter of her slaves have but one-fourth African blood in their veins; half of her slaves are half white. The Ethiopian is changing his skin. Beneficent "effect of the climate"—and Democratic institutions! By the laws of Virginia, it is a crime punishable by imprisonment, to deny the master's right to hold his slave; it was lately proposed in her Legislature, to exclude from the jury-box all persons guilty of this opinion. Her present law provides that men of three-fourths white descent shall be free—it is now proposed to enslave all who have less than nine-tenths Caucasian blood; so the blood of "Jefferson and Sally," uncontaminated by any new African admixture, must pass through yet four other slave-breeding Presidents before it is entitled to freedom! New York has 862,507 children at her public schools. Virginia makes it a crime to teach writing and reading to slaves. Her highest literature is partisan newspapers and speeches; her noblest men are nothing but party politicians; her chief manufacture is slaves—children of her own Caucasian loins, begotten for exportation. She stocks the plantations of Alabama and the bagnios of New Orleans. Shall we establish in Nebraska the institutions of Virginia? Let the North answer.

I know Northern politicians say, "slavery will never go there!" Do they believe their own word? They believe it! In 1820, they said it could not go to Missouri; then, there were but 10,222 therein; now 87,422! more than a quarter of all the slaves in the United States are north of 36° 30'. Desperate men from the slave States of the Atlantic and the Mississippi, too miserable to reach California, will find their El Dorado in Nebraska, take slaves there and work their lives out! It will be a better breeding State than Virginia herself.

Congress, it is said, has no right to legislate for the people of the territory against slavery. It must be left to the inhabitants thereof. There are 485,000 square miles,—not 1000 men, not two hundred voters. Shall two hundred squatters entail slavery on a country as large as all Germany, Switzerland, France, Belgium, and Holland? Is it "democratic" for Congress to allow two hundred stragglers in the wilderness, cheating the Indians, swearing, violent, half of them unable to write or read,—is it democratic in Congress to allow these vagabonds of the wilderness to establish the worst institution which Spain brought out of the middle ages; which Western Europe casts off with scorn; which Russia treads under her feet; which Turkey rejects with indignation,—and spread this over a country larger than the whole Roman empire when Julius Cæsar was cradled in his mother's arms? If it is so, let me go back and, O most Imperial Nicholas! let me learn political justice from thee, thou last great tyrant of the Western world!

Suppose we grant this,—will that be the end? Suppose slavery flows into Nebraska,—is that all? This is the tenth time that slavery has demanded a great wrong, and the North has said, "Yes, I will do it." Each time it has been a greater and worser wrong. Our great enemy demands sacrifices, not of interests but of principle; the sacred principle of natural right, allegiance to the Eternal God. "Grant it," say they, "or we will dissolve the Union." Presently the cry will be raised again, "Save the Union! Oh! save the Union." "The Union is in danger—this hour!" will be rung again in our deceived ears. Suppose it is granted. Only once in seventy years has the Southern demand been rejected,—when she asked to put slavery into Oregon. But the conscience of the North,—there is not much of it,—not enough to act, only to grumble, or perchance to swear. The conscience of the North complains. "Stop that agitation, or I will dissolve the Union at once," says the South. Then the North says again, "Hush! Save the Union!" and there will not be a whisper from Whig or Democrat. The Church has got its mean mouth sewed up with an iron thread.

Then the South will demand again, "Grant us this demand, or we will dissolve the Union!"—and the same thing goes over and over again. Do you think the North fears a dissolution of the Union? As much as I fear that this handful of flowers shall rise and strike the life out of my soul. *No! No!* Think not of that. Is it love of country which prompts the Northern sacrifice of conscience? No! never! Never, no! It is love of the dollar. It is love of the power of the majority, of the slave-holder's power; not love of man, but love of money. While the North can make money by the Union, there is no danger of dissolution!

Grant this, and see what follows. I omit the probable acts of individual States, over which Congress has no direct control.

I. The South will claim that the master has a right to take his slaves into a free State—spite of its laws to the contrary—and hold them there—first, for a definite time, say seven years; next, for an indefinite period in perpetuity. That will restore slavery to the North and enable the sons of New England to return to their native land with their "chattels personal." Perhaps it will require no Act of Congress to do this—and "supersede" the Ordinance of 1787, or declare it "inoperative and void." The whole may be done any day by the Supreme Court of the United States; any day when the President shall say, "Down with you, judges. Do as you are bid." Whigs and Democrats can do all things through money, which strengtheneth them! will the North consent? Why not, nothing is so supple as the Northern neck.

II. Then the South will seek more slave territory. Here is what is wanted:—a part of Mexico,—the Gadsden treaty stipulates for about 89,000,000 acres, eight States as large as Massachusetts; Cuba, which the slave power has long coveted; Porto Rico; Hayti, which the Democratic Christians hate with such bitterness; Jamaica and the other West Indies; the Sandwich Islands; other parts of the Northern and Southern continent. Slavery must be put in all these places. Will the North consent? Why not? habit makes all things easy. What an excellent "field for religious enterprise" Hayti would be, if this Republic should restore slavery to St Domingo! Conquer your prejudices!

III. Then she will seek to restore the African slave-trade. Here are the steps. 1. to authorize any State to import slaves; 2. to authorize any individual to do so in spite of the adverse laws of any State, which will be declared "inoperative and void," or "superseded." I can foresee the arguments for the measure—Whig and Democratic—Yes, the theological arguments, drawn from the Bible, from "conscience and the Constitution." Some future Unitarian Doctor of Divinity, I suppose, for a "consideration" will be afraid of a "dissolution of the Union," and solve the problem of human destination by offering to sacrifice his own brother, sister, wife, daughter, mother! Will the North consent? Why stop at the thirteenth demand and not at the first, at the ninth? Is it worse to steal Heathen men in Africa than Christian babies in Virginia? Worse to steal the son of Pumbo Jumbo than the daughters of Jefferson! Why should not the North consent—all the slaves are to be voluntary "Missionaries for civilization and Christianity!" What is there which the North will not consent to?

Some of you may live long enough to see all this. The Union has been in danger five times, and five times saved by sacrifice of those principles which lie at the basis of the nation, and are its glory. Is that too sad a prophecy, even to be spoken? It is not worse for the fifty years to come, than for the fifty years past; it is only the history of the last fifty years.

In 1775, what if it had been told the men all red with battle at Lexington and Bunker Hill,—" your sons will gird the Court House with chains to kidnap a man; Boston will vote for a Bill which puts the liberty of any man in the hands of a commissioner, to be paid twice as much for making a slave as for declaring a freeman; and Boston will call out its soldiers to hunt a man through its streets!" What if on the 19th of April, 1775, when Samuel Adams said, "Oh! what a glorious morning is this!" as he heard the tidings of war in the little village where he passed the night,—what if it had been told him,—" that on the 19th of April, seventy-six years from this day, will your city of Boston land a poor youth at Savannah, having violated her own laws, and stained her magistrates' hands, in order to put an innocent man in a slave-master's jail?" What if it had been told him that Ellen Craft must fly out of democratic Boston, to monarchic, theocratic, aristocratic England, to find shelter for her limbs, her connubial innocence, and the virtue of her woman's heart? I think Samuel would have cursed the day in which it was said a man-child was born, and America was free! What if it had been told Mayhew and Belknap, that in the pulpits of Boston, to defend kidnapping should be counted to men as righteousness? They could not have believed it .They did not know what baseness could suck the Northern breast, and still be base.

Who is to blame? The South? Well, look and see! In the House of Representatives there are eighty-eight Southern men; there are one hundred and forty-four from the North. In the Senate, the South has thirty, the North thirty-two. But out of the two and thirty Northern Senators, not twelve men can be found to protest against this wicked Bill. The President is a Northern man; the Cabinet has the majority from the North; the committee of Senators who reported this Bill has a majority of Northern men; its chairman is a Northern man.

The very men who enacted the Fugitive Slave Law turn pale; but what do they do? They do nothing! Where is the North? Where has it been these fifty years back?—at the feet of the South. Where are the Northern ideas—where is the Northern conscience, the Northern right! Oh, tell me, where? Is it in your Legislature? Listen! See if you can hear any faint breathings of the great Northern heart, that fought the war of Independence. At least, it is in the cities. Listen! In Boston, the "great men" who control Church and State—they have called conventions, have they? prepared resolutions—got them ready—had preliminary meetings—have they? Nothing of it. There is not a mouse stirring amongst them. It is all right, I suppose, in the little towns? There is the Northern heart—a great conscience, that says, "Give me liberty or give me death!"—"Resistance to tyrants is obedience to God!" Listen to Massachusetts! Can you hear anything? Well, I am a minister. It is in the pulpits of the North, perhaps. Hark! The Bible rustles, as that Southern wind, heavy with slavery, turns over its leaves rich in benedictions; and I hear the old breath come up again—"Thou shalt love thy neighbour as thyself"—"Inasmuch as ye have not done it unto one of the least of these my brethren, ye have not done it unto me." Is that the voice of the pulpit? Oh, no! That is the voice of a Hebrew peasant; a poor woman's son. In his own time, they said "He hath a devil." They hung him as a "blasphemer," an "infidel." That is not the pulpit's voice. Listen again. Here it is: "I would send back my own mother." That is the answer of the American pulpit. Eight and twenty thousand Protestant ministers! The foremost sect of them all debated, a little while ago, whether it should have a Litany, and on what terms it should admit young men to the communion table—allow them to drink "grocers' wine," and eat "bakers' bread," on the "Lord's day," in the "Lord's house;" and never dared to lift that palsied hand, in which was once the fire and blood of Channing, against the world's mightiest sin. Eight and twenty thousand Protestant ministers, and not a sect that is opposed to slavery! Oh, the Church! the Church of America! False to the great prophets of the Old Testament, the great world's Prophet of the New; false to the fathers whose bloody knees once kissed the Rock of Plymouth!

The Northern conscience, the Northern religion, the Northern faith in God—where is it? Is it in the midst of the people—the young men and the young women; in your hearts and in my heart? Let us see. Let our actions speak. Now is the time; a month hence may be too late; ay, a week, and the deed may be done. Let us, at least, be manly, and do our part.

Well, let us contend bravely against this wicked device of men who are the enemies alike of America and mankind. I call on all men who love man and love God, to oppose this extension of slavery. Talk against it, preach against it, print against it—by all means, act against it. Call meetings of the towns to oppose it, of the Congressional districts, of the State, yea, of all the free States. Make a fire in the rear of your timid servants in Congress. Let us fight manfully, contesting the ground inch by inch, till at last we are driven back to the Rock of Plymouth. There let us gather up the wreck of the old ship which brought over the three churches of Plymouth, Salem, Boston,—whose children have so often proved false,—therewith let us build new our Mayflower, make Plymouth our Delft-haven, launch again upon the sea, sailing to Greenland or to Africa, by prayer to lay other deep foundations, and in the wilderness to build up the glorious liberty of the sons of God.

But we shall not toil in vain. Slavery is nothing. It exists only by a whim. Theocracy is nothing. Monarchy is nothing, Aristocracy nothing; America has no "Pope," no "King," no "Noble;" a breath unmakes them as a breath once made. Slavery is no more if we say it; the monster dies. In one day the North could annihilate all the slavery which depends on the Federal Government—abolish it on the Federal soil, the capital, and the territories; abolish the American slave-trade, declare it piracy, or other felony. That would be only common legislation. The next day we could abolish it in the slave States. That would be revolution.

America has one great enemy—slavery, our deadliest foe. Do you believe it is always to last? I tell you no! O young America! are you sure there is no law higher than love of money and power? sure there is no justice? no God? Quite sure of that? Men have sometimes been mistaken who reckoned without that Host.

Political economy is against slavery; it is a poor tool to work with. Compare Kentucky and Ohio, Virginia with Pennsylvania and New York! Do you believe that shifty Americans will always use the poor, rude instrument of the savage? They love riches too well. How weak slavery makes a nation! In time of war how easy it would be for the enemy to raise up the 385,000 slaves of South Carolina against the 283,000 whites! Where would then be the "chivalry" of that mediæval State?

Slavery hinders the education and the industry of the people; it is fatal to their piety. Think of a religious kidnapper! a Christian slave-breeder! a slave-trader loving his neighbour as himself, receiving the "sacraments" in some Protestant church from the hand of a Christian apostle, then the next day selling babies by the dozen, and tearing young women from the arms of their husbands, to feed the lust of lecherous New Orleans! Imagine a religious man selling his own children into eternal bondage! Think of a Christian defending slavery out of the Bible, and declaring there is no higher law, but Atheism is the first principle of Republican government!

"Slavery is the sum of all villanies;" what can save it? Things refuse to be mismanaged for ever. All the world is against us. It is only in America that slave-trading, slave-breeding is thought Christian and Democratic. Mr Slatter, who had become rich by trading in the souls of men, and famous for preserving the Union, in his slave-pen at the capital of the Christian Republic, once entertained the President of the United States at his costly house in Baltimore;—I forget whether it was Southern Mr Polk, or Northern Mr Fillmore; slavery has thrown down the partition-wall between Whig and Democrat. What European despot would have eaten salt with a man whose business was to sell misery by the wholesale, and to retail the agony of women? Even the mediæval Pope, the slave of stronger despots, who appropriately sends us his red-handed Bedini, to be lauded by aspirants for the Presidency—would shrink from this. No Russian despot has his sons as slaves to wait on him at table. You must come to America to find a Cossack President who could boast that honour! Do you believe this wickedness is always to continue? Can the Anglo-Saxon become Spanish? New England like Bolivia, Peru, Laguira, Mexico? The wheels of time turn not back. We cannot break the continuity of human history. See how mankind marches towards freedom, each step a revolution. See what has been done in four hundred years, for the freedom of man in Italy, France, Germany, Switzerland, Holland, or even in Spain! Lay down your ear to the great deep of humanity, and hearken to the ground-swell which goes on therein. That roar of mighty waters, does it whisper security to the tyrant? The next four hundred years what shall it do against Theocracy, Monarchy, Aristocracy, Despotocracy?

See what the Anglo-Saxon in Europe has done for freedom since the first James! Compare the England of 1854 with the England of 1604. What a growth of liberal institutions; of freedom in the people! England loving liberty, loving law, goes on still building up the Cyclopæan walls of humanity, the bulwark of freedom for mankind. See what the same Anglo-Saxon has done in America. Compare the colonies of 1754 with the States of 1854. What a progress! Are we to stop here?

See what Massachusetts has done. Slavery was always a contradiction in the consciousness of New England. So in 1641, Massachusetts enacted that "there shall never be any bond-slavery, villanage, or captivity amongst us, unless it be lawful captives taken in just wars," &c. In 1646, the colony bore "witness against the heinous and crying sin of man-stealing," and restored to Guinea some captives wickedly taken thence. But yet slavery existed, and cruel laws afflicted its victims. Listen to the following. In 1636, "it is ordered that no servant shall be set free—until he have served out the time covenanted:" that "when any servants shall run away from their masters . . . it shall be lawful for the next magistrate, or the constable and two of the chief inhabitants where no magistrate is, to press men and boats or pinnaces at the public charge, to pursue such persons by sea or land, and bring them back by force of arms." In 1703, a law forbade negro, mulatto, or Indian servants or slaves " to be found abroad in the night time after nine o'clock." They were "to be openly whipped by the constable." If a negro or mulatto should strike any person of the English,—he was to be " severely whipped at the discretion of the justices." In 1705, a duty of four pounds was levied on each slave imported, and a drawback allowed in case he was "exported within the space of twelve months." Marriage between white and black was illegal; a fine of fifty pounds punished the officer who joined the parties. It is not a hundred years since slaves were sold in Massachusetts; children were torn from their parents; the charms of young women were advertised in the public print. In less than a hundred years, two slaves were burned alive on Boston Neck for poisoning their master. Now Massachusetts has torn these wicked laws from her Statute-book. It is only Boston which turns a black boy out of her public school. Do you think the Northern men love slavery, the people love it? In all the parties there are noble men who hate American slavery. They know it is a wicked thing; they despise their politicians who seek to perpetuate it, and loathe the purchased priests who justify the iniquity in the name of God! Each of the nine sacrifices to slavery has been unpopular at the North. Only the politicians approved them. The Constitution was adopted with difficulty. New England hated its inauguration of slavery as a power in the Republic. The Fugitive Slave Bill of 1793—why, even Washington did not venture to pursue his slave by its authority and seize her. She was safe even in the native State of Webster and of Pierce! The Mexican war was unpopular. It was not "with alacrity" that the North obeyed the wicked act of 1850. Boston saw her saddest day when she kidnapped Thomas Sims. It could not be done but with chains round the Court House, judges crawling under, and a regiment of flunkeys billeted in Faneuil Hall. If the question of the enslavement of Nebraska were this day put to the vote of the people, in nineteen twentieths of all the towns of the North, nineteen twentieths of the voters would say No. The people are right; though, alas, not very earnest. There are a few politicians, also, who hate slavery. There are noble ministers of all sects save the Catholic, true to their high calling, honouring the great Philanthropist they worship, who hate American slavery, and preach against it in spite of the Pharisee, the Sadducee, and the hypocrite, who thereupon tighten against the minister the strings of the parish purse. I have no words to tell how much I honour such men! True ministers of Christ, they put the churches of commerce to continual shame. I never knew of a Catholic priest who favoured freedom in America; a slave himself, the mediæval theocracy eats the heart out from the celibate monk!

Slavery is one great enemy of America, but there is one other foe—corrupt politicians fillibustering for the Presidency, defending slavery out of the New Testament, volunteering to shoulder their musket and shoot down men claiming their unalienable rights; politicians who deny God's higher law, who call upon us to conquer our prejudices against wickedness, inaugurating Atheism as the first principle of government. In 1788, they put slavery into the Constitution; in 1850, they enacted iniquity into law; and in 1854, they are about their old work "saving the Union." Shall such men always prevail? the mediæval Catholic against the free minister of piety! the corrupt politician fillibustering for office against the people—the American idea in their heads, and humanity in their hearts! Even the Catholic shall learn.

Slavery must die. See how monarchy withdrew in front of White Hall in 1648! How slavery disappeared from St Domingo in 1790! Shall American slavery end after that sort, or as it ended in New England; as Old England put it down in Jamaica? Down it must. God does not forget. His justice is wrought into the world's great heart. See what changes perplex the monarchs of the world—with what strides mankind goes forward! The fourth tyrant must follow to the same tomb with the rest. It is for you and me to slay him!

Half a million immigrants annually find a shelter on our shores. "Westward the course of empire takes its way." Ay, it will come eastward—and Asia already begins to send us her children. What a noble destination is before us if we are but faithful. Shall politicians come between the people and the eternal right—between America and her history! When you remember wh̄ . our fathers have done; what we have done—substituted a new industrial for a military state, the self-rule of this day for the vicarious government of the middle ages; when you remember what a momentum the human race has got during its long run—it is plain that slavery is on the way to end.

As soon as the North awakes to its ideas, and uses its vast strength of money, its vast strength of numbers, and still more gigantic strength of educated intellect, we shall tread this monster underneath our feet. See how Spain has fallen—how poor and miserable is Spanish America. She stands there a perpetual warning to us. One day the North will rise in her majesty, and put slavery under our feet, and then we shall extend the area of freedom. The blessing of Almighty God will come down upon the noblest people the world ever saw—who have triumphed over Theocracy, Monarchy, Aristocracy, Despotocracy, and have got a Democracy—a government of all, for all, and by all—a Church without a bishop, a State without a king, a community without a lord, and a family without a slave.

AN ADDRESS

ON THE

CONDITION OF AMERICA,

BEFORE

THE NEW YORK CITY ANTI-SLAVERY SOCIETY,
AT ITS FIRST ANNIVERSARY,

HELD AT THE BROADWAY TABERNACLE, MAY 12, 1854.

LADIES AND GENTLEMEN :—I shall ask your attention, this evening, to some few thoughts on the present condition of the United States in respect to slavery. After all that has been said by wise, powerful, and eloquent men in this city, this week, perhaps I shall have scarce anything to present that is new.

As you look on the general aspect of America to-day, its main features are not less than sublime, while they are likewise beautiful exceedingly. The full breadth of the continent is ours, from sea to sea, from the great lakes to the great gulf. There are three million square miles, with every variety of climate, and soil, and mineral; great rivers, a static force, inclined planes for travel reaching from New Orleans to the Falls of St Anthony, from the mouth of the St Lawrence to Chicago; smaller rivers, a dynamic force, turning the many thousand mills of the industrious North. There is a coast most richly indented, to aid the spread of civilization. The United States has more than twelve thousand miles of shore line on the continent; more than nine thousand on its islands; more than twenty-four thousand miles of river navigation. Here is the material groundwork for a great state—not an empire, but a commonwealth. The world has not such another.

There are twenty-four millions of men; fifteen and a half millions with Anglo-Saxon blood in their veins—strong, real Anglo-Saxon blood; eight millions and a half more of other families and races, just enough to temper the Anglo-Saxon blood, to furnish a new composite tribe, far better, I trust, than the old. What a human basis for a state to be erected on this material groundwork!

On the Eastern slopes of the continent, where the high lands which reach from the Katahdin mountains in Maine to the end of the Appalachians in Georgia—on the Atlantic slopes, where the land pitches down to the sea from the 48th to the 28th parallel, there are fifteen States, a million square miles, communicating with the ocean. In the South, rivers bear to the sea rice, cotton, tobacco, and the products of half-tropic agriculture; in the North, smaller streams toil all day, and sometimes all night, working wood, iron, cotton, and wool into forms of use and beauty, while iron roads carry to the sea the productions of temperate agriculture, mining, and manufactures.

On the Western slope, where the rivers flow down to the Pacific Ocean from the 49th to the 32nd parallel, is a great country, almost eight hundred thousand square miles in extent. There, too, the Anglo-Saxon has gone; in the South, the gold-hunter gathers the precious metals, while the farmer, the miner, and the woodman collect far more precious products in the North.

In the Great Basin between the Cordilleras of the West and the Alleghanies, where the Mississippi drains half the continent to the Mediterranean of the New World, there also the Anglo-Saxon has occupied the ground—twelve hundred thousand square miles; in the South to rear cotton, rice, and sugar; in the North to raise cattle and cereal grasses, for beast and for man.

What a spectacle it is! A nation not eighty years old, still in its cradle, and yet grown so great. Two hundred and fifty years ago, there was not an Anglo-Saxon on all this continent. Now there is an Anglo-Saxon commonwealth twenty-four millions strong. Rich as it is in numbers, there are not yet eight men to the square mile.

All this is a Republic; it is a Democracy. There is no born priest to stand betwixt the nation and its God; no Pope to entail his "nephews" on the Church; no bishop claiming divine right to rule over the people and stand betwixt them and the Infinite. There is no king, no born king, to ride on the nation's neck. There are noble-men, but none noble-born to usurp the land, to monopolize the government and keep the community from the bosom of the earth. The people is priest and makes its own religion out of God's revelation in man's nature and history. The people is its own king to rule itself; its own noble to occupy the earth. The people make the laws and choose their own magistrates. Industry is free; travel is free; religion is free; speech is free; there are no shackles on the press. The nation rests on industry, not on war. It is formed of agriculturists, traders, sailors, miners—not a nation of soldiers. The army numbers ten thousand—one soldier for every twenty-four thousand men. The people are at peace; no nation invades us. The government is firmly fixed and popular. A nation loving liberty, loves likewise law; and when it sets a plant of liberty, it fences it all round with law as high up as the hands can reach. We annually welcome four hundred thousand immigrants who flee from the despotism of the Old World.

The country is rich—after England, the richest on earth in cultivated lands, roads, houses, mills. Four million tons of shipping sail under the American flag. This year we shall build half a million tons more, which, at forty dollars a ton, is worth twenty millions of dollars. That is the ship crop. Then, the corn crop is seven hundred millions of bushels of Indian corn. What a harvest of coal, copper, iron, lead, of wheat, cotton, sugar, rice, is produced!

Over all and above all these there rises the great American political idea, a "self-evident truth,"—which cannot be proved—it needs no proof; it is anterior to demonstration; namely, that every man is endowed by his Creator with certain unalienable rights, and in these rights all men are equal; and on these the government is to rest, deriving its sole sanction from the governed's consent.

Higher yet above this material groundwork, this human foundation, this accumulation of numbers, of riches, of industry—as the cross on the top of a tall, wide dome, whose lantern is the great American political idea—as the cross that surmounts it rises the American religious idea—one

God; Christianity the true religion; and the worship of God by love; inwardly it is piety, love to God,—outwardly love to man—morality, benevolence, philanthropy.

What a spectacle to the eyes of the Scandinavian, the German, the Dutchman, the Irishman, as they view America from afar! What a contrast it seems to Europe. There liberty is ideal; it is a dream; here it is organic, an institution; one of the establishments of the land.

That, ladies and gentlemen, is the aspect which America presents to the oppressed victims of European despotism in Church and in State. Far off on the other side of the Atlantic, among the Apennines, on the plains of Germany and in the Sclavonian lands, I have met men to whom America seemed as this fair-proportioned edifice that I have thus sketched out before your eyes. But when they come nearer, behold, half the land is black with slavery. In 1850, out of more than two hundred and forty hundred thousand Americans, thirty-two hundred thousand were slaves—more than an eighth of the population counted as cattle; not as citizens at all. They are only human material, not yet wrought into citizens:—nay, not counted *human*. They are cattle, property; not counted men, but animals and no more. Manhood must not be extended to them. Listen while I read to you from a Southern print. It was recommended by the Governor of Alabama that the Legislature should pass a law prohibiting the separation of families; whereupon the *Richmond Enquirer* discourses thus: " This recommendation strikes us as being most unwise and impolitic. If slaves are property, then should they be at the absolute disposal of the master, or be subject only to such legal provisions as are designed for the protection of life or limb. If the relation of master and slave be infringed for one purpose, it would be difficult to fix any limit to the encroachment." They are property, no more, and must be treated as such, and not as men.

Slavery is on the Atlantic slopes of the continent. There are one million six hundred thousand slaves between the Alleghany range and the Atlantic coast. Slavery is in the central basin. There are a million and a half of slaves on the land drained by the Mississippi. Spite of law and constitution, slavery has gone to the Pacific slopes, travelling with the gold-hunter into California. The State whose capital county "in three years committed over twelve hundred murders" has very appropriately legalized slavery for a limited time. I suppose it is only preliminary to legalizing it for a time limited only by the Eternal God. In the very capital of the Christian Democracy there are four thousand purchased men. In the Senate-house, a few years ago, a Mississippi Senator belched out his imprecations against that one New Hampshire Senator who has never yet been found false to humanity. Mr Foote was a freeman, a citizen, and a "Democrat;" and while, in the halls of Congress, he was threatening to hang John P. Hale on the tallest pine tree in Mississippi, there toiled in a stable, whose loft he slept in by night, one of that Senator's own brothers. The son of Mr Foote's father was a slave in the capital of the United States, while his half-brother—by the father's side—threatened to hang on the tallest pine in Mississippi the only Senator that New Hampshire sent to Washington who dared be true to truth and free for freedom.

But a few years ago, Mr Hope H. Slatter had his negro market in the capital of the United States; one of the greatest slave-dealers in America. He was a member also, it is said, of a "Christian church." The slave-pen is a singular institution for a democratic metropolis, and the slave-trader a peculiar ornament for the Christian church in the capital of a democracy. He grew rich, went to Baltimore, had a fine house, and once entertained a "President of the United States" in his mansion. The slave-trader and the democratic President met together—Slatter and Polk! fit guest and fitting host!

In all the three million square miles of American land there is no inch of free soil, from the St John's to the Rio Gila, from Madawasca to San Diego. The star-spangled banner floats from Vancouver's Island by Nootka Sound to Key West on the South of Florida, and all the way the flag of our Union is the standard of slavery. In all the soil that our fathers fought to make free from English tyranny, there is not an inch where the black man is free, save the five th----sand miles which Daniel Webster surrendered to Lord A------rton by the treaty of 1842. The symbol of the Union is a fetter. The President should be sworn on the auction-block of a slave-trader. The New Hampshire

President, in his Inaugural, declared publicly his allegiance to the slave power—not to the power of Northern mechanics, free farmers, free manufacturers, freemen; but allegiance to the slave power; he swears special protection to no property but "property" in slaves; specific allegiance to no law but the Fugitive Slave Bill; devotion to no right but the slaveholder's "right" to his property in man.

The supreme court of the United States is a slave court; a majority of the Senate and of the House of Representatives the same. It has been so this forty years. The majority of the House of Representatives are obedient to the lords of the lash; a majority of Northern politicians, especially of that denomination which is called "dough-faces," are only overseers for the owner of the slave. Mr Douglas is a great overseer; Mr Everett is a little overseer.

The nation offers a homestead out of its public land; it is only to the white man. What would you say if the Emperor of Russia offered land only to nobles; the Pope only to priests; Queen Victoria only to lords? Each male settler in Utah, it seems, is to have four hundred and eighty acres of land, if he is not married, and a hundred and sixty more, I believe, according to one proposition, for every wife that he has got. But if he have the complexion of the only children that Madison left behind him, he can have no land at all.

Even a Boston school-house is shut against the black man's children. The arm of the city government slams the door in every coloured boy's face. His father helps pay for the public school; the son and daughter must not come in.

In the slave States, it is a crime to teach the slave to read and write. Out of four millions of children of America at school in 1850, there were twenty-six thousand that were coloured. There were more than four hundred thousand free coloured persons, and there were more than two hundred and fourteen thousand thereof under the age of twenty; of these, there were at school only twenty-six thousand—one child in nine! Out of three and a quarter millions of slaves, there was not one at school. It is a crime by the statute in every slave State to teach a slave to spell "God." He may be a Christian; he must not write "Christ." He must worship the Bible; he must not read it! It is a crime even in a Sunday school to teach a child the great letters which spell out "Holy Bible." I knew a minister, he was a Connecticut man, too, who went off from New Orleans because he did not dare to stay; and he did not dare to stay because he tried to teach the slave to read in his Sunday school. He went back to Connecticut, whence he will, perhaps, go as a missionary to China or Turkey, and find none to hinder his Christian work.

At the North, the black man is shut out of the meetinghouse. In heaven, according to the theology of America, he may sit down with the just made perfect, his sins washed white "in the blood of the Lamb;" but when he comes to a certain Baptist church in Boston, he cannot own a pew. And there are few churches where he can sit in a pew. The rich and the poor are there; the one Lord is the Maker of them all; but the church thinks He did not make the black as well as the white. Nay; he is turned out of the omnibus, out of the burial-ground. There is a burial-ground in this State, and in the deed which conveys the land it is stipulated that "no coloured person or convict" can ever be buried there. He is turned out of the graveyard, where the great mother of our bodies gathers our dust when the sods of the valley are sweet to the soul. Nowhere but in the jail and on the gallows has the black man equal rights with the white in our American legislation!

The American Press—it is generally the foe of the slave, the advocate of bondage.

In Virginia, it is felony to deny the master's right to own his slaves. There is an old law re-enacted in the revision of the Virginia statutes, which inflicts a punishment of not more than one year's confinement on any one guilty of that offence. It was proposed in the Virginia Legislature, last winter, that if a man had conscientious objections to holding slaves, he should not be allowed to sit on any jury where the matter of a man's freedom was in question. Nor is that all. There is a law in Virginia, it is said, that when a man has three quarters white blood in his veins, he may recover his freedom in virtue of that fact. It is well known that at least half the slaves in Virginia are half white and one quarter of them three quarters white. Accordingly, it was proposed in one of their newspapers that this old law should be repealed, and another substituted providing that no man should recover his freedom in consequence of his complexion, unless he had more than nine tenths white blood in his veins.

The slave has no rights; the ideas of the Declaration of Independence are repudiated; he is not "endowed by his Creator" with "certain unalienable rights" to "life, liberty, and the pursuit of happiness."

Listen to what a Southern editor says. I am quoting now from one of the most powerful Southern journals, printed at the capital of Virginia, the Richmond Examiner, and the words which I read were written by the American Chargé d'Affairs at Turin. He says: "The foundation and right of negro slavery is in its utility and the fitness of things; it is the same right by which we hold property in domestic animals." The negro is "the connecting link between the human and brute creation." "The negro is not the white man. Not with more safety do we assert that a horse is not a hog. Hay is good for horses—but not for hogs; liberty is good for white men, but not for negroes." "A law rendering perpetual the relation between a negro and his master is no wrong, but a right."

Then in reply to some writer in the Tribune, who had asked, "Have they no souls," he says, "They may have souls, for aught we know to the contrary; so may horses and hogs." Then, when somebody quotes the Bible in behalf of the rights of men, he answers: "The Bible has been vouchsafed to mankind for the purpose of keeping us out of hell-fire and getting us into heaven by the mysteries of faith and the inner life; not to teach us government, political economy," &c.

The American Church repudiates the Christian religion when it comes to speak about the African. It does not apply the golden rule to the slave. The "servants" of the New Testament, in the Greek language, were "slaves," and the American Church commands them to be obedient to their masters. There must be no marriage—the affectional and passional union of one man and one woman for life—only transient concubinage. Marriage is inconsistent with slavery, and the slave wedlock in the American Church is not a sacrament. "Manifest destiny" is the cry of politicians, and that demands slavery : "The will of God" is the cry of the priests, and it demands the same thing. I am not speaking of ministers of Christianity; they are a very different sort of men, and preach a very different creed from that—only of the ministers in the churches of commerce. According to the popular theology of all Christendom, Jesus Christ came on earth to seek and to save that which is lost. The Good Physician does not go among the whole, but among the sick. If he were to come here to seek to relieve the slave, the leading men in the American denominations would tell him he came before he was called; he ran before he was sent; that it was no mission from God to break a single American fetter, nor to let the oppressed go free. Is not the "Constitution" above "Conscience," and the Fugitive Slave Bill more holy than the Bible; the commissioner of more authority than Christ?

> "Oh, Faith of Christians, hast thou wandered there
> To waft us home the message of despair,
> Then bind the palm *thy sage's brow to suit*
> *Of blasted leaf and death-distilling fruit.*"

Such is the aspect of America when the immigrant comes near and looks the nation in the face. What a spectacle that is to put along-side of the other! Europe repudiates bondage—Scandinavia, Holland, France, England. Since Britain emancipated her slaves, the present Emperor of Russia has set free over seven millions of slaves that belonged to his own private domain, and established more than four thousand schools, free for those seven millions of emancipated slaves; and did he not fear an outbreak in a country where "revolution is endemic," he would set free the other five and thirty millions that occupy his soil to-day. And when he enlarges his territory, he never extends the area of bondage, only the area of what in Russia is freedom.

What a spectacle! A country reaching from sea to sea, from the Gulf of tropic heat to Lake Superior's artic cold, and not an inch of free soil all the way! Three millions of square miles, and not a foot where a fugitive from slavery can be safe! A Democracy, and every eighth man bought and sold!

It is the richest nation in the world, after England; yet, we are so poor that every eighth man is unable to say that he owns the smallest finger on his feeblest hand. So poor are we amid our riches, that every eighth woman is to such an extent a pauper that she does not own the baby she has borne; nor even the baby that she bears. Maternity is put up at public vendue, and the auctioneer says, "So much for the mother and so much for the hopes and expectations of another life that is to be born!"

America calls herself "the best-educated nation in the world," and yet, in fifteen Democratic States, it is a felony by statute to teach a child to know the three letters which spell "God." What a spectacle is that!

Nor is this all; but able men, well educated and well endowed, come forward to teach us that slavery is not only no evil, but is "right as a principle," and is "divine"—is a "part of the divine revelation" which the great God miraculously made to man. What a spectacle!

Four hundred thousand immigrants come here openly every year, and a thousand fugitives flee off by night, escaping from American despotism. They go by the Underground Railroad, shut up in boxes smaller than a coffin, or, as lately happened, riding through the storms of Ocean in the fore-chains of a packet-ship, wet by every dash of the sea, and frozen by the winter's wind. Far off in the South the spirit of freedom came in the Northern blast to the poor man, and said to him, "It is better to enter into freedom halt and maimed rather than, having two hands and two feet, to continue in bondage for ever;" and he puts himself in the fore-chains of a packet-ship, and, half frozen, with the loss of two of his limbs, he reaches the North, and thanks God that he has still one hand and one foot to enter into freedom with. Alas, he is carried back, halt and maimed, to die; then he goes from bondage to that other Commonwealth, where even the American slave is free from his master, and Democrats "cease from troubling."

America translates the Bible—I am glad of it, and would give my mite thereto—into a hundred and forty-seven different tongues, and sends missionaries all over the world; and here at home are three and a quarter millions of American men who have no Bible, whose only missionary is the overseer.

In the Hall of Independence, Judge Kane and Judge

Grier hold their court. Two great official kidnappers of the middle States hold their slave-court in the very building where the Declaration of Independence was decreed, was signed, and thence published to the world. What a spectacle it is! We thought, a little while ago, that Judge Jeffries was a historical fiction; that Scroggs was impossible; we did not think such a thing could exist. Jeffries is repeated in Philadelphia; Scroggs is brought back to life in New York and Boston and various Northern towns. What a spectacle is that for the Swiss, the German, and the Scandinavian who come here!

Do these immigrants love American slavery? The German, the Swiss, the Scandinavian hate it. I am sorry to say there is one class of men that come here who love it; it is the class most of all sinned against at home. When the Irishman reaches America, he takes ground against the African. I know there are exceptions, and I would go far to honour them; but the Irish, as a body, oppose the emancipation of the blacks as a body. Every sect that comes from abroad numbers friends of freedom—except the Catholic. Those who call themselves infidels from Germany do not range on the slaveholder's side. I have known some men who take the ghastly and dreadful name of Atheist; but they said "there is a law higher than the slaveholder's statute." But do you know a Catholic priest who is opposed to slavery? I wish I did. There are good things in the Catholic faith—the Protestants have not wholly outgrown it yet. But I wish I could hear of a single Catholic priest of any eminence who ever cared anything for the freedom of the most oppressed men in America. I have heard of none.

Look a little closer. The great interests prized most in America are commerce and politics. The great cities are the head-quarters of these. Agriculture and the mechanic arts are spread abroad all over the country. Commerce and politics predominate in the cities. New York is the metropolis of commerce; Washington of politics.

What have been the views of American commerce in respect to freedom? It has been against it; I am sorry to say so. In Europe commerce is the ally of freedom, and has been so far back that the memory of man runs not to the contrary. In America, the great commercial centres, ever since the Revolution, have been hostile to freedom. In Massachusetts we have a few rich men friendly to freedom—they are very few; the greater part of even Massachusetts capital goes towards bondage—not towards freedom. In general, the chief men of commerce are hostile to it. They want first money, next money, and money last of all; fairly if they can get it—if not, unfairly. Hence, the commercial cities are the head-quarters of slavery;. all the mercantile capitals execute the Fugitive Slave Bill — Philadelphia, New York, Boston, Buffalo, Cincinnati; only small towns repudiate man-stealing. The Northern capitalists lend money and take slaves as collateral; they are good security; you can realize on it any day. The Northern merchant takes slaves into his ships as merchandise. It pays very well. If you take them on a foreign voyage, it is "piracy;" but taken coastwise, the domestic slave-trade is a legal traffic. In 1852, a ship called the "Edward Everett" made two voyages from Baltimore to New Orleans, and each time it carried slaves, once twelve, and once twenty.

A sea captain in Massachusetts told a story to the commissioners sent to look after the Indians, which I will repeat. He commanded a small brig, which plied between Carolina and the Gulf States. "One day, at Charleston," said he, "a man came and brought to me an old negro slave. He was very old, and had fought in the Revolution, and had been much distinguished for bravery and other soldierly qualities. If he had not been a negro, he would have become a captain at least, perhaps a colonel. But, in his old age, his master found no use for him, and said he could not afford to keep him. He asked me to take the revolutionary soldier and carry him South and sell him. I carried him," said the man, "to Mobile, and I tried to get as good and kind a master for him as I could, for I didn't like to sell a man who had fought for his country. I sold the old revolutionary soldier for a hundred dollars to a citizen of Mobile, who raised poultry, and he set him to tend a hen-coop." I suppose the South Carolina master, "a true gentleman," drew the pension till the soldier died. "How could you do such a thing?" said my friend, who was an anti-slavery man. "If I didn't do it," he replied, "I never could get another bale of cotton, nor a box of sugar, nor anything to carry from or to any Southern port."

In politics, almost all the leading men have been servants of slavery. Three "major prophets" of the American Republic have gone home to render their account where "the servant is free from his master, and the wicked cease from troubling, and the weary are at rest." Clay, Calhoun, Webster; they were all prophets of slavery, all against freedom. No men of high political standing and influence have ever lived in this country who were fallen so low in the mire of slavery as they during the last twenty years. No political footprints have sunk so deep into the soil—all their tracks run towards bondage. Where they marched, slavery followed.

Our Presidents must all be pro-slavery men. John Quincy Adams even, the only American politician, thus far, who inherited a great name and left it greater, as President did nothing against slavery that has yet come to light; said nothing against it which has yet come to light. The brave old man, in his latter days, stirred up the nobler nature in him, and amply repaid for the sins of omission. But the other Presidents, a long line of them—Jackson, Van Buren, Harrison,—they are growing smaller and smaller,—Tyler, Polk, Taylor, who was a brave, earnest man, and had a great deal of good in him,—and now they began rapidly to grow very small,—Fillmore, Pierce—can you find a single breath of freedom in these men? Not one. The last slave President, though his cradle was rocked in New Hampshire, is Texan in his latitude. He swears allegiance to slavery in his inaugural address.

Is there a breath of freedom in the great federal officers —secretaries, judges? Ask the Cabinet; ask the supreme court; the federal officers. They are, almost without exception, servants of slavery. Out of forty thousand government officers to-day, I think thirty-seven thousand are strongly pro-slavery; and of the three thousand who are at heart anti-slavery, we have yet to listen long before we shall hear the first anti-slavery lisp. I have been listening ever since the fourth of March, 1853, and have not heard a word yet. In the English Cabinet there are various opinions on important matters; here the administration is a unit, a unit of bondage. In Russia, a revolutionary man sometimes holds a high post and does great service; in America, none but the servant of slavery is fit for the political functions of Democracy. I believe in the United States there is not a single editor holding a government office who says anything against the Nebraska Bill. They do not dare. Did a Whig office-holder oppose the Fugitive Slave Bill or its enforcement? I never heard of one. The day of office, like the day of bondage, "takes off half a man's manhood," and the other half it hides! A little while ago, an anti-slavery man in Massachusetts carried a remonstrance against the Nebraska Bill, signed by almost every voter in his town, to the postmaster, and asked him, "Will you sign it?" "No, I shan't," said he. "Why not?" Before he answered, one of his neighbours said, "Well, I would not sign it if I were he." "Why not?" said the man. "Because if he did, he would be turned out of office in twenty-four hours; the next telegraph would do the business for him." "Well," said my friend, "if I held an office on that condition, I would get the biggest brass dog-collar I could find and put it round my neck, and have my owner's name on it, in great, large letters, so that everybody might see whose dog I was."

In the individual States, I think there is not a single anti-slavery governor. I believe Vermont is the only State with an anti-slavery supreme court; and that is the only State which has not much concern in commerce or manufactures. It is a State of farmers.

For a long time the American Government has been controlled by slavery. There is an old story told by the Hebrew rabbis, that before the flood there was an enormous giant, called Gog. After the flood had got into the full tide of successful experiment, and every man was drowned except those taken into the ark, Gog came striding along after Noah, feeling his way with a cane as long as a mast of the "Great Republic." The water had only come up to his girdle. It was then over the hill-tops and was still rising—raining night and day. The giant hailed the Patriarch. Noah put his head out of the window, and said, "Who is there?" "It is I," said Gog. "Take us in; it is wet outside!" "No," said Noah, "you're too big; no room. Besides, you're a bad character. You would be a very dangerous passenger, and would make trouble in the ark; I shall not take you in. You may get on top if you like;" and he clapped to the window. "Go to thunder," said Gog; "I will ride, after all." And he strode after him, wading through the waters; and mounting on the top of the ark, with one leg over the larboard and the other over the starboard side, steered it just as he pleased, and made it rough weather inside. Now, in making the Constitution, we did not care to take in slavery in express terms. It looked ugly. We allowed it to get on the top astride, and now it steers us just where it pleases.

The slave power controls the President, and fills all the offices. Out of the twelve elected Presidents, four have been from the North, and the last of them might just as well have been taken by lot at the South anywhere. Mr Pierce, I just now said, was Texan in his latitude. His conscience is Texan; only his cradle was of New Hampshire. Of the nine judges of the supreme court, five are from the slave States; the chief-justice is from the slave States; all slave judges. A part of the Cabinet are from the North—I forget how many; it makes no difference; they are all of the same Southern complexion; and the man who was taken from the furthest North, I think is most Southern in his slavery proclivities.

The nation fluctuates in its policy. Now it is for internal improvements; then it is against them. Now it is for a bank; then a bank is "unconstitutional." Now it is for free trade; then for protection; then for free trade again —"protection is altogether unconstitutional." Mr Calhoun turned clear round.—When the North went for free trade and grew rich by that, Calhoun did not like it, and wanted protection: he thought the South would grow rich by it. But when the North grew rich under protection, he turned round to free trade again. Now the nation is for giving away the public lands. Sixteen millions of acres of "swamp lands" are given, within seven years, to States. Twenty-five millions of the public lands are given away gratuitously to soldiers—six millions in a single year. Forty-seven millions of the public lands to seventeen States for schools, colleges, &c. Forty-seven thousand acres for deaf and dumb asylums. And look; just now it changes its policy, and Mr Pierce is opposed to granting any land—" it is not constitutional "—to Miss Dix, to make the insane sober and bring them to their right minds. He may have a private reason for keeping the people in a state of craziness, for aught I know.

The public policy changes in these matters. It never changes in respect to slavery. Be the Whigs in power, slavery is Whig; be the Democrats, it is Democratic. At first, slavery was an exceptional measure, and men tried to apologize for it and excuse it. Now it is a normal principle, and the institution must be defended and enlarged.

Commercial men must be moved, I suppose, by commercial arguments. Look, then, at this statement of facts. Slavery is unprofitable for the people. America is poorer for slavery. I am speaking in the great focus of American commerce—the third city for population and riches in the Christian world. Let me, therefore, talk about dollars. America, I say, is poorer for slavery. If the three and a quarter millions of slaves were freemen, how much richer would she be! There is no State in the Union but it is poorer for slavery. It is a bad tool to work with. The educated freeman is the best working power in the world.

Compare the North with the South, and see what a difference in riches, comfort, education. See the superiority of the North. But the South started with every advantage of nature—soil, climate, everything. To make the case plainer, let me take two great States, Virginia and New York. Compare them together.

In geographical position, Virginia has every advantage over New York. Almost everything that will grow in the Union will grow somewhere in Virginia, save sugar. The largest ships can sail up the Potomac a hundred miles, as far as Alexandria. The Rappahannock, York, James, are all navigable rivers. The Ohio flanks Virginia more than three hundred miles. There are sixty miles of navigation on the Kanawha. New York has a single navigable stream with not a hundred and fifty miles of navigation, from Troy to the ocean. Virginia has the best harbour on the Atlantic coast, and several smaller ones. Your State has but a single maritime port. Virginia abounds in water power for mills. I stood once on the steps of the Capitol at Washington, and within six miles of me, under my eyes, there was a water power greater than that which turns the mills of Lawrence, Lowell, and Manchester, all put together. In 1836, it did not turn a wheel; now, I am told, it drives a grist-mill. No State is so rich in water power. The Alleghanies are a great water-shed, and at the eaves the streams rush forward as if impatient to turn mills. Virginia is full of minerals—coal, iron, lead, copper, salt. Her agricultural resources are immense. What timber clothes her mountains! what a soil for Indian corn, wheat, tobacco, rice! even cotton grows in the southern part. Washington said the central counties of Virginia were the best land in the United States. Daniel Webster, reporting to Virginians of his European tour, said, he saw "no lands in Europe so good as the valley of the Shenandoah." Virginia is rich in mountain pastures favourable to sheep and horned cattle. Nature gives Virginia all that can be asked of nature. What a position for agriculture, manufactures, mining, commerce! Norfolk is a hundred miles nearer Chicago than New York is, but she has no intercourse with Chicago. It is three hundred miles nearer the mouth of the Ohio; but if a Norfolk man wants to go to St Louis, I believe his quickest way lies through New York. It is not a day's sail further from Liverpool; it is nearer to the Mediterranean and South American ports. But what is Norfolk, with her 23,000 tons of shipping and her fourteen thousand population? What is Richmond, with her twenty-seven thousand men—ten thousand of them slaves? Nay, what is Virginia herself, the very oldest State? Let me cypher out some numerical details.

In 1790, she had 748,000 inhabitants; now she has 1,421,000. She has not doubled in sixty years. In 1790, New York had 340,000; now she has 3,048,000. She has multiplied her population almost ten times. In Virginia, in 1850, there were only 452,000 more freemen than sixty years before; in New York, there were 2,724,000 more freemen than there were in 1790. There are only 165,000 dwellings in Virginia; 463,000 in New York. Then the Virginia farms were worth $216,000,000; yours, $554,000,000; Virginia is wholly agricultural, while you are also manufacturing and commercial. Her farm tools were worth $7,000,000; yours, $22,000,000. Her cattle, $33,000,000; yours, $73,000,000. The orchard products of Virginia were worth $177,000; of New York, $1,762,000. Virginia had

478 miles of railroad; you had 1826 miles. She had 74,000 tons of shipping; you had 942,000. The value of her cotton factories was not two millions; the value of yours was four and a quarter millions. She produced $841,000 worth of woollen goods; you produced $7,030,000. Her furnaces produced two millions and a half; yours produced eight millions: her tanneries $894,000; yours, $9,804,000. All of her manufactures together were not worth $9,000,000; those of the city of New York alone have an annual value of $105,000,000. Her attendance at school was 109,000; yours, 693,000.

But there is one thing in which Virginia is far in advance of you. Of native Virginians, over twenty years old, who could not read the name of "Christ," nor the word "God"—free white people who cannot spell "Democrat"—there were 87,383. That is, out of every five hundred free white persons, there were one hundred and five that could not spell PIERCE. In New York there are 30,670—no more; so that out of five hundred persons, there are six that cannot read and write. Virginia is advancing rapidly upon you in this respect. In 1840, she had only 58,787 adults who could not read and write; now 28,596 more. So you see she is advancing!

Virginia has 87 newspapers; New York 428. The Virginia newspaper circulation is 89,000; the New York newspaper circulation is 1,622,000. The Tribune—and I think it is the best paper there is in the world—has an aggregate circulation of 110,000; 20,000 more than all the newspapers of Virginia. Virginia prints every year 9,000,000 copies of newspapers, all told. New York prints 115,000,000. The New York Tribune prints 15,000,000—more than the whole State of Virginia put together. Such is the state of things counted in the gross, but I think the New York quality is as much better as the quantity is more.

Virginia has 88,000 books in libraries not private; New York 1,760,000,—more than twenty times as much. Virginia exports $3,500,000 worth each year; New York $53,000,000. Virginia imports $426,000; New York $111,000,000. But in one article of export she is in advance of you—she sends to the man-markets of the South about $10,000,000 or $12,000,000 worth of her children every year; exports slaves! The estimated value of all the property real and personal in the State of Virginia, including slaves, is $430,701,882; of New York $1,080,000,000, without estimating the value of the men who own it. Virginia has got 472,528 slaves. I will estimate them at less than the market value—at $400 each; they come to $189,000,000. I subtract the value of the working people of Virginia, and she is worth not quite $242,000,000. Now, the State of New York might buy up all the property of Virginia, including the slaves, and still have $649,000,000 left; might buy up all the real and personal property of Virginia, except the working men, and have $838,000,000 left. The North appropriates the rivers, the mines, the harbours, the forests, fire and water—the South kidnaps men. Behold the commercial result.

Virginia is a great State—very great! You do not know how great she is. I will read it to you presently. Things are great and small by comparison. I am quoting again from the Richmond Examiner (March 24, 1854). "Virginia in this confederacy is the impersonation of the well-born, well-educated, well-bred aristocrat" [well born while the children of Jefferson and the only children of Madison are a "connecting link between the human and brute creation;" well educated, with twenty-one per cent. of her white adults unable to read the vote they cast against the unalienable rights of man; well bred, when her great product for exportation is—the children of her own loins! Slavery is a "patriarchal institution;" the democratic Abrahams of Virginia do not offer up their Isaacs to the Lord; that would be a "sacrifice," they only sell them. So]; "she looks down from her elevated pedestal upon her *parvenu*, ignorant, mendacious Yankee vilifiers, as coldly and calmly as a marble statue; occasionally she condescends to recognize the existence of her adversaries at the very moment when she crushes them. But she does it without anger, and with no more hatred of them than the gardener feels towards the insects which he finds it necessary occasionally to destroy." "She feels that she is the sword and buckler of the South—that it is her influence which has so frequently defeated and driven back in dismay the Abolition party when flushed by temporary victory. Brave, calm, and determined, wise in times of excitement, always true to the slave power, never rash or indiscreet, the waves of Northern fanaticism burst harmless at her feet; the contempt for her Northern revilers is the result of her consciousness of her influence in the political world. She makes and unmakes Presidents; she dictates her terms to the Northern Democracy and they obey her. She selects from among the faithful of the North a man upon whom she can rely, and she makes him President." This latter is true! The opinion of Richmond is of more weight than the opinion of New York. Slavery, the political Gog on the outside, steers the ark of commercial Noah, and makes it rough or smooth weather inside, just as he likes.

"In the early days of the Republic, the superior sagacity of her statesmen enabled them to rivet so firmly the shackles of the slave, that the Abolitionists will never be able to unloose them."

"A wide and impassable gulf separates the noble, proud, glorious Old Dominion from her Northern traducers; the mastiff dares not willingly assail the skunk!" "When Virginia takes the field, she crushes the whole Abolition party; her slaughter is wholesale, and a hundred thousand Abolitionists are cut down when she issues her commands!"

Again (April 4th, 1854), "A hundred Southern gentlemen, armed with riding-whips, could chase an army of invading Abolitionists into the Atlantic."

In reference to the project at the North of sending Northern Abolitionists along with the Northern slave-breeders to Nebraska, to put freedom into the soil before slavery gets there, the Examiner says: "Why, a hundred wild, lank, half-horse, half-alligator Missouri and Arkansas emigrants would, if so disposed, chase out of Nebraska and Kansas all the Abolitionists who have figured for the last twenty years at Anti-slavery meetings."

I say slavery is not profitable for the nation nor for a State, but it is profitable for slave-owners. You will see why. If the Northern capitalist owned the weavers and spinners at Lowell and Lawrence, New England would be poorer; and the working-men would not be so well off, or so well educated; but Undershot and Overshot, Turbine Brothers, Spindle & Co., would be richer and would get larger dividends. Land monopoly in England enfeebles the island, but enriches the aristocracy. How poor, ill-fed, and ill-clad were the French peasants before the Revolution;

how costly was the *château* of the noble. Monopoly was bad for the people ; profitable for the rich men. How poor are the peasants in Italy ; how wealthy the Cardinals and the Pope. Oppression enriches the oppressor; it makes poorer the down-trodden. Piracy is very costly to the merchant and to mankind ; but it feeds the pirate. Slavery impoverishes Virginia, but it enriches the master. It gives him money—commercial power,—office—political power. The slave-holder is drawn in his triumphal chariot by two chattels; one, the poor black man, whom he "owns legally ;" the other is the poor white man, whom he " owns morally " and harnesses to his chariot. Hence these American lords of the lash cleave to this institution—they love it. To the slave-holders, slavery is money and power !

Now the South, weak in numbers, feeble in respect to money, has continually directed the politics of America just as she would. Her ignorance and poverty were more efficacious than the Northern riches and education. She is in earnest for slavery ; the North not in earnest for freedom ; only earnest for money. So long as the Federal Government grinds the axes of the Northern merchant, he cares little whether the stone is turned by the freeman's labour or the slave's. Hence, the great centres of Northern commerce and manufactures are also the great centres of pro-slavery politics. Philadelphia, New York, Boston, Buffalo, Cincinnati, they all liked the Fugitive Slave Bill ; all took pains to seize the fugitive who fled to a Northern altar for freedom ; nay, the most conspicuous clergymen in those cities became apostles of kidnapping ; their churches were of commerce, not Christianity. The North yielded to that last most insolent demand. Under the influence of that excitement she chose the present Administration, the present Congress. Now see the result ! Whig and Democrat meet on the same platform at Baltimore. It was the platform of slavery. Both candidates—Scott and Pierce—gave in their allegiance to the same measure ; it was the measure which nullifies the first principles of American Independence—they were sworn on the Fugitive Slave Bill. Whig and Democrat knew no " higher law," only the statute of slave-holders. Conscience bent down before the Constitution. What sort of a government can you expect from such conduct ? What Representatives ? Just what you have got. Sow the wind, will you? then reap the whirlwind. Mr Pierce said in his Inaugural, "I believe that involuntary servitude is recognized by the Constitution;" "that it stands like any other admitted right. I hold that the Compromise measures [that is, the Fugitive Slave Bill] are strictly constitutional and to be unhesitatingly carried into effect." The laws to secure the master's right to capture a man in the free States "should be respected and obeyed, not with a reluctance encouraged by abstract opinions as to their propriety in a different state of society, but cheerfully and according to the decision of the tribunal to which their exposition belongs." These words were historical,—reminiscences of the time when "no higher law" was the watchword of the American State and the American Church; they were prophetic —ominous of what we see to-day.

I. Here is the Gadsden Treaty which has just been negotiated. How bad it is I cannot say; only this: If I am rightly informed, a tract of 39,000,000 acres, larger than all Virginia, is "reannexed" to the slave soil which the "flag of our Union" already waves over. The whole thing, when it is fairly understood by the public, I think will be seen to be a more iniquitous matter than this Nebraska wickedness.

II. Then comes the Nebraska Bill, yet to be consummated. While we are sitting here in cold debate, it may be the measure has passed. From the beginning I have never had any doubts that it would pass. If it could not be put through this session—as I thought it would—I felt sure that before this Congress goes out of office, Nebraska would be slave soil. You see what a majority there was in the Senate; you see what a majority there is in the House. I know there is an opposition—and most brilliantly conducted, too, by the few faithful men; but see this: The Administration has yet three years to run. There is an annual income of sixty millions of dollars. There are forty thousand offices to be disposed of—four thousand very valuable. And do you think that a Democratic Administration, with that amount of offices, of money and time, cannot buy up Northern doughfaces enough to carry any measure it pleases? I know better. Once I thought

that Texas could not be annexed. It was done. I learned
wisdom from that. I have taken counsel of my fears. I
have not seen any barrier on which the North would rally
that we have come to yet. There are some things behind
us. John Randolph said, years ago, "We will drive you
from pillar to post, back, back, back." He has been as
good as his word. We have been driven "back, back,
back." But we cannot be driven much further. There is
a spot where we shall stop. I am afraid we have not come
to it yet. I will say no more about it just now—because
not many weeks ago I stood here and said a great deal.*
You have listened to me when I was feeble and hollow-
voiced; I will not tax your patience now, for in this, as in
a celebrated feast of old, they have "kept the good wine
until now!" (alluding to Mr Garrison and Mr Phillips who
were to follow).

If the Nebraska Bill is defeated, I shall rejoice that iniquity is foiled once more. But if it become a law—there
are some things which seem probable

1. On the Fourth of March, 1857, the "Democrats" will
have "leave to withdraw" from office.

2. Every Northern man who has taken a prominent
stand in behalf of slavery will be politically ruined. You
know what befell the Northern politicians who voted for the
Missouri Compromise; a similar fate hangs over such as
enslave Nebraska. Already, Mr Everett is, theologically
speaking, among the "lost;" and of all the three thousand
New England ministers whose petition he dared not present, not one will ever pray for his political salvation.

Pause with me and drop a tear over the ruin of Edward
Everett, a man of large talents and commensurate industry, very learned, the most scholarly man, perhaps, in the
country, with a persuasive beauty of speech only equalled
by this American [Mr PHILLIPS], who therein surpasses him;
he has had a long career of public service, public honour—
Clergyman, Professor, Editor, Representative, Governor,
Ambassador, President of Harvard College, Senator, alike
the ornament and the auxiliary of many a learned society
—he yet comes to such an end.

"This is the state of man; to-day, he puts forth
The tender leaves of hope; to-morrow, blossoms,

---

* See above, p. 245, *et seq.*

And bears his blushing honours thick upon him;
The third day comes a frost, *Nebraska's* frost;
And, when he thinks, good easy man, full surely,
His greatness is a ripening, nips his root,
And then he falls————.

"Oh how wretched
Is that poor man that hangs on public favours!
There is betwixt that smile he would aspire to,
That sweet aspect of voters, and their ruin,
More pangs and fears than wars or women have;
And when he falls, he falls like Lucifer,
Never to hope again!"

Mr Douglas also is finished; the success of his measure is his own defeat. Mr Pierce has three short years to serve; then there will be one more Ex-President—ranking with Tyler and Fillmore. Mr Seward need not agitate,

————"Let it work
For 'tis the sport to have the enginer
Hoise with his own petar."

III. The next thing is the enslavement of Cuba. That is a very serious matter. It has been desired a long time. Lopez, a Spanish fillibuster, undertook it and was legally put to death. I am not an advocate for the garroté, but I think, all things taken into consideration, that he did not meet with a very inadequate mode of death, and I believe such is the general opinion, not only in Cuba, but in the United States. But Young America is not content with that. Mr Dean, a little while ago, in the House, proposed to repeal the neutrality laws—to set fillibusterism on its legs again. You remember the President's message about the "Black Warrior"—how black-warrior-like it was; and then comes the "unanimous resolution" of the Louisiana legislature asking the United States to interfere and declare war, in case Cuba should undertake to emancipate her slaves. Senator Slidell's speech is still tingling in our ears, asking the Government to repeal the neutrality laws and allow every pirate who pleases to land in Cuba and burn and destroy. You know Mr Soulé's conduct in Madrid. It is rumoured that he has been authorized to offer $250,000,000 for Cuba. The sum is enormous; but when you consider the character of this Administration and the Inaugural of President Pierce, the unscrupulous abuse made of public money, I do not think it is a very extraordinary supposition.

But this matter of getting possession of Cuba is something dangerous as well as difficult. There are three conceivable ways of acquiring it.

One is by buying, and that I take it is wholly out of the question. If I am rightly informed, there is a certain Spanish debt owing to Englishmen, and that Cuba is somehow pledged as a sort of collateral security for the Spanish Bonds. I take it for granted that Cuba is not to be bought for many years without the interference of England, and depend upon it England will not allow it to be sold for the establishment of slavery; for I think it is pretty well understood by politicians that there is a regular agreement entered into between Spain on the one side and England on the other, that at a certain period within twenty-five years every slave in Cuba shall be set free. I believe this is known to men somewhat versed in the secret history of the two Cabinets of England and of Spain. England has the same wish for land which fires our Anglo-Saxon blood. She has islands in the West Indies; the More in Cuba is only a hundred miles from Jamaica. If we get Cuba for slavery, we shall next want the British West Indies for the same institution. Cuba filled with fillibusters would be a dangerous neighbour to Jamaica.

The second way is by fillibustering; and that Mr Slidell and Mr Dean want to try. The third is by open war. Now fillibusterism will lead to open war, so I will consider only this issue.

I know that Americans will fight more desperately, perhaps, on land or sea, than any other people. But fighting is an ugly business, especially with such antagonists as we shall have in this case. It is a matter well understood that the Captain-General of Cuba has a paper in his possession authorizing him discretionally to free the slaves and put arms in their hands whenever it is thought necessary. It is rather difficult to get at the exact statistics of Cuba. There has been no census since 1842, when the population was estimated at a million. I will reckon it now at 1,300,000 —700,000 blacks, and 600,000 whites. Of the 700,000 blacks, half a million are slaves and two hundred thousand freemen. Now, a black freeman in Cuba is a very different person from the black freeman in the United States. He has rights. He is not turned out of the omnibus, nor the meeting-house, nor the graveyard. He is respected by the law; he respects himself, and is a formidable person; let the blacks be furnished with arms, they are dangerous foes. And remember there are mountain fastnesses in the centre of the island; that it is as defensible as St Domingo; and has a very unhealthy climate for Northern men. The Spaniard would have great allies: the vomito is there; typhoid, dysentery, yellow fever, the worst of all, is there. A Northern army even of fillibusters would fight against the most dreadful odds. "The Lord from on high," as the old Hebrews say, would fight against the Northern men; the pestilence that swept off Sennacherib's host would not respect the fillibuster.

That is not all. What sort of a navy has Spain? One hundred and seventy-nine ships of war! They are small mostly, but they carry over 1400 cannon, and 24,000 men —15,000 marines and 9000 sailors. The United States has seventy-five ships of war; 2200 cannon, 14,000 men —large ships, heavy cannon. That is not all. Spaniards fight desperately. A Spanish armada I should not be very much afraid of; but Spain will issue letters of marque, and a Portuguese or Spanish pirate is rather an uncomfortable being to meet. Our commerce is spread over all the seas; there is no mercantile marine so unprotected. Our ships do not carry muskets, still less cannon, since pirates have been swept off the sea. Let Spain issue letters of marque, England winking at it, and Algerine pirates from out the Barbary States of Africa, and other pirates from the Brazilian, Mexican, and the West Indian ports, would prowl about the coast of the Mediterranean and over all the bosom of the Atlantic; and then where would be our commerce? The South has nothing to fear from that. She has no shipping. Yes, Norfolk has 28,000 tons. The South is not afraid. The North has four million tons of shipping. Touch the commerce of a Northern man, and you touch his heart.

England has conceded to us as a measure just what we asked. We have always declared, "free ships make free goods." England said "Enemies' goods make enemies' ships." Now she has not affirmed our principle; she has assented to our measure. That is all you can expect her to do. But if we repeal our neutrality laws and seek to get Cuba in order to establish slavery there, endangering the interests of England and th. freedom of her coloured citizens, depend upon it, England will not suffer this to be done without herself interfering. If she is so deeply immersed in European wars that she cannot interfere directly, she will indirectly. But I have not thought that England and France are to be much engaged in a European war. I suppose the intention of the American Cabinet is to seize Cuba as soon as the British and Russians are fairly fighting, thinking that England will not interfere. But in "this war of elder sons" which now goes on for the dismemberment of Turkey, it is not clear that England will be so deeply engaged that she cannot attend to her domestic affairs, or the interest of her West Indies. I think these powers are going to divide Turkey between them, but I do not believe they are going to do much fighting there. If we are bent on seizing Cuba, a long and a ruinous fight is a thing that ought to enter into men's calculations. Now let such a naval warfare take place, and how will your insurance stock look in New York, Philadelphia, and Boston? How will your merchants look when reports come one after another that your ships are carried in as prizes by Spain, or sunk on the ocean after they have been plundered? I speak in the great commercial metropolis of America. I wish these things to be seriously considered by mercantile men. Let the Northern men look out for their own ships.

But here is a matter which the South may think of. In case of foreign war, the North will not be the battle-field. An invading army would attack the South. Who would defend it—the local militia, the "chivalry" of South Carolina, the "gentlemen" of Virginia, who are to slaughter a hundred thousand Abolitionists in a day? Let an army set foot on Southern soil, with a few black regiments; let the commander offer freedom to all the slaves, and put arms in their hands; let him ask them to burn houses and butcher men; and there would be a state of things not quite so pleasant for "gentlemen" of the South to look at. "They that laughed at the grovelling worm and trod on him, may cry and howl when they see the stoop of the flying and fiery-mouthed dragon!" Now, there is only one opinion about the valour of President Pierce. Like the sword of Hudibras, it cut into itself,

"—— for lack
Of other stuff to hew and hack."

But would he like to stand with such a fire in his rear? Set a house on fire by hot shot, and you do not know how much of it will burn down.

IV. Well, if Nebraska is made a slave territory, as I suppose it will be, the next thing is the possession of Cuba. Then the war against Spain will come, as I think, inevitably. But even if we do not get Cuba, slavery must be extended to other parts of the Union. This may be done judicially, by the Supreme Court—one of the most powerful agents to destroy local self-government and legalize centralization; or legislatively, by Congress. Already slavery is established in California. An attempt, you know, was made to establish it in Illinois. Senator Toombs, the other day, boasted to Mr John P. Hale, that it would "not be long before the slave-holder would sit down at the foot of Bunker Hill monument with his slaves." You and I may live to see it—at least to see the attempt made. A writer in a prominent Southern journal, the Charleston Courier (of March 16, 1854), declares "that domestic slavery is a constitutional institution, and cannot be prohibited in a territory by either territorial or congressional legislation. It is recognized by the Constitution as an existing and lawful institution ... and by the recognition and establishment of slavery *eo nomine* in the District of Columbia, under the constitutional provision for the acquisition of and exclusive legislation over such a capitoline district; and by that clause also which declares that the citizens of each State shall be entitled to all the privileges and immunities of citizens in the several States." "The citizens of any State ... cannot be constitutionally denied the equal right ... of sojourning or settling ... with their man-servants and maid-servants ... in any portion of the wide-spread Canaan which the Lord their God hath given them, there to dwell unmolested in person or property." Admirable exposition of the Constitution! The free black man must be shut up in jail if he goes from Boston in a ship to Charleston, but the slave-holder may bring his slaves to Massachusetts and dwell there, unmolested with his property in men. South Carolina has a white population of

274,567 persons, considerably less than half the population of this city. But if South Carolina says to the State of New York, with three million men in it, Let us bring our slaves to New York, what will the "Hards" and the "Softs" and the "Silver Greys" answer? Gentlemen, we shall hear what we shall hear. I fear that not an office-holder of any note would oppose the measure. It might be carried with the present Supreme Court, or Congress, I make no doubt.

But this is not the end. After the Gadsden Treaty, the enslavement of Nebraska, the extension of slavery to the free States, the seizure of Cuba, with other islands—San Domingo, &c.,—there is one step more—THE RE-ESTABLISHMENT OF THE AFRICAN SLAVE TRADE.

A recent number of the *Southern Standard* thus develops the thought: "With firmness and judgment we can open up the African slave emigration again to people the whole region of the tropics. We can boldly defend this upon the most enlarged system of philanthropy. It is far better for the wild races of Africa themselves." "The good old Las Casas, in 1519, was the first to advise Spain to import Africans to her colonies.... Experience has shown his scheme was founded in wise and Christian philanthropy... The time is coming when we will boldly defend this emigration [kidnapping men in Africa and selling them in the 'Christian Republic'] before the world. The hypocritical cant and whining morality of the latter-day saints will die away before the majesty of commerce.... We have too long been governed by psalm-singing schoolmasters from the North.... The folly commenced in our own Government uniting with Great Britain to declare slave-importing piracy."... "A general rupture in Europe would force upon us the undisputed sway of the Gulf of Mexico and the West Indies.... With Cuba and St Domingo, we could control the ... power of the world. Our true policy is to look to Brazil as the next great slave power. ... A treaty of commerce and alliance with Brazil will give us the control over the Gulf of Mexico and its border countries, together with the islands; and the consequence of this will place African slavery beyond the reach of fanaticism at home or abroad. These two great slave powers ... ought to guard and strengthen their mutual interests.

". . We can not only preserve domestic servitude, but we can defy the power of the world." . . . " The time will come that all the islands and regions suited to African slavery, between us and Brazil, will fall under the control of these two powers. . . . In a few years there will be no investment for the $200,000,000 . . . so profitable . . . as the development . . . of the tropical regions" [that is, as the African slave-trade]. . . . "If the slave-holding race in these States are but true to themselves, they have a great destiny before them."

Now, gentlemen and ladies, wh   to blame that things have come to such a pass as th..   The South and the North; but the North much more than the South, very much more. Gentlemen, we let Gog get upon the ark; we took pay for his passage. Our most prominent men in Church and State have sworn allegiance to Gog. But this is not always to last; there is a day after to-day—a FOR-EVER behind each to-day.

The North should have fought slavery at the adoption of the Constitution, and at every step since; after the battle was lost then, we should have resisted each successive step of the slave power. But we have yielded—yielded continually. We made no fight over the annexation of slave territory, the admission of slave States. We ought to have rent the Union into the primitive townships sooner than consent to the Fugitive Slave Bill. But as we failed to fight manfully then, I never thought the North would rally on the Missouri Compromise line. I rejoice at the display of indignation I witness here and elsewhere. For once New York appears more moral than Boston. I thank you for it. A meeting is called in the Park to-morrow. It is high time; though I doubt that the North will yet rally and defend even the line drawn in 1820. But there are two lines of defence where the nation will pause, I think— the seizure and occupation of Cuba, with its war so destructive to Northern ships; and the restoration of the African slave-trade. The slave-breeding States, Maryland, Virginia, Kentucky, Tennessee, Missouri, will oppose the last; for if the Gulf States and the future tropical territories can import Africans at one hundred dollars a head, depend upon it, that will spoil the market for the slave-breeders of America. And, gentlemen, if Virginia cannot sell her own children, how will this "well-born, well-educated, well-bred aristocrat" look down on the poor and ignorant Yankee, when the "gentlemen" of the Old Dominion do not bring a high price in the flesh market. No, this iniquity is not to last for ever! A certain amount of force will compress a cubic foot of water into nine-tenths of its natural size; but beyond that, the weight of the whole earth cannot make it any smaller. Even the North is not infinitely compressible. When atom touches atom, you may take off the screws.

Things cannot continue long in this condition. Every triumph of slavery is a day's march towards its ruin. There is no higher law, is there? "He taketh the wise in their own craftiness." "The counsel of the wicked is carried,"—ay, but it is carried headlong.

Only see what a change has come over our spirit just now. Three years ago, Isaiah Rynders and Hiram Ketchum domineered over New York. Those gentlemen who are to follow me, and whom you are impatient to hear, were mobbed down in this city two years ago; they could not find a hall which would be leased to them for money or love, and had to adjourn to Syracuse to hold their convention. Look as this assembly now.

A little while ago all the leading clergymen were in favour of the Fugitive Slave Bill; now three thousand of New England's ministers remonstrate against Nebraska. They know there is a fire in their rear, and, in theological language, it is a fire that "is not quenched;" it goeth not out by day; and there is no night there. The clergymen stand between eternal torment on one side, and the "little giant of slavery" on the other. They do not turn back! Two thousand English clergymen once became non-conformists in a single day. Three thousand New England ministers remonstrated against the enslavement of Nebraska. When the "gentlemen of the Old Dominion" find their sons and daughters do not bring a high price in the flesh-markets of the South, they will doubt the "divinity of slavery."

Now is the time to push and be active, call meetings, bring out men of all parties, all forms of religion; agitate, agitate, agitate. Make a fire in the rear of the Government and the Representatives. The South is weak—only united. The North is strong in money, in men, in education, in the justice of our great cause—only not united for freedom. Be faithful to ourselves and slavery will come down, not slowly, as I thought once, but when the people of the North say so, it shall come down with a great crash!

Then when we are free from this plague-spot of slavery—the curse to our industry, our education, our politics, and our religion—we shall increase more rapidly in numbers, and still more abundantly be rich. The South will be as the North—active, intelligent; Virginia rich as New York, the Carolinas as active as Massachusetts. Then by peaceful purchase, the Anglo-Saxon may acquire the rest of this North American continent,—for the Spaniards will make nothing of it. Nay, we may honourably go further South, and possess the Atlantic and Pacific slopes of the Southern continent, extending the area of freedom at every step. We may carry thither the Anglo-Saxon vigour and enterprise, the old love of liberty, the love also of law; the best institutions of the present age—ecclesiastical, political, social, domestic.

Then what a nation we shall one day become! America, the mother of a thousand Anglo-Saxon States, tropic and temperate, on both sides the Equator, may behold the Mississippi and the Amazon uniting their waters, the drainage of two vast continents in the Mediterranean of the Western World; may count her children at last by hundreds of millions—and among them all behold no tyrant and no slave! What a spectacle—the Anglo-Saxon family occupying a whole hemisphere, with industry, freedom, religion! It is our function to fulfil this vision; we are the voluntary instruments of God. Shall America scorn the mission He sends her on? Then let us all perish, and may Russia teach justice to mankind!

THE END.

JOHN CHILDS AND SON, PRINTERS.

www.ingramcontent.com/pod-product-compliance
Lightning Source LLC
Chambersburg PA
CBHW021155230426
43667CB00006B/405